ESSAYS IN

AMERICAN HISTORY

DEDICATED TO

FREDERICK JACKSON TURNER

NEW YORK
PETER SMITH
1951

THESE ESSAYS ARE DEDICATED BY THE AUTHORS, HIS
FORMER PUPILS AT THE UNIVERSITY OF WISCONSIN,

· TO

FREDERICK JACKSON TURNER

ON THE OCCASION OF HIS PRESIDENCY OF THE
AMERICAN HISTORICAL ASSOCIATION,
1909—1910

INTRODUCTION

SPONTANEOUS movements are hard to explain. Perhaps they need no explanation. Certainly a volume of essays on American history which in a large sense has written itself out of the love and respect of the authors for the scholar and friend to whom it is dedicated, needs but little by way of introduction to this generation of American students of history. To all others it preserves and transmits, by its very existence, that part of a scholar's work which is hardest to measure and record—his power to kindle his spirit and his love of scholarship in other men. Beyond the measure usually allotted to men of his own rank in scholarship and productive power, Professor Turner has manifested this most precious gift of the gods to the teachers of men. The office of president of the American Historical Association is a recognition by the larger constituency of American scholars in his chosen field of the permanent contributions of Professor Turner to the literature of that discipline. It has seemed to the narrower circle of those who, as students, have felt the stimulation of his personality, who have tasted at first hand of the fruits of his learning, and under his guidance have learned the methods of the craft, that there could be no more proper occasion than his presidency of this society and no more fitting form than this volume for acknowledging their obligations to him in whose workshop they learned the methods by which historical truth is sought.

Speaking for the many students of Professor Turner who are now interested in fields allied to history or in historical work other than American, and by reason of a self-denying ordinance are not contributors to this volume, the editor takes this occasion to acknowledge on behalf of the represented to those who represent, their appreciation of the zeal and thoroughness with which the contributors have done their work in the short time assigned them. They have made the volume possible and have reduced editorial work to the minimum. A like word should be said for the publishers and for the many friends of Professor Turner whose advice and assistance have helped to give form to this volume.

In their special fields these essays, it seems to one whose pleasure it was to be their first reader, are each a permanent contribution either in substance, point of view, or interpretation, to the literature of American history. If this is in a measurable degree the judgment of less prejudiced readers, then they will be, in full measure, such a tribute as his former students would offer to Frederick Jackson Turner, teacher, scholar, and friend.

GUY STANTON FORD.

CONTENTS

ESSAYS IN AMERICAN HISTORY

SOME ACTIVITIES OF THE CONGREGA-
TIONAL CHURCH WEST OF THE
MISSISSIPPI [1]

THREE institutions have been characteristic of the New England settler, wherever he has made his home,—the Congregational Church, the public school or the academy with its culminating point in the Congregational college, and the town-meeting. The first of these institutions had its inception in what might be called a second " Protestant Revolt," since it grew up as the expression of a widespread demand for more liberty in creed and ritual than an increasingly conservative established church of England permitted. Born in England, the Congregational Church grew to its full stature on New England soil, uncramped by the swaddling bands of an ecclesiastical and political system which viewed conformity and uniformity as necessities of the body politic, and variation from the type of either as anarchy and ruin. Founded upon a Calvinistic basis, the sermon the center of the service, an educated ministry speaking to an educated people was a necessity of the existence and of the growth of the Congregational Church. Hence the public school became an indispensable accompaniment of that church, thus providing that enlightened constituency which could alone

[1] See also Mathews, L. K., *The Expansion of New England* (Boston, 1909). The material for this essay was obtained in the Congregational Library, housed in the Congregational House of Boston. There is a large mass of correspondence which must be investigated at the headquarters of the American Home Missionary Society in New York City, as well as similar material in the headquarters of missionary organizations of other denominations, especially the Presbyterian, before the study can be completed.

maintain its principles and hold fast to an unwavering conviction of the truth of its dogmas. Beyond the school must come the college, which should provide the additional training for the educated man who was not only to minister to each of these groups of people, but also to convince those outside his field, whether of his own race or some other, of the rightness of that creed in which he himself so fervently and profoundly believed. Among such a people, with such a ministry, democracy was the only tenable political theory and practice; and out of a conviction of its necessity and the right of possessing it, together with the accident, as it were, of remoteness and isolation from a larger body politic, developed its expression in the town-meeting. Though these three institutions are found in their original form only in New England itself, their variations have been in a way immaterial in the face of the fact that their fundamental principles have been repeatedly used in new communities, though the superstructure erected upon these foundations has been no exact copy of the original form. Indeed, a superficial glance perceives no vital connection between local government in the Rocky Mountain states and that in Massachusetts; or between a state university of the Mississippi Valley and the denominational college such as Yale or Wellesley originally was. But although the more obvious characteristics may have been well-nigh obliterated in making the newer institution fit more plastic communities and ideals which may be broader but are certainly less definite, the type viewed in the large is the same. The Congregational college, for example, ceases to fit men almost exclusively for the ministry or the missionary field, and sends out both men and women to take a prominent place in their communities as Christian citizens. It ceases to call itself sectarian if it may thereby increase its constituency and spread its influence farther. It may be turned over by its trustees to the state for a university supported by legislative appropriation. It may decide that in order to share the advantages of a pension fund which will provide its poorly paid faculty with dignified poverty in their old age, it can dispense with its essentially sectarian views as to the church affiliations of its trustees, president, and faculty, and proclaim itself broadly Christian and not at all denominational. In spite of all these changes or any of them, its New England origin remains, and it is with this New England origin of church and school that the present study concerns itself.

All through the colonial period the missionary spirit of the Congregational Church had expressed itself in founding towns, churches, and schools. Just before the Revolution, in 1774, the Congregational churches of Connecticut, in their General Association, voted to send missionaries to the latest settlements in Vermont and New York, whither Connecticut pioneers had been thronging.[2] But the stirring events of the next quarter-century prevented any large contributions of either money or men to the movement. It was only when the Revolutionary War had become a matter of past history, when the new national government had been set upon its feet, and when the peril from foreign aggression had apparently been overcome, that the missionary spirit was born anew. Stayed only temporarily by the conflict between the colonies and the mother-country, the tide of emigration to the frontier had flowed out in unprecedentedly great floods after 1783. Into the western parts of Massachusetts and Connecticut, into the three northern New England states, into central and western New York and Pennsylvania, into the Appalachian valleys, into the back-country of Virginia, the Carolinas, and Georgia, and over into the new Northwest and

[2] Walker, Williston, *A History of the Congregational Church in the United States,* pp. 311, 312.

Southwest Territories,—in every direction the outposts of civilization were advanced far beyond the frontiers of 1775. Settlers went singly, in families, and in colonies. The differentiation between seaboard and back-country had meantime become clearly marked; and the new governments, both state and federal, had concerned themselves largely with questions of adjustment of representation and taxation, and with internal improvements in the matter of roads, bridges, ferries, and even canals. Yet the back-country often felt itself misunderstood and unappreciated, and pleaded its poverty as an excuse and a cause for the discontent it loudly voiced. On the other hand, to the older communities the rural districts seemed rude and uncivilized, uneducated and godless; and out of this poverty on the one hand, and comparative plenty on the other, was born anew the missionary spirit which had stirred New England since the beginning. This time·it was directed, not alone toward the education and conversion of the Indian, but toward the education and conversion of their own brethren on the frontier, where scarcity of money, coupled with a declining sense of their necessity, had delayed the formation of schools and churches, and thus retarded the development of that peculiar kind of Christian civilization which the older parts of New England had developed. The movement found expression almost simultaneously all over New England, though Connecticut in 1798 led the way. In that year the General Association of Congregational Churches in that state organized itself as a Missionary Society, " to Christianize the Heathen in North America, and to support and promote Christian knowledge in the new settlements within the United States." [3] To stimulate interest in these home missions an official organ, known as the *Con-*

---

[3] *Ibid.*, p. 312. It concerned itself less with the conversion of the Indian and more with the new settlements.

necticut Evangelical Magazine, was established in 1800, and in 1802 the society received a charter from the Connecticut legislature.[4] A similar society, known as the Congregational Missionary Society in the Counties of Berkshire and Columbia, had in 1798 been formed to take care of poor churches in western Massachusetts and eastern New York. In 1799 the Massachusetts Missionary Society was founded on the same lines as that in Connecticut, and four years later established its *Massachusetts Missionary Magazine.*[5] Then followed similar societies in New Hampshire (1801), Maine (1807), and Vermont (1807), but these confined their work almost wholly to the large opportunity which lay at their hand in their own newer communities.[6] So great was the zeal for the work that other local societies were formed outside the large state ones;—as the one in 1802 in Hampshire County of Massachusetts, the Piscataqua Missionary Society of eastern New Hampshire (1804), and the Evangelical Missionary Society of Worcester and Middlesex counties of Massachusetts (1807).[7] Some of these organizations sent missionaries as far west as New York and Ohio, besides helping weak churches near home. These were the beginnings of the home missionary movement of the Congregational Church. The great work done east of the Mississippi River must, however, be passed over in order to trace a few phases of its labors beyond that great artery.

---

[4] *Ibid.*

[5] *Ibid.,* p. 313.

[6] Clark, J. B., *Leavening the Nation,* p. 31. Missionary societies made up exclusively of women had their inception in these years. The Boston Female Society for Missionary Purposes, the Female Cent Institution of New Hampshire (1804), by which its members pledged a cent a week for missions; and many other " cent associations " all through New England were pioneer societies. See Walker, p. 313.

[7] *Ibid.*

With the acquisition of the Louisiana Purchase in 1803 enormous tracts of land with few or no inhabitants save native Indians were added to the territory of the United States. The area of settled territory consisted of a few towns, scarcely more than trading-posts, scattered up the west bank of the Mississippi with long distances between them, or. lying a few miles from the mouths of the larger tributaries of that river. The settlers were for the most part French, though there were here and there such wanderers as Moses Austin, a native of Durham, Connecticut, who had gone in 1799 to the region which became Missouri. The expeditions of Lewis and Clark, and of Pike, made better known the possibilities of the newly acquired region, and settlers from those states and territories bordering on the Mississippi began to make their way to the trading-posts and settlements already in existence. Soon the missionaries who were laboring to build up churches in Illinois and the neighboring states made tours of investigation across the river, while the home missionary societies in New England sometimes sent special messengers to bring back reports of the number of settlers and their needs. The Missionary Societies of Connecticut and Massachusetts together sent Rev. Samuel J. Mills and Rev. John F. Schermerhorn on a tour which occupied the years 1812 and 1813, and covered a long strip of territory lying along the western bank of the Mississippi. They reported that the settlements in Missouri were scattered, confined almost wholly to the banks of rivers, and contained perhaps 20,000 souls, of whom two-fifths were Americans, the rest French. They found a few Baptists, a few Methodist preachers, and a hundred or more families which had been Congregationalists or Presbyterians, many of them Connecticut-born.[8] Moses Austin's colony was then at Mine au Breton, near the present town of

[8] *Report of Rev. John F. Schermerhorn*, pp. 32, 33.

Potosi (Missouri), and Mr. Austin himself sent for Mr. Mills to preach in the settlement. Other pioneer missionaries of these early days were Rev. Salmon Giddings, whose work was done from 1815 to 1827 in Missouri; Rev. Elias Cornelius, Jr., in 1817-1818 in Louisiana;[9] Rev. H. Hull, in 1819-1820 in Louisiana; Rev. John Matthews, in 1819-1823 in Missouri; and Rev. Timothy Flint, whose experiences from 1815 to 1818 in Ohio and Missouri he detailed at length in his *Recollections*.[10] One of the most faithful workers was Rev. C. S. Robinson, born in 1791 in Granville, Massachusetts, a graduate of Williams College and of Andover Theological Seminary, who went to St. Charles (Missouri) as a missionary and preached there until his death.[11] Rev. Salmon Giddings, mentioned above, in 1817 gathered nine families (including five from Massachusetts and one from Connecticut) into the first Presbyterian church in St. Louis.[12]

[9] See Edwards, B. B., *Memoir of the Rev. Elias Cornelius* (2d edition, 1834), especially pp. 95-104, 108, 109. He paved the way for the founding of the first Presbyterian Church in New Orleans, though he was a Congregationalist.

[10] All these were sent out by the Missionary Society of Connecticut. A complete list of their missionaries from the founding of the society till its union with the American Home Missionary Society in 1880, is given in the *Annual Report of the Directors of the Missionary Society of Connecticut* (1880). Many of these reports consist so largely of financial statistics that they have little value for historical purposes. For Rev. Timothy Flint, see his *Recollections of the Last Ten Years in the Mississippi Valley,* and his *History and Geography of the Mississippi Valley.*

[11] See "Memoir of Rev. C. S. Robinson" in *The American Pastor's Journal,* 1 Sept., 1829.

[12] Roy, J. E., "Congregationalism in the Northwest," in Dunning, A. E., *Congregationalism in America,* p. 425. This is but one of many instances where Presbyterian churches were made up of a Congregational pastor and members. The one Connecticut family in Rev. Salmon Giddings' church mentioned in the text was that of the parents of Stephen Hempstead, second governor of the State of Iowa. See Roy, J. E., as above, and Shambaugh, B., *Messages and Proclamations of the Governors of Iowa,* I., p. 423.

But the tide of emigration between 1800 and 1840 was flowing most strongly into the sections known earlier as the "Northwest Territory" and the "Southwest Territory." Moreover, it proceeded for the most part along the parallels of latitude running out from the most densely populated of the older states, though all streams mingled and crossed one another on both sides of the Ohio River.[13] Missionary effort would naturally be directed in large measure to those quarters where the opportunity seemed greatest; by far the greater part of money and men was used east of the Mississippi. The Missouri compromise diverted the streams of pioneers from the southern states to the lands across the Mississippi and south of Iowa; but even there the population was still concentrated for the most part along the rivers, nor had it as yet proceeded far inland. It was still an unsettled, shifting population also; the colony which Rev. S. J. Mills had found at Mine au Breton had moved in 1819 to Texas, and had begun its dramatic life there. That the Congregational Church made little history in the far west until after 1830 is attributable not only to the conditions controlling emigration from New England and New York as a whole, but to two other important factors:—in the north, the church had become in the newer parts of the country in large measure absorbed by the Presbyterian Church through the "Plan of Union"; in the south it was unpopular, because of its strong antipathy to slavery. About 1822 a keen realization of these facts, together with the menace of the rising Unitarian agitation, led to new activity on the part of the Congregational Church both in and out of New England.[14] The founding in 1826 of the American Home

---

[13] See maps of New England settlement in Mathews, L. K., *Expansion of New England*.

[14] Professor Walker's view is that this denominational awakening came first in the West, where the Presbyterian Church had grown very strong,

Missionary Society, a general organization of the whole church, was significant of this new vigor; while it did not in any sense supersede the state organizations, it attempted to work on a larger scale and to unify all missionary effort.

One of the most interesting and important manifestations of this " denominational awakening " was a movement for " lay emigration," as it was called. Rev. Asa Turner, the father of Congregational home missions in Iowa, felt strongly the need of Christian laymen on the frontier. Born in Templeton, Massachusetts, of " migratory stock," [15] he was educated at Amherst Academy, Yale College, and Yale Theological Seminary. Before he left New England to begin his first Illinois pastorate at Quincy, he urged that groups of families should accompany home missionaries to their new fields, to help in church, public school, and Sunday school, " fixing the character of towns, . . . spreading the moral power of New England, and effectually aiding to save the West." [16] He wrote to a friend in 1830: " It is of vast importance to settle a minister in each county as soon as possible. . . . This is the object: to place one missionary in every county, and six or eight pious families . . . without any loss to New England. . . . I mean to bring on a colony with me." [17] And he did take about twenty people west with him in 1833. Rev. Aratus Kent, a missionary in the lead-mining region about Galena, Illinois, had the same idea. He, too, wrote in 1830: " A half dozen families of the right stamp, in company with the missionary, in many cases would render his labors doubly efficient. . . . Every new missionary then should have his little colony selected to accompany

and later in New England. If this is true, it is like many other frontier movements which have reacted upon an older, less volatile, and more complacent community.

[15] Magoun, G. F., *Asa Turner and His Times,* p. 16.

[16] *Ibid.,* p. 116.

[17] Quoted in *ibid.,* p. 117.

him, or pledged to follow and settle around him." [18] Other
home missionaries undoubtedly held similar views.[19]

One of the best illustrations of the practical working
of this idea of " lay emigration "—which was, after all,
only a later phase of the colony plan which New England
pioneers had followed from time to time since 1620 [20]—is
found in the settlement of Denmark, Lee County, Iowa.
Rev. Asa Turner lectured in New Ipswich, New Hampshire, on " The Advantages of Western Farming," and
the need of Christian laymen on the frontier.[21] So impressed was his audience that a committee was sent ahead
(1836) to locate claims, and selected the site of Denmark.
Families from New Ipswich and Lyndeborough in New
Hampshire, Hartford and Enosburgh in Vermont, with
one from Damariscotta in Maine, laid out the town, and
when, in 1838, the Congregational church of thirty-two
members was formed, its pastor was Rev. Asa Turner.
Within a short time every New England state but one was
represented in the town, and it became a center of New
England influence. One of their historians says:

". . . They acted like a well-ordered family, Father Turner
at the head. They met in church meetings to determine on the
policy to be followed, no matter whether it was the candidate
to be voted for at the election, or the charity to be given to the
many applicants they had." [22]

Their school and church meetings were at first held in the
same building, but in 1843 an academy was opened, and

[18] *The Home Missionary* [Magazine], October, 1830, pp. 117, 118.

[19] Magoun, G. F., *Asa Turner and His Times*, p. 117. The subject of
lay emigration has not been investigated, so far as the author knows. It
seems quite probable that one would find a number of towns whose
foundations were laid in this way.

[20] See Mathews, L. K., *Expansion of New England*, for a number of
these colonies which moved as organized churches.

[21] Adams, E., *The Iowa Band*, p. 192. Also Magoun, G. F., *sup. cit.*, pp.
184, 185.

[22] Hawkins, T., in the *Iowa Historical Record*, July, 1892, p. 329.

already they dreamed of a college.   Davenport secured a better location for the latter, and in 1848 Iowa College, a Congregational outpost of higher education, was established there.[23]

From this transplanted New England colony sprang the great work of the Congregational Church in Iowa.   In the spring of 1843 there was read to students of Andover Theological Seminary a letter from Deacon Houston of Denmark, urging that ministers be sent to the frontier. Then followed the formation of that group of Andover men known as " The Iowa Band," pledged to home missionary work in Iowa Territory.   Of the twelve who pledged themselves thus, nine were from New England, two from New York, and one from Illinois.[24] Of the nine who actually went, seven were from New England, one from New York, and one from Illinois.[25]   They met at Albany in October (1843), went by railroad to Buffalo, by steamboat to Chicago, and across Illinois in emigrant wagons loaded with supplies.   At the Mississippi River they divided, one party striking across to Davenport, then to Burlington, and on to Denmark, the other proceeding directly to Burlington.   From Denmark they went to the various small settlements which called them,[26] but throughout their lives tried to meet once a year to renew their friendship.

Other Congregational missionaries preceded and fol-

[23] Walker, W., *History of the Congregational Church in the U. S.*, p. 374.

[24] This last was Rev. Edwin B. Turner.   He came from Monticello, Illinois, a town settled largely by New Englanders, and had been educated at Illinois College, itself a child of Yale College.

[25] Their historian was of their number—Rev. Ephraim Adams, author of *The Iowa Band* (revised edition, 1902).   Constant use has been made of it for the facts given in the text above.   The last survivor of the band, Rev. William Salter, died only a few days ago (August, 1910).

[26] In the appendix of the revised edition (1902) of *The Iowa Band* there is a map of their churches.

lowed the " Iowa Band ": Rev. A. B. Hitchcock of Great
Barrington, Massachusetts, who preached from 1841 to
1843 in Davenport; Rev. Oliver Emerson, Jr., of Lynn-
field, Massachusetts, but graduated at Waterville College
in Maine, who went in 1841 to Iowa; Rev. Reuben Gaylord of Norfolk, Connecticut, who preached in Iowa from
1844 until he went in 1855 as the first Congregational minister to Nebraska; Rev. Julius A. Reed, of East Windsor,
Connecticut, who conducted a private school in Natchez,
Mississippi, from 1831 to 1833, and went to Iowa in 1844;
and Rev. J. C. Holbrook of Brattleboro, Vermont, who
settled in 1845 in Dubuque.[27]   It is no matter for wonder
that in 1870 the Congregational churches in Iowa numbered 189, with about 10,000 members, and 181 ministers.
Twenty years later there were over 30,000 members in
more than 300 churches.[28]   The large New England element in the state might account partially for these large
numbers; but the far-reaching influence of the " Iowa
Band," of other Congregational home missionaries, and of
Iowa College cannot be emphasized too strongly.   The
idea of a Congregational college was, as has been shown,
in the minds of the Denmark settlers; the school had begun in struggling fashion in 1848 in Davenport; but the
first aid which set it on its feet came from the east in
1853,—a gift of $5,080, from Deacon P. W. Carter of
Waterbury, Connecticut.[29]   The Davenport site not
proving a wise choice, the college was moved in 1859 to
its present site, Grinnell.   This town was itself of New
England origin, planned by and named for Josiah B. Grinnell, who was born in 1821 in New Haven, Vermont.
Mr. Grinnell was forced to forego his plan for entering
the ministry, and determined to devote his life to further-

[27] See Magoun, G. F., *Asa Turner and His Times,* pp. 199-217.
[28] Adams, E., *The Iowa Band,* pp. 78, 100.
[29] *Ibid.,* p. 110.

ing Christian interests as a layman might.   Falling under the influence of Horace Greeley, he decided to go west, and advertised in both the *New York Tribune* and the *New York Independent* for " correspondence with parties desirous of educational facilities, and of temperance and Congregational affinities, who wished to settle on some Western railroad, or one projected." [30]   In an article in the *Independent* he put forth a plea for emigration in colonies.   " Organized emigration," he said, " becomes a Christian duty, if a new home is sought." [31]   The town of Grinnell was settled in 1853, and six years later became the permanent home of Iowa (now Grinnell) College.[32]

Meanwhile settlement was progressing not only in the eastern half of Iowa, but on the Missouri slope in the west.   In 1848 a colony from Oberlin, Ohio, led by Deacon George A. Gaston, who had served his apprenticeship from 1840 to 1845 as a missionary of the American Board among some Missouri River Indians, settled in what became the town of Tabor.[33]   Near this colony in 1849 settled a few Congregational families who had left Illinois to go to California.   They made a camp and then a town on the banks of the Missouri opposite the mouth of the Big Platte River.[34]   Here they formed a church of ten members, a sister church to the one of eight members in Tabor.   The Tabor colony desired also to found a college, and as early as 1852 consecrated ground for that purpose.   In 1858 another party, thirty-eight in number,

[30] Grinnell, J. B., *Men and Events of Forty Years*, p. 87.

[31] *Ibid.*, p. 89.

[32] Mr. Grinnell maintains in his memoirs that it was not a *bona fide* colony, since all the land entries were in his name, and he himself took the risks. But to all intents and purposes it was as real a Congregational colony as was Denmark. Mr. Grinnell himself speaks of it as a colony. See *Men and Events of Forty Years*, pp. 94, 109.

[33] Dunning, *Congregationalists in Iowa*, p. 376.

[34] The settlement was called Civil Bend, but its post office now is Gaston. See Adams, E., *The Iowa Band*, pp. 146, 147.

came from Oberlin, and the same year the Tabor Literary Institute was incorporated, the germ of the later Tabor College.   It was in Tabor that John Brown spent some time preparing for his work in Kansas; and two members of the " Yale Dakota Band," missionaries to Dakota in 1881, came from this little colony.[35]

While Iowa was passing through the pioneer stage other fields were opening to missionaries.   In Missouri the Presbyterian Church had been more popular than the Congregational because of the uncompromising attitude of the latter toward slavery.   The larger part of the Missourians were southerners, but here and there were little groups of settlers whose New England birth made them adhere to the faith of their childhood.   Nathan Trumbull and his wife from Monson, Massachusetts, Colonel Cyrus Russell and his wife, with their nine children, from Somers, Connecticut, and Augustus Pease and his wife, neighbors of Colonel Russell in New England,—all these had made their way in 1837-8, when the Iron Mountain excitement was at its height, to Arcadia (now Ironton) in Missouri.[36] In 1841 these families formed a Congregational church; but there was not another in the state until Rev. Truman M. Post, " father of Missouri Congregationalism," gathered one together in 1852 in St. Louis.[37]   Dr. Post was born in Middlebury, Vermont, was graduated at Middlebury College, and also taught there.   He then became a professor in Illinois College, and was pastor of the Congregational church in Jacksonville until 1847, when he went to St. Louis to become pastor of the Third Presbyterian church.   He was determined, however, to form a

[35] Dunning, A. E., *Congregationalists in America,* pp. 376, 377.   It is obvious that the paragraphs above are but the beginning of a study of New England in Iowa.

[36] Punchard, G., *History of Congregationalism,* V., p. 153.

[37] There were New England Congregationalists in Missouri long before this, but they affiliated with the Presbyterians.

Congregational church, and did so in 1852.   He continued as pastor of that church until his death, thirty-four years later.   In 1859 he went to Hannibal, 150 miles away, to preach the sermon at the first service in the Congregational church there.[38]   But the growth of Congregationalism in Missouri was slow until after 1865.   More than one reason might be assigned for the difficulty missionaries found in holding congregations together.   In 1850 one missionary deplored the fact that " the churches had begun to feel the drain of emigration to Oregon and California." [39]

During the same decades that part of Minnesota which bordered on the Mississippi River was being taken up by settlers from the states near by, from New England, and from the Middle States.   The Indians were still in possession of the largest part of the territory, as they were of the Dakotas and Montana.   In 1835 the American Board sent missionaries to the Indians around Fort Snelling; but for the next fifteen years the Presbyterians held the field.   By 1851, however, enough Congregationalists had made homes in that region for the formation of a Congregational church,—to-day the " First Church " of Minneapolis.   So rapidly did the denominational missionaries make headway that the Congregational churches in Minnesota in 1858 numbered thirty.   Rev. Richard Hall, who had gone to the territory in 1850, wrote seven years later that the population had grown greatly since his arrival, especially the New England element, which he considered " unquestionably . . . destined to constitute the main staple of the population. . . . It promises, indeed, to predominate here in a more marked and decisive manner

[38] For references to Dr. Post's work see Magoun, G. F., *Asa Turner and His Times*, p. 110; Walker, W., *History of the Congregational Church in the United States*, p. 377.

[39] Hill, T., in *Thirtieth Annual Report* (1856) *of the American Home Missionary Society*, p. 77.

than in any Western state yet formed." He added that already the territory was called " the New England of the West." [40]   In the decade between 1850 and 1860 the population jumped from 6,000 to 172,000. The fact that there were as yet no railroads kept settlements close to the rivers;—one can almost locate them by the spread of the Congregational missionary churches, of which in 1860 there were forty-three.   The largest ones were located in St. Anthony (now Minneapolis), Excelsior, Winona, Faribault, Northfield, Lake City, Spring Valley, Owatonna, Austin, Glencoe, Zumbrota, Wabasha and St. Paul.[41] From that decade dates the great strength of Congregationalism in Minnesota, which became, with Iowa, its greatest stronghold in the western Mississippi Valley.

In yet another quarter was the tide of emigration flowing after 1835,—into the little known country lying north of California.   Interest in that section was aroused among New Englanders when Captain Robert Gray, of Tiverton, Rhode Island, sailing in command of a Boston ship, had in 1792 discovered the mouth of the Columbia River.[42] The expedition of Lewis and Clark had stimulated the interest already awakened; but the remoteness of the Oregon country, the difficulty of making a way over the plains and mountains which lay between the settled area along the Mississippi River and that distant territory, together with the hostile attitude maintained by the fur-trading companies toward settlements, had effectually prevented emigration into the region.   In 1835 the American Board sent out Dr. Marcus Whitman, a missionary physician, and Rev. Henry H. Spalding, with their wives. They arrived in Oregon in 1836, and were followed in 1838 by

[40] Hall, R., in *Annual Report* (1857) *of the American Home Missionary Society*, pp. 84, 85.

[41] Hadden, A., *Congregationalism in Minnesota*, p. 11.

[42] For Jefferson's early interest in this region see Sparks, J., *Life of John Ledyard*, p. 153 ff. (ed. of 1828).

Rev. Cushing Eels, who formed at Oregon City in 1844 the first permanent Congregational church. Four years later a " General Association of Congregational Churches " in Oregon was formed, and in the same year Tualatin Academy was founded by the church missionaries. In 1853 the first institution for higher education in this section opened its classes—Pacific University at Forest Grove.[43] The attitude of the General Association toward the work it had to do is best illustrated by a resolution passed in 1866:

> " *Resolved,* That the idea and practice of our fathers, that education is the handmaid of religion, and that the school and college should go hand-in-hand with the church, should be a living, practical idea with us in Oregon, while laying foundations here." [44]

The Congregational missionaries had been working nearly a quarter of century—since Oregon had become unquestionably a part of the United States—to make those New England ideas realities in their field.

All parts of the country felt the drain upon their population when, in 1848, gold was discovered in California. By all the old trails,—the Santa Fé, the Salt Lake, and even by the Oregon trail, as well as by water to the Isthmus or around the Horn,—emigrants poured into the territory so recently wrested from Mexico. The treaty of 1848 had given the overland approaches to the Pacific Coast entirely and without question into the hands of the United States, and the Mormon settlements in Utah, while not always friendly to emigrants, nevertheless afforded a half-way station that made the coast seem more accessible. But it needed an extraordinary reason to direct the tide of

[43] Walker, W., *History of the Congregational Church in the United States,* p. 378.
[44] Punchard, G., *History of Congregationalism,* V., pp. 403, 404, citing *Minutes of the General Association . . . of Oregon,* 1866, p. 7.

emigration strongly to California while good and cheap land was still plentiful in regions nearer the settled area to the east, and this reason the gold discoveries supplied. Even before the rush from the east had begun, Rev. Timothy D. Hunt, a Yale graduate, had reached San Francisco; but it was of the new arrivals that in 1849 he formed the first Congregational church in California. The same year the second church of the denomination was gathered in Sacramento. In 1850 Rev. Mr. Blakeslee, also a missionary, tried to interest people in the establishment of a Congregational college near San José; but the removal of the capital to Sacramento put an end to his plan for the moment.[45] Rev. Tyler Thacher, a New England Congregationalist, reached California in the latter part of 1851, and located at Marysville, intending to open a private school and also preach in the neighborhood. His school was not a success, but he continued to preach on Sundays and work on his ranch during the week.[46] In 1853 seven home missionaries and their families came to San Francisco, among whom was Henry Durant of Byfield, Massachusetts, the seat of Dummer Academy. He began at once to work for an academy and a college, and was aided by both Presbyterians and Congregationalists. Contra Costa Academy was opened, with Mr. Durant as principal. It grew into the College of California, then became the state university, with Mr. Durant its first president.[47] These were the foundation-stones of higher education in northern California; not for nearly forty years was Pomona College founded to represent the efforts of Congregationalism for higher education in southern California.

When the " gold rush " to California began, there was

[45] Punchard, G., *History of Congregationalism*, V., pp. 386, 387.
[46] *Ibid.*, p. 379.
[47] *Ibid.*, pp. 382, 383.

but little settlement beyond the Missouri River, save for
a few towns (really only trading-posts) along its western
bank.   Within the next few years settlers straggled into
what are now the states of Kansas and Nebraska, but they
were mostly from Missouri, Kentucky, and Tennessee.
In March, 1854, the Kansas-Nebraska bill became a law,
and at once work began on organized lines by both northern and southern sympathizers to gain these new territories
for their own cause.   During 1854-55 ten companies
(about 1,500 persons in all) were sent out by the Massachusetts association alone.   One of the largest went to
Lawrence, Kansas, where, on September 23, 1854, Rev.
Mr. Lum, a Congregational minister, preached the first
sermon in the town, and the next month organized the first
Congregational church in Kansas.[48]   On March 1, 1855,
a colony was organized in Hampden County, Massachusetts, and started almost immediately for Kansas. They
had intended to go to Lawrence, but changed their minds
and founded a town called Hampden in the Neosho Valley, near the present town of Burlington.   Their minister
preached his first sermon April 29, 1855; but town and
church had a precarious existence until 1865, when Burlington became the county seat, whereupon most of the Hampden colony moved there, and their first town died.[49]   Other
towns had a different history; there were enough of them
containing Congregational churches to form a General
Association in 1855.[50]   The Maine Missionary Society put

[48] Ibid., V., p. 346. Walker, W., History of the Congregational Church
in the United States, p. 391.
[49] Andreas, A. T., History of the State of Kansas, pp. 647, 663.
[50] The eight towns whose churches formed the association were Osawa-
tomie, Zeandale, Topeka, Council City (Burlingame), Hampden,
Lawrence, Manhattan, Kanwaka. See Punchard, sup. cit., V., p. 348.
Some figures as to the birthplace of Kansans from New England are found
in an article by Wilder, D. W., in Kansas Hist. Coll., IX., pp. 507, 508,
note on p. 508.

forth an earnest plea in 1856 for extra funds to carry on
church work in all parts of the country, but especially in
Kansas. "*Our* Home Missionary work," says the report,[51] "may be regarded as embracing the whole land.
In what part of it are not the sons and daughters of Maine
to be found? The portion of its annual receipts which
this Society shall deposit in the Treasury in New York, for
the benefit of the mighty West, will go to the support of
missionaries from Maine, in preaching the Gospel to hear-
ers from Maine. In the Territory of Kansas there are
emigrants from Maine . . . ready to do their part . . .
on the side of order, law, and liberty." So imperative did
the need for missionaries seem that four young men (two
from New Hampshire and two from Michigan), students in Andover Theological Seminary, organized in 1856
a "Kansas Band," similar in purpose to the "Iowa Band"
mentioned above.[52] They, as well as other missionaries,
preached to Congregational churches not made up exclusively of New Englanders; but their most cordial welcome
was in such towns as Manhattan; Hartford, named for
Hartford in Connecticut by one of its founders, Harvey D.
Rice; Burlington, named for Burlington, Vermont; and
Lawrence, named for A. A. Lawrence of Boston.[53] Man-

[51] "Trustees' Report," in *Annual Report* (No. 30) *of the American
Home Missionary Society,* 1856, p. 61.

[52] Clark, *Leavening the Nation,* p. 109. Two other significant steps were
taken by the Congregational Church in 1852 and in 1854. In the former
year a convention met in Albany, N. Y., to which came 463 pastors
and lay representatives from seventeen states, to consider the condition
and needs of the church as a whole. Among other requests one was made
for $50,000 to erect "meeting-houses" in Ohio, Michigan, Wisconsin, Il-
linois, Missouri, Iowa, and Minnesota. See Walker, W., *sup. cit.,* pp.
382, 383. In 1854 a convention of lay and clerical delegates representing the Congregational churches of Michigan, Indiana, Illinois, Wisconsin,
Missouri, and Iowa, met in Chicago and organized the Chicago Theological Seminary to train up ministers for service in those states and other
portions of the west. See *ibid.,* p. 389.

[53] For names of Kansas towns and their origin, see Calver, W. R., in
Kansas Hist. Coll., VII., pp. 476, 479, 480.

hattan had a literary society, a circulating library, a weekly
debating society, and an association for establishing a college almost as soon as the town was settled.   In 1859
the cornerstone of their " Blue Mont College " was laid;
in 1863, when it was turned over to the state for an agricultural college, its first president was Joseph Denison,
born in Bernardston, Massachusetts.[54]   The first steps
towards founding a college under the auspices of the
General Association of Congregational Churches in
Kansas were taken in 1857.   But a year of drought, the
disturbed conditions preceding the Civil War, followed
by the five years of conflict, prevented further action until
1865, when Lincoln College opened its doors in Topeka.
A gift of $25,000 from Deacon Ichabod Washburn of
Worcester, Massachusetts, led in 1868 to a change in its
name; and Washburn College has ever since been supported especially by Congregationalists of Massachusetts
and Connecticut.[55]

New England settlers began to leave for Nebraska in
July and August, 1854.   In 1855 Rev. Reuben Gaylord,
who had been for seventeen years a home missionary in
Iowa, went to Omaha to see what were the spiritual needs
of that region.   He preached on Sunday, and after the
service was asked by a Mr. Richardson, a native of Vermont, who had been a lieutenant-governor in Michigan,
to stay as pastor of a Congregational church if one could
be formed.   The following May Mr. Gaylord returned to
Omaha and began his ministry with a church of eight mem-

[54] Humphrey, J., in *Kansas Hist. Coll.,* IV., p. 292; also see Walters,
J. D., in *ibid.,* VII., p. 169 and note.   Isaac T. Goodnow, superintendent
of public instruction in Kansas from 1863 to 1867, a native of Whitting-
ham, Vermont, was one of the founders of Blue Mont College and of the
State Agricultural College. See *Columbian History of Education in
Kansas* (Topeka, 1893), p. 7.

[55] Dunning, A. E., *Congregationalists in America,* p. 375.

bers—the first Congregational society in Nebraska.[56] During the remaining months of the year he established four more, at Bellevue, Florence, Fort Calhoun, and Fontanelle. The Fontanelle church of twenty-four members was made up of colonists from Quincy, Illinois, who in platting their town the previous year had set off a tract of one hundred acres for a college. As some of the leading members of the colony were Baptists, it was at first intended to represent that denomination; but later the site was offered to the Congregationalists, who then founded " Nebraska University." At least three other towns wanted a college, but the American Home Missionary Society determined to encourage but one college for their denomination in Nebraska, and frowned down other plans. When the one college was moved to Crete in 1873, it became Doane College, as it is to-day.[57]

Although the Civil War checked the flow of emigration to the west, it did not stop it.[58] The discovery of gold in the Bannack and neighboring regions in the early sixties drew settlers from Missouri, Kentucky, and Virginia by way of the Missouri River and its upper tributaries, or through Utah, to make the first settlements in Montana and Idaho. The early capital of Montana was first named Varina, for the wife of Jefferson Davis, and then Virginia City. New England emigrants and pioneers from the middle west came in during the later years of the war, and " the ' cause,' while waning after Vicksburg and Get-

[56] Punchard, sup. cit., V., p. 358.

[57] Ibid., V., pp. 364, 365, 366. Later still Gates College had a precarious existence at Neligh, but has now become merely an academy.

[58] Nor did it quench missionary zeal even temporarily. In 1861 the trustees of the Maine Missionary Society reported to the American Home Missionary Society that they were interested in sending missionaries to "the sons of Maine on Puget Sound [who were] . . . calling upon ministers from the East—their fatherland—to come over and help them." See Thirty-fifth Annual Report of the American Home Missionary Society (1861), p. 65.

tysburg, was still triumphant in the gulches of Montana." [59]
Though southern influence was strongest in Montana as in
Idaho till many years later, a trace of New England influence may here and there be found; such as the naming
of Billings, Montana, for Frederick Billings of Vermont,
after he had given $10,000 to build the first church in the
town.

South of Montana, in Colorado, one finds a different
history. There in 1863, at Central City, the first Congregational church within its borders was founded, with one
deacon from Worcester and another from Cambridgeport
in Massachusetts, while a third came from Norridgewock
in Maine. The Denver church was organized in 1864,
as was the one in Boulder; the one in Colorado Springs
dates its history from 1874, with the founding also of
Colorado College. [60]

But emigration to the west during the Civil War,
great as its volume was, was the exception, not the rule; [61]
and it was but natural that when the conflict ended there
should come at once a tremendous outpouring of population into sparsely settled or entirely unoccupied lands.
Foreign immigration took place at an unheard-of rate, and
Germans and Scandinavians by hundreds of families made
their way to the farming communities of Wisconsin, Iowa,
Minnesota, the Dakotas, Kansas, Nebraska, Missouri, and
even to Montana. The native-born Americans, who maintained an influence out of proportion to their numbers,

[59] Crooker, J. H., in the *New England Magazine*, February, 1900, pp.
741, 742, 744. Also Clark, *Leavening the Nation*, p. 148.

[60] Clark, *Leavening the Nation*, pp. 156, 157. Also Dunning, *Congrega-
tionalists in America*, p. 379. The town had been founded by General
William J. Palmer and a colony in 1871. For General Palmer's ideas see
Wray, H. R., "A Unique Western City," in the *Pioneer Edition* of the *El
Paso County* [Colorado] *Democrat*, December, 1908.

[61] For emigration and immigration during the Civil War, see Fite, E. D.,
Social and Industrial Conditions in the North During the Civil War, especially chapters I. and II.

turned more easily to manufacturing, railroad-building, cattle-raising, and mining, leaving the foreigners to fill in the stratum of agricultural laborers, depleted as this class was by the drain of Americans into the more skilled industries.

Minnesota, whose population of 250,000 in 1865 grew to 400,000 in 1870, was a goal for both kinds of pioneers. It continued, however, to develop along the lines of New England tradition which had been in evidence before 1860. New Congregational churches were established every year after 1863, and in 1866 the first movement was made toward founding a college.   In 1867 a preparatory school was opened at Northfield, long a New England town and a stronghold of Congregational principles; in 1870-71 the college department was organized and named for William Carleton of Massachusetts, who gave it $50,000.[62]   By 1880 there were 130 Congregational churches in the state; 80 new ones were planted during the next ten years; and in 1890, of the twenty-five cities in the state having a population of 2,000 or over, all but five had Congregational churches.[63]   The centers of Congregational influence— and they were all in their early days centers of New England influence—were Winona, with two churches of that denomination; Duluth, with three; St. Paul, with eight, and ten missions; and Minneapolis, with sixteen, and twelve missions.[64]

Turning again to Missouri, it was not until after 1864 that Congregationalism found much favor outside the immediate circle of Dr. Post's influence; yet by 1870 Hannibal, which had had a Congregational church since 1859,

[62] Hadden, A., *Congregationalism in Minnesota,* pp. 11, 12.
[63] *Ibid.,* p. 12. These five were Albert Lea, Moorhead, Hastings, Red Wing, and St. Peter.
[64] *Ibid.,* p. 12. Dr. Hadden gives a valuable map showing the location of Congregational churches in 1890 in *ibid.,* p. 17, with a key on pp. 14, 15, 16.

had become a center of sixteen churches, all founded within six years.[65]   The founding of Drury College at Springfield in 1873[66] was a sign of the increasing strength of the denomination.

Iowa continued to be a stronghold of Congregationalism, and of home missionary zeal.   One of its workers wrote in 1872:[67] " We hope and pray that our churches may prove to be centers of such spiritual life and power, that we may merit the application which we now scarcely dare accept for ourselves—the Massachusetts of the West."

As has been said, emigrants were making their way into the Dakotas, hitherto an Indian stronghold.   The first settlers entered by the southeastern corner, and there made their homes.   They were mostly from Maine, but were closely followed by families from Wisconsin, and afterward by those from all the New England states. Among the earliest arrivals was Rev. Joseph Ward, born in Perry, New York, in 1838, of New England parentage.[68] He went to southeastern Dakota as a home missionary, organized in 1868 a Congregational church at Yankton, and laid his plans at once for a college.   When in 1881[69] he saw his dream realized, he became the president of the new Yankton College, and for eight years had his hand

---

[65] Punchard, *sup. cit.*, V., p. 162.

[66] Dunning, *Congregationalists in America*, p. 378.   Besides its own academy, Drury College has maintained a close connection with three other academies in Arkansas and Missouri.

[67] Pickett, J. W., in *Forty-sixth Annual Report of the American Home Missionary Society* (1872).

[68] Clark, *Leavening the Nation*, p. 129.   Dr. Clark says: "Perry was itself a colony from the Berkshire Hills of western Massachusetts. . . . His [Ward's] parents had emigrated from Massachusetts to the far west of central New York, at an early day; . . . and their son turned his steps toward the newer West." *Ibid.*

[69] A "Yale Dakota Band" went out in 1881, but I have not investigated its *personnel* or its work.

at its helm.   It was to Dr. Ward and the New England
element that much of the distinct character of southeastern
Dakota was due.   In northern Dakota the first Congregational church was not established until 1881.[70]

West of the crest of the Rocky Mountains there were
in 1864 but twenty-six Congregational churches.   In 1897
California had 184, Washington 106, and Oregon 51.[71]
The Seattle church, first of the denomination in Washington, was founded in 1870; the Reno church, first in Ne-
vada, in 1871; the Salt Lake City church, first in Utah,
in 1874; while the pioneer churches in Arizona at Prescott
and in New Mexico at Albuquerque were founded in
1880.[72]   In 1882 aid was asked for the Albuquerque
church, which was reported also as being without a pastor.[73]
Montana and Idaho had no Congregational churches until
1882; and Wyoming had but one—in Cheyenne—from
1869 until 1884.[74]   In 1890 a group of young men just
graduated from Yale Divinity School formed a " Yale
Washington Band," like the Iowa, the Kansas, and similar groups of missionaries.   One of their number, Rev.
S. B. L. Penrose, became later the president of Whitman College.[75]

The antipathy of the south toward the Congregational
church has been mentioned.   In all the southern states
there were in 1866 but twelve churches of that denomination.   In 1894 there were 441, of which 130 were mainly
negro.[76]   The work among the freedmen was of course

[70] It was in Fargo, on the Minnesota border. See Walker, W., *sup. cit.*,
p. 391.
[71] Dunning, *Congregationalists in America*, p. 407.
[72] Walker, W., *sup. cit.*, p. 391.
[73] *Second Annual Report of the New West Education Commission*, May,
1882, p. 22.
[74] Dunning, *Congregationalists in America*, p. 407.
[75] Clark, *Leavening the Nation*, pp. 209, 210.
[76] Dunning, *Congregationalists in America*, p. 408.

very great, as has been also that among the "mountain whites"; but many of these 311 churches have on their roll of members many New Englanders who have moved into the south since 1865, because of the great business opportunities which an industrially reconstructed South have opened. With the building of railroads and telegraph lines, with the growth of factories nearer the fields of cotton production, with the greatly diversified industrial life of the cities, the old lines of migration have ceased to draw New Englanders exclusively into the north and northwest, but have made possible a crossing and re-crossing of the lines of both northern and southern settlement. The greater wealth of individual families, moreover, has produced the "winter colonies" in Florida, Louisiana, Georgia, the Carolinas, and Virginia, and it is to this element—people who go to the South for but a portion of the year—that many Congregational churches as well as those of other creeds look for their support. The same condition is found in California, Arizona, and New Mexico, as we shall see in a brief survey of the educational work done in the last fifty years by the Congregational Church and its societies.

Besides giving their support to public schools in the towns they have helped to build, New England Congregationalists have, especially since their "denominational awakening" about 1822, taken keen interest in sectarian education. The foundations were often laid, as has been shown, by the establishment of an academy. Typical cases are two schools in Utah and New Mexico.[77] In the winter of 1877-78 President Edward P. Tenney and Rev. Charles R. Bliss of Colorado College, met in the Congre-

[77] The account which follows is taken from a manuscript entitled, "A Fragment of History," by Rev. Charles R. Bliss, in the Congregational Library, Congregational House, Boston, under *New West Education Commission Papers.*

gational House in Boston, and there laid plans for establishing during the following summer two academies.
These were to be situated at Salt Lake City and at Santa
Fé, for the following objects :—" Primarily to benefit the
people of those territories, and secondarily to build up
feeders to Colorado College." The type of each school
was that " of the old New England academy." Colorado
College sent a principal to each city, and in September,
1878, the schools were opened. In 1879 another of the
same group was opened in Albuquerque, in 1881 another
in Trinidad, and a few years later a fifth in Las Vegas.
At the same time there was a preparatory school in Colorado Springs, as a department of Colorado College. In
Iowa as late as 1883 the demand for such schools was set
forth in the following words : " One academy, like the New
England grammar school, in every county is a growing
necessity. For example, Denmark Academy, in Lee
County, has promoted the higher education of more persons than all the colleges in Iowa." [78] But throughout the
country west of the Mississippi River the prevailing system of education, beginning with the elementary school,
continuing in the free high school, and ending in the state
university, all supported by general taxation and under
state or local control, has led to a partial abandoning of
the academy idea. The policy in recent years has been
to disband the sectarian preparatory schools as soon as
public high schools became competent to do the work,
excepting where the academy was needed as a " feeder "
for the denominational college. [79] The large funds at the
disposal of the state universities, moreover, have often put

[78] Howe, S. S., *Annals of Iowa*, April, 1883, p. 55.

[79] For instance, the academies at Albuquerque and Las Vegas were dis-
banded in 1896. The Presbyterians have often had an academy in the
same town, doing the same work; and the unnecessary expense entailed
upon the educational societies of the Congregational Church has also
been a potent factor in closing the academies.

the denominational college at a great disadvantage in the matter of equipment, and funds have been put at the disposal of the colleges that would formerly have been used for academies. The Congregational colleges throughout the west have been almost without exception missionary enterprises at the beginning, and many have continued to be dependent upon the gifts of eastern Congregationalists. A list of these colleges, with the dates of their founding, is significant not only of the history of the denomination, but also of the story of advancing population.[80]

COLLEGE	LOCATION	DATE OF ESTABLISH- MENT
Iowa (now Grinnell) College	Grinnell, Iowa	1859
Washburn College	Topeka, Kansas	1865
Carleton College	Northfield, Minnesota	1867
Doane College [81]	Crete, Nebraska	1873
Drury College	Springfield, Missouri	1873
Colorado College	Colorado Springs, Colorado	1874
Yankton College	Yankton, South Dakota	1881
Gates College [82]	Neligh, Nebraska	1881
Whitman College	Walla Walla, Washington	1883
Rollins College	Winter Park, Florida	1885
Fargo College	Fargo, North Dakota	1887
Redfield College	Redfield, South Dakota	1888
Pomona College	Claremont, California	1889
Lake Charles College [83]	Lake Charles, Louisiana	1890
Northland College	Ashland, Wisconsin	1906

[80] The list is taken from Walker, W., *History of the Congregational Church in the United States,* p. 391, and Dunning, *Congregationalists in America,* pp. 378-391.

[81] Named for Col. Thomas Doane, of Charlestown, Mass., a member of the same church as Wm. Carleton, for whom Carleton College was named.

[82] Now only an academy.

[83] Given up in 1901 or 1902. The only woman's college beyond the Mississippi is Mills College, near Oakland, California, founded by Dr. Mills and his wife, the latter a graduate of Mount Holyoke Seminary.

As the denominational college has come to be for both men and women a training-school in Christian citizenship, and as the requirements for entrance to the ministry have become higher, the theological seminary or "divinity school" has become differentiated from the college, and is sometimes a separate institution. Of these schools but one lies beyond the Mississippi River—the Pacific Theological Seminary, opened in 1869 in Oakland, California. Never a large institution, it has, however, been an important factor in setting and maintaining on the Pacific Coast a high standard of preaching, of ministerial work, and of missionary enterprise.

Some tentative conclusions appear from the brief study given above:

1. The Congregational Church has sometimes accompanied, sometimes followed settlement; it has almost never preceded it. It has made its way most quickly and easily in communities where there have been found together the four most typical New England institutions,—the church, the preparatory school (public or private), the college, and the town-meeting. All four are, as was said at the beginning of this study, part of one political, social, and religious system. Therefore the Congregational Church has become most influential where there has settled the greatest number of persons with New England background.

2. The peculiarity in the organization of the Congregational Church—the absolute independence of each group of members—has made it difficult for the denomination to maintain itself except in churches of some size. This accounts for the colony idea, the necessity for "lay emigra-

Dr. and Mrs. Mills had been missionaries in the Hawaiian Islands, and returned to the United States after many years' service to "do for the far West what Mount Holyoke Seminary does for the East." (See Dunning, *sup. cit.*, p. 385). Mills Seminary, now Mills College, has always had Congregational affiliations.

tion," which would result in transplanting a group of families with their minister at their head. In farming communities or in small towns the Presbyterians gained ground, and finally in some parts of the country supplanted the Congregationalists entirely. The rise of the Congregational missionary societies was in large part due to a general desire to prevent Presbyterianism from growing, and at the same time to help small and isolated churches.

3. The conservatism of the Church has made it cling to its original ideas—especially to the belief in the religious education of young men and young women, and to the inherent democracy of its organization and practice. Hence the necessity for the denominational college and the denominational preparatory school, both to be planted in the midst of Congregational communities.

4. With all its conservatism, the ideals of the Congregational Church are shifting with the changing ideals of our country. For ten years the American people have been growing more sensitive to the presence in their midst of social, political, and industrial wrongs, and they have become more and more determined to right those wrongs. The Church has felt this moral awakening, and in response to it has broadened its creeds, increased its work on the philanthropic and humanitarian sides, and sought to " democratize " its membership by sweeping all classes into its fold. The denominational college has broadened its scope as a part of the same movement.

5. The history of the Congregational Church is bound up inseparably with the history of the whole country, and cannot be studied apart from the large movements which have affected the United States from ocean to ocean. Any impetus to emigration into the west has carried New Englanders and the Congregational Church with it; any check to the movement towards the frontier has held them both back. Small groups set here and there as they have

been in the past and are to-day, they are, nevertheless, integral parts of the large group, the American people, and they can only be understood when they are studied in their relations to that larger group.

Lois Kimball Mathews.

OREGON PIONEERS AND AMERICAN DIPLOMACY

THE settlement of diplomatic questions, if such a settlement is to be permanent and satisfactory, must be upon the basis of facts whose logic cannot be denied by the nations most interested. It is upon these facts that national convictions ultimately depend irrespective of whether or not they influence or dominate the course and conclusion of the diplomatic negotiations over boundary disputes. In the formation of public opinion on the merits of such territorial controversies, possession is not only nine points of the law—it is the law. It is then a happy conjunction when the negotiations are between the diplomats of governments which are quickly and fully responsive to public opinion. The natural opportunism of diplomacy is made to square with the facts in the case, and the results of treaties are consequently more likely to make for peace and a permanent solution.

Some of the principles just stated are exceptionally well illustrated in the history of the negotiations between the United States and England over the question of the Oregon boundary. The issue in that instance, first formally raised in 1815, was discussed by representatives of the two powers in the years 1818, 1824, 1826, and again in 1842, always without success beyond the bare adoption of a mode for postponing safely its final determination. This failure is not chargeable to incompetency or dereliction on the part of the negotiators on either side, but simply to the state of facts as regards the relations of the parties to each other and to the territory in question.

In 1818 the Oregon boundary question was associated with that of the boundary from the Lake of the Woods to the Rocky Mountains. The United States was especially concerned about the latter question, while Great Britain was very willing to leave the former open for subsequent discussion.[1] Each party had its views as to what would be a satisfactory boundary from the Rocky Mountains to the Pacific, and these views failed to coincide, but neither party was ready to insist on a final partition at the time, and doubtless each hoped to reap some advantage from delay. The opportune moment had not arrived. Similarly, on the later occasions, 1824, 1826, and 1842, the negotiations ostensibly begun in the expectation that the pending dispute might be terminated, were in each case hopeless from their inception because it was well understood that neither party was ready to yield anything toward closing the gap between their rival claims. Discussion, under the circumstances, was little more than a pompous mode of marking time.

George Canning, in 1824, had laid down the principles which would govern England in the case, definitely announcing that no boundary other than the Columbia River could be accepted.[2] To this policy the British govern-

[1] See report of British Negotiators, Board of Trade, October 20, 1818, to Viscount Castlereagh, in *Public Record Office, F. O. America, No. 138,* " it appeared to us impossible, at the present moment, permanently to define any boundary in that quarter [west of the Rocky Mountains]. Under these circumstances we thought it most advisable to accede to an article which will appear in the inclosed protocol in the hope that by thus leaving the country in question open to the trade of both nations for a limited period we substantially secured to Great Britain every present advantage which could have flowed from its actual possession; and the arrangement appeared also to us to remove all prospect of immediate collision without precluding any further discussion for a definitive settlement.

[2] *F. O. America, No. 191.* Canning to the British plenipotentiaries May 31, 1824. Their proposal was to extend the boundary by the forty-

ment adhered with a doggedness sufficiently characteristic, until the final stage of the negotiations of the period 1842 to 1846, when, with seeming inconsistency, they agreed to accept with slight modifications the offer our government had made as early as 1818, namely, to run the boundary along the forty-ninth parallel to the sea. The year 1846 was therefore apparently the opportune time for effecting the boundary settlement, and it would be possible to explain pretty fully, on the basis of circumstances as they operated on the one nation and on the other, why this was true. In the present paper, however, we shall content ourselves with an effort to trace with some detail the influence upon the negotiations of one noteworthy fact—the forward movement of American pioneer farmers into the Oregon territory during the period of debate over the boundary.

But a preliminary word is required upon the allied topic of the influence of the Oregon fur-trade in determining the earlier attitude of the respective claimants to the question of delimiting the territory. The region of country watered by the Columbia and its far-spreading tributaries remained during a full third of the nineteenth century a fur-traders' preserve. The magnificent enterprise of John Jacob Astor in the years 1810 to 1814, by which it was hoped to bring it definitely under American control, was brought to a disastrous ending through the stress of war, and so the British Northwest Company, from Canada, was left from the latter date in almost undisturbed possession of the trade from Alaska to California. At the periods of the earlier negotiations these British interests dominated the region.[3] Canning, in 1824, called attention to that

ninth parallel from the Rockies to the northeasternmost branch of the Columbia, thence down that river to the sea.

[3] See a forthcoming article by the writer to appear in the *American Historical Review* for January, 1911, under the title, " The British Attitude Toward the Oregon Question, 1815 to 1846."

fact as " a circumstance of no small moment." [4]   There is
evidence to show that in their original assertion of national rights over the Columbia region in 1815 to 1817,
the British government acted in response to stimuli applied
by the Northwest Company,[5] and the statement of Canning quoted above testifies to the interest the government
manifested in the fur company's occupation of the territory
as late as 1824.[6]   It was in part to guard the privilege of
that company's trade, by way of the Columbia, with the
interior, that Canning was so insistent on holding the Columbia as the boundary from the point at which the forty-
ninth parallel crosses the river to its mouth.[7]   When we
discover, as we do, that the same argument for that
boundary was reiterated at each successive negotiation, and
that even in the final treaty of June, 1846,—though the
more northerly boundary was conceded by Britain,—the
right of her subjects trading in the country to navigate the
river throughout its course was insisted on, we begin to
understand how significant to that government was the
fact that their subjects were actually in the territory, and
were making a commercial use of it.[8]

[4] Letter of May 31, 1824. *F. O. America, No. 191.*

[5] See letter of Simon M'Gillivray, a chief partner of the Northwest
Company, to Mr. Bagot, British minister at Washington, dated New
York, November 15, 1817, together with its enclosure. *F. O. America,
No. 123.* M'Gillivray affirms that it was his company that induced the
government to send a warship to the Columbia during the war in order
to oust the Astor party, the Northwest Company being prepared at that
time to engage in the trade of the Oregon country.

[6] It was now the Hudson's Bay Company in fact, although Canning in-
advertently calls them the " Associated Merchants," a name signifying the
Northwest Company.

[7] See his instructions, May 31, 1824, to the British plenipotentiaries.
F. O. America, No. 191.

[8] In 1826 the British negotiators were governed by Canning's instructions of 1824. In 1842 Lord Ashburton, on opening the negotiation at
Washington, promptly informed Mr. Webster that he " could make no arrangement in the matter which did not give us the joint use of the northern

The American government, no less than the British, was spurred to activity by the fur-trading interest. It was probably Astor's representations that put the government on its guard against the possible loss of Astoria at the peace of 1814,[9] and it was the influence of the Astor partners, in a measure at least, that incited John Floyd of Virginia to inaugurate the congressional agitation for taking possession of the Columbia and for creating in that region an Oregon Territory, an agitation which was fundamental in the history of American expansion to the Pacific.[10] And when the Astor influence subsided, there were not wanting other American trading interests to make their desires relative to Oregon known at the nation's capital.[11]

The beginnings of the pioneer movement into the Oregon country need not be discussed here, but they are well known to fall within the fourth decade of the nineteenth century. Following closely in the footsteps of the mis-

branch of the Columbia River." Ashburton to Aberdeen, April 25, 1842. *F. O. America, No. 379.* Aberdeen himself often expressed these views.

[9] See Astor to Jefferson, October 18, 1813, in *MSS. Jefferson Papers,* in Washington. Also Gallatin, *Writings,* II., p. 505. Monroe, as Secretary of State, first called official attention to Astoria in a dispatch to the American peace commissioners March 22, 1814. *Am. State Papers, F. R.,* III., p. 731.

[10] Floyd made a report to the House of Representatives, January 25, 1821, of which Professor E. G. Bourne wrote: "This pioneer report, urging the occupation of the Pacific Northwest, in its expression and embodiment of the ideas and impulses that were to shape the progress of events, bears the same relation to Oregon that Richard Hakluyt's famous *Discourse on Western Planting* bears to the foundation of the English colonies in America" (*Qtly. Ore. Hist. Soc.,* VI., p. 263). The report is reprinted in the *Quarterly,* VIII., 51 ff.

[11] See letter of Smith, Jackson, and Sublette to the secretary of war, dated at St. Louis, October 29, 1830. These men, representing the Rocky Mountain Fur Company, demanded the abrogation of the treaty of joint-occupation of 1818 respecting Oregon, and the opening of the region to the American traders. The letter is reprinted in the *Quarterly of the Oregon Historical Society,* V., pp. 395-398. See also the *Journals and Letters of Nathanael J. Wyeth,* published by the Oregon Historical Society.

sionary enterprise directed toward the Indians of the region the movement quickly assumed an independent character, and by the year 1843 had gained considerable momentum.[12] Coming thus late in the history of the negotiation, we would expect to discern its influence in a marked form only in the final stage of the controversy. Therefore, despite oft-repeated American prophecies of such an event,[13] it is not surprising to find the British government for the first time taking account of the possibility of an American pioneer occupation of the Oregon country during the negotiation of 1843. Lord Ashburton, writing from Washington to Lord Aberdeen after the opening of that negotiation, expressed his conviction that the Americans were chiefly interested in securing a good harbor on the Pacific, not in acquiring the country for purposes of settlement. "At present," said he, "they have few if any settlers there, and as they have located the great body of Indian tribes which they have forced back from the countries east of the Mississippi, on the headwaters of the Missouri towards the Rocky Mountains and the Pacific, it will not be easy for their western settlements to spread in the usual manner in that direction for many years to come."[14]

Had Lord Ashburton been aware that at the very moment of writing the above prediction, a company of more than one hundred emigrants was setting out from the Missouri frontier for Oregon, he would perhaps have modified this opinion. The Indians in fact offered no serious obstacle to the movement of Americans from the more settled districts to the western slope; and though the lands

---

[12] See Schafer, Joseph, *A History of the Pacific Northwest*, Chapters X., XI., and XII.

[13] See Floyd's report, 1821, *sup. cit.*, note 12. J. Q. Adams, instructing Richard Rush in 1823 about a proposal for an Oregon treaty with Britain, spoke of the high probability that the United States would one day plant a colony in Oregon. *Am. State Papers, F. R.,* V., p. 792.

[14] Ashburton to Aberdeen, April 25, 1842. *F. O. America, No. 379.*

they roamed over were almost inconceivably extensive, yet
a trail was soon worn across its entire breadth—spite of
the enormous physical difficulties the country presented—
over which wagons bearing pioneer families could readily
pass from the lower Missouri to the lower Columbia.[15]
The "Oregon fever," as it was called in the west, was
beginning to rage along the border,[16] and each successive
year was destined to witness an augmentation of the parties
assembling for the all-summer journey to the Pacific.

However, it is hardly to be wondered at that Ashburton was unacquainted with the conditions producing the
movement toward Oregon from the western border of the
United States.   In truth, the resident British ministers of
this period, Mr. H. S. Fox and Mr. Richard Pakenham,
who might be expected to have more complete information
than a special envoy remaining but for a few busy weeks,
never became fully aware of what the spring emigrations
to the far west really meant, and Pakenham insisted almost to the last on minimizing their importance.[17]   For-

[15] The emigration of 1842 started with wagons, which at Fort Hall
were exchanged for pack animals. But the great emigration of 1843,
nearly 1000 persons, opened a road all the way to the Columbia.

[16] A gentleman writing from Iowa Territory, March 4, 1843, says:
"Just now Oregon is the pioneer's land of promise. Hundreds are already prepared to start thither with the spring, while hundreds of others
are anxiously awaiting the action of Congress in reference to that country, as a signal for their departure. Some have already been to view the
country and have returned with a flattering tale of the inducements it
holds out. They have painted it to their neighbors in the brightest colors;
these have told it to others; the Oregon fever has broken out, and is now
raging like any other contagion." In *National Intelligencer,* April 18,
1843.

[17] Pakenham to Aberdeen, September 28, 1844. *F. O. America, .No. 408,*
suggesting a further term of joint-occupation, says: "For, let the Americans say what they like, it is impossible that emigration can take place
on a large scale from the United States to the Oregon Territory, until the
population in the Western states becomes far more densely packed than
it is at present, and in the meantime I think that our position in that part
of the world would be at least as comfortable as it is at present."

tunately for both parties, the British government was able to secure from the officers of the Hudson's Bay Company from their own military and naval officers data which enabled them to estimate the real significance of the pioneer movement as a local factor in determining the destiny of the Oregon country.

In November, 1841, Sir George Simpson, governor of the Hudson's Bay Company's territories in America, visited the Columbia and the Willamette—as well as the Puget Sound country, California, Hawaii, and Alaska—and wrote to the London office a detailed description of conditions there at that time.[18]   Simpson found in the Willamette Valley a flourishing community of French and American settlers, the latter, under the leadership of the Methodist Mission,[19] giving direction to affairs.   British subjects were as yet the more numerous party, but the American section of the community showed a " strong feeling of nationality," and they were already threatening trade rivalry and entering upon a struggle with the Company for the possession of the valuable water privilege at Willamette Falls.[20]

We do not know the precise time at which the government was put in possession of Simpson's information,[21] but Sir Robert Peel, the premier, may have been aware of the conditions he described as early as July, 1842.   At all

[18] See Letters of Sir George Simpson, *Am. Hist. Rev.*, XIV., pp. 73-79; also p. 86 ff.

[19] The Methodists established the first of the Oregon missions in the Willamette Valley in 1834, the leader being Rev. Jason Lee.   By the time of Simpson's visit these missions had developed into a virtual colony.

[20] See *Am. Hist. Rev.*, XIV., p. 80; also p. 82.

[21] His semi-official dispatch dated Woahoo, March 10, 1842, was delivered to Lord Aberdeen by Sir John H. Pelley, governor of the Hudson's Bay Company, in person prior to the 27th of August, 1842.   Doubtless the substance of Simpson's other letters was communicated orally at the same time.   See Pelley to Aberdeen, January 23, 1843.   *Am. Hist. Rev.*, XIV., p. 71.

events, Edward Everett, the American minister at London, writing to Mr. Webster on the first day of August, reported a conversation recently held with Peel in regard to the progress of the Ashburton-Webster negotiations, in the course of which Peel remarked " he was sorry to perceive that there was little prospect of agreeing as to the boundary west of the Rocky Mountains;—but that now was the time to adjust it, before the settlement of the country increased the difficulty of an arrangement." [22] We know that Simpson's letters were all fully before the cabinet by January, 1843, and that Simpson sought personal interviews with leading British statesmen at the same time.[23] It is, therefore, certain that when the British government offered to reopen the discussion of the Oregon question after the conclusion of the treaty of Washington[24] they did so with some knowledge of the local situation on the Columbia. This knowledge doubtless contributed to produce the keen appreciation which they showed of the various movements in Congress for stimulating emigration into Oregon and for erecting an American territory there.[25]

[22] No. 19. Everett to Webster, August 1, 1842. By the Britannia, August 4, 1842. Copied from *Archives of the Am. Embassy,* London, Vol. VII. This may possibly have been merely a reflection of the difficulties encountered in connection with the northeastern boundary on account of the settlement of the country by British and Americans.

[23] Letters of Sir George Simpson, *Am. Hist. Rev.,* XIV., pp. 71-73. Pelley writes Aberdeen January 23, 1843, inclosing significant extracts from all of Simpson's letters. He says Sir George is in London, and he asks that he (Pelley), accompanied by Simpson, may be granted an interview with Aberdeen.

[24] See Aberdeen to Fox, October 18, 1842, instructing him to propose to the United States to reopen the Oregon negotiation, and his letter to Fox of August 18, 1843, again instructing him to prepare to reopen the question. *Correspondence relative to the Oregon Territory* (London, 1846), pp. 3, 5.

[25] When the Linn bill for those purposes was introduced in the United States Senate, early in the year 1843, Lord Aberdeen wrote to Mr. Fox in-

In the negotiation which was opened in Washington between Mr. Calhoun, secretary of state, and Mr. Richard Pakenham—afterward Sir Richard—in August, 1844, the subject of the emigration of pioneers into Oregon was brought forward publicly by way of enforcing the American argument. Calhoun had expressed the view while a senator in Congress during the discussion of the Linn bill, January 24, 1843, that the Oregon question, if left to itself, would be settled by the process of emigration into that country. "Time," said Mr. Calhoun on that occasion, "is acting for us; and, if we shall have the wisdom to trust its operation, it will assert and maintain our right with resistless force, without costing a cent of money or a drop of blood. There is often, in the affairs of government, more efficiency and wisdom in non-action, than in action. All we want to effect our object in this case is 'a wise and masterly inactivity.' Our population is rolling towards the shores of the Pacific, with an impetus greater than what we realize. . . . It will soon—far sooner than anticipated —reach the Rocky Mountains, and be ready to pour into the Oregon Territory, when it will come into our possession without resistance, or struggle; or if there should be resistance, it would be ineffectual. We would then be as much stronger there, comparatively, than Great Britain, as she is now stronger than we are; and it would then be as idle in her to attempt to assert and maintain her ex-

structing him to protest against its enactment into law. The idea was to dissuade the president from signing it, should Congress send it up to him. Aberdeen to Fox, February 3, 1843. *F. O. America, No. 390.*

When Fox asked Webster whether Tyler could be relied upon to veto the bill, Webster replied: "What the President will do or will not do, in any given case, no one can venture to guess, for he is a man whose conduct is determined by no intelligible motive or principle."

Aberdeen wrote to Pakenham October 7, 1843, saying the Oregon question "is growing daily in importance and demands the attention of the governments of both countries." *Lord Aberdeen MSS.,* at the Red House, Ascot, in care of Lord Stanmore.

clusive claim to the territory against us, as it would now be in us to attempt it against her.[26]

These opinions of the South Carolina senator became significant when, a little more than a year later, he was appointed by Mr. Tyler secretary of state to succeed Mr. Upshur, and Mr. Pakenham was careful to make his government aware of them.[27] When the negotiation opened after many delays, the informal discussion soon developed that Mr. Calhoun was disposed to emphasize strongly the fact that population was already pushing into Oregon from the American frontier. Just before Calhoun presented his formal statement respecting the American claims, Pakenham wrote to Aberdeen: "My idea is that in the paper which he is about to produce, great stress will be laid on the fresh interest which the United States have acquired in the question by the introduction of an American population into the disputed Territory. . . . This circumstance he will, I dare say, appeal to as strengthening the American claim on the ground of contiguity.[28] The statement, when it came, did not in any way disappoint these expectations, for in it Calhoun wrote: "Our well-founded claim, grounded on contiguity, has greatly strengthened during the same period [since 1818] by the rapid advance of our population towards the territory: its great increase

[26] *Cong. Globe, 1st Sess., 27th Cong.,* XII., p. 139.

[27] See Pakenham to Aberdeen, June 27, 1844. *F. O. America, No. 406.* He incloses a copy of Calhoun's speeches, refers to that on the Linn bill, and summarizes Calhoun's argument in favor of leaving the settlement of the Oregon question "to time." Calhoun, he says, has often repeated to him (Pakenham) in conversation the same argument.

[28] No. 17. Pakenham to Aberdeen, August 29, 1844. *F. O. America, No. 407.* This letter, down to the paragraph here partly quoted, is printed in *Correspondence Relating to the Oregon Territory,* p. 11. The printed portion concludes: "It now remains to be seen what new arguments he is prepared to bring forward, either to give strength to the claim of this country, as originally presented, or to invalidate that of Great Britain."

especially in the Valley of the Mississippi, as well as the greatly increased facility of passing to the territory by more accessible routes; and the far stronger and rapidly swelling tide of population that has recently commenced flowing into it,—an emigration estimated at not less than 1,000 during the past, and 1,500 during the present year, has flowed into it. . . . There can be no doubt, now, that the operation of the same causes which impelled our population westward from the shores of the Atlantic across the Alleghany to the Valley of the Mississippi will impel them onward with accumulating force across the Rocky Mountains into the Valley of the Columbia, and that the whole region drained by it is destined to be peopled by us.[29]

We see, therefore, that at this point the pioneer movement into Oregon gave a decided turn to the negotiation, introducing what Calhoun regarded as a vital new argument for the American claim. And, while it is true that the British negotiator, as in duty bound, contested Calhoun's argument, insisting that emigration of Americans into Oregon after the adoption of the joint-occupation agreement could not affect the question of their territorial right,[30] yet emigration was precisely one of those facts which have a practical effect irrespective of laws or of treaties. On the one hand it made it impossible that any material concession as to the boundary should come from the American government, and, on the other, it would tend to convince Great Britain of the importance of a prompt settlement of the dispute.

The effect upon the American government is sufficiently revealed by the attitude of Calhoun just cited, the declaration of a similar faith by President Tyler,[31] and the threat-

---

[29] Inclosure in Pakenham's No. 17, *Correspondence Relative to Oregon Territory*, pp. 13-19, especially pages 18 and 19.

[30] No. 17. Pakenham's statement of the British case. *Ibid.*, p. 20.

[31] See his letter to Calhoun, October 7, 1845, where he says he re-

ened advance to more aggressive positions on the part of President Polk after an election which turned in some measure on the question of our title to " the whole of Oregon "—a title boisterously asserted in many western communities where the Oregon country was coming to be regarded as a " land of promise " by the pioneering class.[32] Pakenham saw very clearly that the government of the United States could never be induced to accept a boundary less favorable than the forty-ninth parallel extended westward to the Pacific, except as to the slight modification at the western end, and this view he impressed upon his government by frequent repetitions.[33]   He noted, meantime, the proposals of the American government to facilitate emigration into Oregon,[34] and finally was under the necessity of reporting that the House of Representatives had passed, by a vote of 140 to 59, the Atchison bill, " For Organizing a territorial government in the Oregon Territory, and for other purposes," which he thought had as its " undisguised object and purport—to subject the Territory in question completely and exclusively to the jurisdiction of the United States." [35]

opened the Oregon negotiation, not because he wished to do so—for he preferred to permit emigration to settle the question—but because both Great Britain and the American west insisted on it.   Correspondence of John C. Calhoun. *Am. Hist. Ass'n Rept.*, 1899, II., p. 1059.

[32] The declaration concerning "the re-occupation of Oregon" in the Democratic platform of 1844 is traceable to the resolutions of an Oregon convention held at Cincinnati in July, 1843, and attended by delegates from most of the states and territories of the Mississippi Valley. The purpose of the convention was to make the government aware of western feeling relative to Oregon. See account of the convention in the *Ohio Statesman*, the numbers for July, 1843.

[33] See his No. 99, August 29, 1844, *F. O. America, No. 407, No. 106,* and September 28, 1844, *ibid., No. 408,* in which he says, " I am afraid there is no chance whatever of inducing him [Calhoun] or any other American negotiator to accept the line of the Columbia River as a frontier." Also his No. 140 of December 29, 1844, *ibid., No. 409,* and other dispatches.

[34] See his No. 134, *F. O. America, No. 409.*

[35] See his No. 140, December 29, 1844, *ibid.,* and his dispatch of February

The relentless attitude of the western members of Congress was well known to the British cabinet early in the year 1845,[36] and produced a feeling of uneasiness which was not disguised in their intimate private communications. On the twenty-third of February, Sir Robert Peel requested Lord Aberdeen to prepare a circular memorandum on American relations, especially the Oregon question, for the benefit of the cabinet. In the course of this letter on the subject Peel said: " You [Lord A.] seem confident that we have the upper hand on the Columbia—that the settlers connected with the Hudson's Bay Company are actually stronger than the settlers, the subjects of the United States, are at present. Have you carefully ascertained this fact? If our subjects are the stronger at this present time, may not their superiority be speedily weakened or destroyed by the accession of fresh strength to the Americans? "[37] In the same letter Peel suggested the advisability of sending a frigate to the Columbia and establishing a small garrison in that region, a proceeding which looked quite as warlike as anything the Americans were proposing in Congress, but which he, of course, could justify as defensive in case the Atchison bill should become law. The immediate effect of Peel's letter to Aberdeen was to set on foot an investigation into contemporary conditions in Oregon. Aberdeen appealed to Governor Pelley of the Hudson's Bay Company, and received the latest information respecting the Oregon settlements in the form of an excerpt from Simpson's report to the Company dated from Red River in the month of June preceding. Simp-

4, 1845, *ibid., No. 424* (referring to his No. 9), in which he gives the vote on the Atchison bill and some account of the amendments to it.

[36] An outline of the Atchison bill as originally presented to the House was sent home by Pakenham, December 29, 1844. The bill as passed February 3, 1845, embodied several amendments calculated to render it less obnoxious to Great Britain.

[37] From private papers of Lord Aberdeen.

son notices the large influx of American settlers in 1843, speaks of the progress of a movement for a provisional government among them, and concludes: " American influence, I am sorry to find, predominates very much, as, out of a population of about 3,000 souls, not more than one-third are British subjects." [38]

Though the Senate did not finally accept the Atchison bill, President Polk's inaugural declaration that he regarded the American claim to the whole of Oregon as " clear and unquestionable" was assumed by the British government to justify precautionary measures. They ordered a warship to the Oregon coast " to give a feeling of security " to British subjects there—and a feeling of a different sort to the Americans [39]—and a little later arranged for a military reconnoissance of the country with a view to a possible armed conflict for its possession.[40] The British frigate *America,* anchored in De Fuca's Strait August 31, 1845. Her captain was Sir John Gordon, brother of Lord Aberdeen, and she carried as one of her younger officers Lieutenant William Peel, a son of the British premier, Sir Robert Peel. Captain Gordon detached Lieutenant Peel and Captain Parke " to examine and procure information of the present state of the New American settlement on the Willamette." While other objects were included in the captain's instructions, this quotation seems to indicate what was uppermost in his mind.[41]

[38] This correspondence, dated February 25 and February 26, 1845, is in *F. O. America, No. 439.*

[39] See Lord Aberdeen's letter to the Admiralty on March 5, 1845. *F. O. America, No. 440.*

[40] See " Documents Relative to Warrè and Vavasour's Military Reconnoissance in Oregon, 1845-6." Edited by Joseph Schafer. *Quarterly of the Oregon Historical Society,* X., pp. 1-99.

[41] See Gordon's letter to Dr. John McLoughlin, chief factor of the H. B. Co. at Vancouver, dated Port Discovery (Puget Sd.) 2d Sept., 1845,

During Captain Gordon's stay of one month in the Puget Sound country, he collected information from three different sources, in addition to his personal observations, on the state of the Oregon country and its settlements. McLoughlin wrote him a long and detailed letter. James Douglas (afterward Sir James), who was McLoughlin's principal associate in the management of the Hudson's Bay Company's business west of the Rockies, visited Gordon and had much conversation with him, while Peel and Parke inspected the Willamette settlements—as well as the Cowlitz Farms and Fort Vancouver—and presented to their captain a formal report covering their observations and conclusions.

McLoughlin's letter, written from Vancouver on the fifteenth of September,[42] testifies to the state of uneasiness created among the British subjects in Oregon by the rapid influx of American settlers and their assumption of practical political control over the country itself. He speaks of the generally peaceable character of the Americans, but mentions his difficulty with the Methodist Mission over land claims,[43] the attempt of an American named William-

a copy of which was transmitted by the Admiralty to the Foreign Office, February 10, 1846. After stating that he has sent an officer for the purpose here described, Captain Gordon says: "I therefore must beg of you in furtherance of this object that you will give him all the assistance in your power, in order that I may transmit a full report to Her Majesty's Government, who are much interested in the question of the Boundary of the North American United States, and determined to insist upon a just and equitable settlement of the Oregon Question." He has been commanded "to assure all British subjects of firm protection," and to prevent encroachment on the part of Americans.

[42] F. O. America, No. 459.

[43] A Mr. Waller, mission representative at Willamette Falls, had set up a claim adverse to McLoughlin to land, including the water-power, and McLoughlin found it necessary to buy out Waller for a substantial sum, paying him "five hundred dollars in cash, five acres of land, twelve building lots, and two lots for a church to the Methodist Mission." See on

son to oust the Hudson's Bay Company from a portion of their lands at Vancouver upon which Williamson proposed to establish his own claim, and one or two minor differences with Americans. McLoughlin also traces the history of the movement for a provisional government which began to take shape among the American settlers in 1842. He explains why the Canadians—British subjects—living in the Willamette Valley, who declined at first to join in that movement, allowed themselves finally to be won over. They felt that with the growth of population some settled form of government became imperative. Lastly, he explains and defends the action of himself and associates, the representatives of the Company, in themselves joining the provisional government as it was reorganized a few weeks before the arrival of the British ship in Oregon waters. They did it to protect the Company's large property interests in Oregon, and to contribute to the general peace and prosperity which would be jeopardized if the local division into a British and American jurisdiction should be perpetuated.[44] McLoughlin concludes the salient part of his letter with the prediction " that, unless active measures are taken by [the British] government, for the protection and encouragement of British influence— this country will pass into their [American] hands, as the overwhelming number of Americans who are from year to year coming to the country will give an American tone and character to the institutions which it will be impossible afterward to eradicate.

" We have lately received intelligence from the interior that a large party of American citizens are on the route

the origin of this claim Simpson's Letters. *Am. Hist. Rev.*, XIV., pp. 82, and note.

[44] Some of these points are more flatly stated by McLoughlin in a letter to his Company, dated August 30, 1845, and transmitted to the Foreign Office almost contemporaneously with the above letter. See *F. O. America*, *No. 459.*

to this country, having about five hundred wagons in their train, with numerous herds of cattle."

What Gordon learned in personal conferences with Douglas must have been much to the same effect, for he concluded from this and other testimony that " the Hudson's Bay Company are very anxious for a settlement of the [Oregon] question. . . ." [45]

The views of Lieutenant Peel, so far as these were written, are found in his report to Captain Gordon, made on his return to the Straits of Fuca, September 27, and in a letter addressed to Mr. Pakenham at Washington on the second of January, 1846. He was then on board ship in the Gulf of Mexico, bound for England, whither he had been dispatched by Gordon for the purpose of conveying all of the information collected in Oregon to the government with the least possible delay and in the fullest manner. He reached London probably on the ninth of February. Of course his oral report to his father, the premier, and to Lord Aberdeen, would be much more exhaustive than his written statements. [46]

Lieutenant Peel showed himself to be cognizant of all the general facts stated by McLoughlin—in addition to the detailed knowledge of local conditions which his survey of the country afforded—and of some things that Mc-

[45] *Ibid.,* Captain Gordon's letter to the Admiralty, dated, At Sea, 19th October, 1845, and transmitted to the Foreign Office February 10, 1846.

[46] Gordon detached Peel at the Sandwich Islands October 22, sending him in an American vessel for Mazatlan " with all the official reports . . . and with a full account of the actual state of the Oregon country and California." He thought it of " serious consequence " to put this information in the government's hands as soon as possible. " By sending Lieutenant Peel direct I trust they will have all possible information inside of three months, and as I directed this officer to visit the new American settlement on the Willamette, the information he would be able to give their Lordships will, I think, be of infinite service. . . ." Captain Gordon to Admiral Seymore, Honolulu, October 22, 1845. *F. O. America, No. 459.*

Loughlin does not mention. In particular, he notes in the report to Captain Gordon that the Oregon settlers, through their new government, had recently sent a memorial to Congress " shewing the dangers and difficulties to which this country is exposed, and praying the government of the United States to extend their jurisdiction over them." [47] And in his letter to Pakenham he expresses the fear that: " The American settlements on the Willamette, running *south,* and those on the Sacramento, running *north,* will . . . very soon unite. Their junction will render the possession of Port San Francisco to the Americans inevitable. . . ." [48] Gordon personally observed that "the head of Puget Sound [had been] lately taken possession of by an American party," and that the country south of the Straits of Fuca was of little value. He appeared to be perfectly reconciled to the idea of settling the boundary at the forty-ninth parallel, but insisted, as did Peel also, that the Straits of Fuca must be left open to the British in common with the Americans, a qualification which would be not at all unfamiliar to Lord Aberdeen. [49]

We thus see that in the year 1845 the British government caused to be made a virtual survey of conditions in Oregon, with special reference to the strength of the American pioneer element which had found lodgment in

[47] *Ibid.* Captain Gordon was anxious that Peel might reach London with his report before this Memorial could be received at Washington. See his letter to Admiral Seymore.

[48] Letter dated from " The Steamship *Trent,* January 2, 1846, between Vera Cruz and the Havana." *F. O. America, No. 459.*

[49] *Ibid.* Gordon's letter to the Admiralty, dated October 19, 1845. See also Lieutenant Peel's letter to Pakenham. Sir George Simpson had insisted on this point as early as March, 1845. See his " Memorandum," printed in *Quarterly of the Oregon Historical Society,* X., p. 13 ff; and Lord Aberdeen himself stated it, probably as a result of Everett's suggestion, in a private letter to Pakenham, dated March 4, 1844. Everett suggested to Aberdeen such a modification of the forty-ninth parallel boundary as early as November 29, 1843. See his dispatch No. 69 of December 2, 1843.

the country.   And the result was overwhelmingly to prove
that all of Oregon south of the Columbia was already fully
occupied by the Americans, who had organized a government which was rapidly effacing local opposition from
British subjects; that Americans were beginning to settle
north of the Columbia as high up as Puget's Sound; and
that the annual immigrations from the Missouri were increasing at a rapid rate, presaging a more complete and
more obstinate adverse possession of the territory in dispute.

These facts, brought fully to the attention of the government early in February, 1846, by the return of Lieutenant Peel as the bearer of dispatches from the Pacific, constituted a new background on which to project the Oregon
question.   What effect it may have produced in detail,
upon the later course of the negotiations, we cannot in the
nature of the case determine,[50] nor is it necessary to do so
in order to warrant the conviction that we have in the
pioneer movement one of the prime conditions affecting
this boundary dispute.   The private remarks of Sir Robert Peel, quoted above,[51] are a sufficient indication of the
significance ascribed to the movement by the British cabinet, while Captain Gordon's report discloses the effect already produced upon the Hudson's Bay Company, repre-

[50] We know that, while Lord Aberdeen as Secretary of State for Foreign Affairs was personally ready at a much earlier time to accept the
boundary of the forty-ninth parallel, with modifications, yet there seem to
have been serious obstacles in the way of the British government proposing
or even acceding to such a compromise. They persistently suggested
arbitration by some friendly power. Their last proposal of that sort
was formally rejected by the United States February 4, 1846, news of
the rejection being received at the Foreign Office, March 3. Thereafter,
as soon as conditions at Washington appeared favorable, Aberdeen himself
proposed the settlement on the forty-ninth parallel, which was accepted.
See on these topics, the author's paper on " The British Attitude Toward
the Oregon Question." *Am. Hist. Rev., sup. cit.*

[51] Page 43.

senting the chief British interest in the country itself. The detailed knowledge of conditions in Oregon interpreted to the British, as nothing else could, the attitude of the American people on this question—the government's adamantine stand against concession,[52] the impatience, not to say insolence, of Congress, and the widespread disposition through the country, and especially in the west, to force the issue even at the hazard of war. Had it been possible for the British government to remain ignorant of the conditions generating this peculiar national psychology, it is conceivable they might have chosen war instead of concession, but these conditions fixed the " irreducible minimum " they would have to yield in order to secure a peaceful settlement. In other words, it was the Oregon pioneer who, fulfilling by his arduous trail-making across the continent in the forties earlier prophesies of American expansion to the Pacific, vindicated his government's pretensions to the forty-ninth parallel boundary on the ground of contiguity, and actually prepared the triumph technically won by American diplomacy.

JOSEPH SCHAFER.

[52] Except on minor points, particularly in running the line around Vancouver's Island instead of across it.

SOME PROBLEMS OF THE NORTHWEST
IN 1779

THE occupation of the northwest by George Rogers Clark and his band of frontiersmen established a claim for the United States to the transmontane territory which the later negotiations of Franklin, Adams, and Jay made effective; but the brilliant diplomacy of these agents might have proved fruitless had the Virginia troops failed in maintaining their position on the distant frontier. Throughout the year following that of the occupation this appeared to the leaders an almost hopeless task on account of the many difficulties confronting them. The soldiers who had followed Clark so gallantly into the wilderness were, like all frontier militia, satisfied with the accomplishment of their immediate task, and now demanded the right of returning to their homes. The pleadings of their leader persuaded only about eighty to remain to secure the results of their enterprise. Colonel Clark was obliged to replace this loss by enlisting the volatile and, in his opinion, untrustworthy French of the villages into the companies of the Illinois battalion. With this small and untried band he prepared to hold the whole territory of the northwest against the forces which the British could muster from Canada.

It had not been expected that the Virginians would thus be isolated, for the Continental Congress had planned to capture Detroit by a force sent out from Fort Pitt. Unfortunately, the successful peace with the Indians as a preliminary to this expedition was followed by the futile acts of General McIntosh, the leader of this expedition, who proved himself unfitted to cope with the conditions of frontier warfare. This failure and the critical situation in the east caused General Washington to abandon, temporarily, active operations in the west on the part of the United States. Thus the British officers of Canada were left a clear field to send their war bands to harry the whole border at will, and also to give their undivided attention to the reconquest of the Illinois country.

Clark, who had throughout the fall of 1778 impatiently awaited the news of the capture of Detroit by the Americans, first heard of General McIntosh's abandonment of that undertaking in December; and almost at the same time he learned that the British had begun the first movement to reconquer the northwest by sending a force of six hundred regulars, French militia, and Indians, under Lieutenant-Governor Hamilton of Detroit, in his direction. By January 29, 1779, the floating rumors of the capture of Vincennes by Hamilton, which had reached Clark, were confirmed by Francis Vigo, a Spanish trader, who had recently come from that post.

It is probable that Clark, when he set out, February 5, on the desperate undertaking to risk all in a single battle for the recapture of Vincennes, contemplated, in the event of a victory, the capture of Detroit.[1] His authority for such an undertaking was complete, for, by the order of Governor Henry of Virginia, the area of his activities had been extended beyond that defined in his original instructions, so as to include the " Enemy's Settlements above or across," as he might think proper.[2] He knew that with Detroit in his possession, the whole northwest would be under his control. He was informed that the British gar-

<hr/>

[1] Clark letter to Mason, November 19, 1779. Printed in English, W. H., *Conquest of the Country Northwest of the River Ohio*, Vol. I., p. 428.

[2] *Draper MSS., 48 J 7.* Patrick Henry to Clark, January 15, 1778.

rison at that post, few in numbers, without adequate stores, and subject to still greater distresses with the cutting off of the supplies from the Illinois country, might be overcome with ease.[3]   This desperate situation was expressed in a communication from Colonel Bolton to General Haldimand at Niagara as follows:

" Captain Lernoult acquaints me that Detroit is capable in peaceable times to supply the garrison with provisions but at this time the inhabitants are so much employed in Convoys and probably will continue so that they have not been able to thrash last years corn, and the great number of cattle furnished for Gov. Hamilton's Expedition as well as for Detroit with what have been consumed by Indians have reduced the numbers so much that a pair of oxen cannot be purchased for less than 1000 Livres and then reckoned a cheap bargain, Flour is 60 Livres a hundred and every article very dear."

Moreover, Clark had won the friendship of the French by his liberal government.   " I made it a point," he wrote, " to guard the happiness and tranquility of the inhabitants, supposing that their happy change, reaching the ears of their Brothers and Countrymen on the Lakes and about Detroit, would be paving my way to that place and a good effect on the Indians.   I soon found that it had the desired effect for the greatest part of the French Gent. and Traders among the Indians declared for us many letters of congratulations were sent from Detroit to the Gent. of the Illinois, which gave me much pleasure."[4]   The news of the French alliance was skillfully used to still further excite their enthusiasm for the American cause. With like purpose, the report was circulated that the Canadian French had been invited by Count D'Estaing to take up arms in behalf of the Americans, that he had promised them his support, and that Spain was about to de-

[3] *Draper MSS., 14 S 128.* Patrick Henry to the Virginia delegates in Congress, November 16, 1778.
[4] *Clark-Mason Letter* in English, *sup. cit.*

clare hostilities against Great Britain.[5]   Oliver Pollock,
agent for Virginia in New Orleans, had already contributed largely to Clark's success through the secret aid
granted him by the Spanish governor, Galvez.   The Spanish lieutenant-governor at St. Louis likewise favored the
Americans and proposed to send Spanish troops to the assistance of the Americans in the event of an attack upon
them.[6]   The Sauk, Fox, Miami, and other tribes of Indians, terrorized at the name of Clark, had bound themselves by treaties and promises to maintain peaceable relations in the future.

On February 25, 1779, Clark concluded his bold march
from the distant Illinois country by the recapture of Vincennes together with Colonel Hamilton and his mixed
troop of British, French, and Indians.   It is with that
event that this study begins.   Interesting as it would be
to recount the details of that military venture, they would
contribute no essential to the effort to trace Clark and his
associates as they faced the problems which arose after
this striking achievement.

The first great undertaking was to be the expedition
against Detroit, " in the execution of which," as Clark
later expressed it, " my very soul was wrapt."[7]   Despite
the seeming certainty of success, Clark did not neglect the
practical means for stimulating the cupidity of his followers and their desire for the new venture.   The goods
brought from Detroit by Hamilton, likewise those seized
from British traders, were divided among Clark's soldiers.
They were thereby aroused to the undertaking of some
new expedition, and their thoughts turned towards Detroit.

Enthusiasm for the enterprise on the part of the people

---

[5] *Draper MSS., 48 J 49.*   Patrick Henry to Clark, December 15, 1778.
[6] *Draper MSS., 14 S 62.*   Clark to Governor Henry, September 16, 1778.
[7] Clark to Jefferson, October 1, 1781.   Draper, *Trip 1860*, VI., p. 73.

of Vincennes was enhanced on the return of Captain Helm with the spoils of his expedition. February 26, accompanied by fifty men, the majority of them French militiamen,[8] Helm had ascended the Wabash to intercept a party of British sent by Hamilton to bring on the stores left at Ouiattanon, one hundred and twenty miles up the Wabash. Besides making prisoners of forty men, Captain Helm had captured seven boats loaded with provisions and Indian goods, amounting to fifty thousand dollars. These spoils were divided among his followers.

With almost as many prisoners as there were men to guard them, Clark sent off Hamilton, seven of his principal officers, and eighteen other prisoners, to the Falls of the Ohio under guard of Captain Williams, Lieutenant Rogers, and twenty-five men. From thence they were to be taken to Williamsburg. Again he showed excellent judgment in his treatment of the French volunteers who had accompanied the British troops. Instead of sending them to Virginia, as they had been led to expect, there to be held during the course of the war, they were discharged on taking the oath of neutrality.[9] A few of them joined Clark's forces. Those returning to Detroit were provided with boats, arms, and provisions. The boats were to be sold upon arrival at their destination, and the money therefrom was to be divided. This act, well calculated to promote Clark's interests among the French at Detroit, was successful.[10] " I after this," wrote Clark, " had spies, disguised as traders, constant to and from Detroit I learned they answered every purpose that I could have wished for, by prejudicing their friends in favor of America." That the Americans would triumph, was a wish openly expressed,

[8] *Bowman's Journal*, Library of Congress, " Letters to Washington, 1779." Fol. 91-102.
[9] *Ill. Hist. Coll's*, I., p. 436.
[10] *Clark-Mason Letter* in English, *sup. cit.*

and children in the streets with cups of water were wont to drink success to Clark.[11]   Clark fully counted on the capture of Detroit.   He assured the paroled prisoners that he would be there nearly as soon as they, and sent by them a copy of the alliance between France and the United States.[12]   " I learned by your letter to Governor Hamilton," he wrote Captain Lernoult, who was in charge at that post, " that you were very busy making new works; I am glad to hear it; as it saves the Americans some expenses in building." [13]

General gloom pervaded the garrisons at Detroit and Michilmackinac when it was learned that Hamilton had been captured, and that two subordinate expeditions of Langlade and Gautier had likewise failed.   Langlade, who had advanced as far as " Milwakee " on his way to assist Hamilton in an attack on the Illinois posts, was forced to return to Mackinac when his Indian followers refused to proceed further.[14]   Gautier, also under orders from Hamilton to join him early in the spring, advanced with 200 Indians over the Fox-Wisconsin course down the Mississippi as far as the mouth of the Rock River.   Learning of Hamilton's capture, he had no alternative but to make his way back to Green Bay.[15]

In anticipation of an attacking party of Americans expected from Pittsburgh the British ordered a new fort built at Detroit, and carpenters were sent to repair the vessels.[16]   Urgent request was made that large re-enforce-

[11] *Draper MSS., 49 J 47.*

[12] *Bowman's Journal,* Library of Congress, "Letters to Washington, 1779." Fol. 91-102.

[13] *Mich. Pioneer and Hist. Coll's,* X., p. 308. For the letter and General Haldimand's comments on its impertinence, see *Draper MSS., 58 J 37, 38.*

[14] *Mich. Pioneer and Hist. Coll's,* IX., pp. 380, 381. He found the Indians about "Milwakee" loyal to the Americans. By July, 1779, most of the Indians of southern Wisconsin favored the Americans.

[15] *Wis. Hist. Coll's,* XI., pp. 126, 127.

[16] *Draper MSS., 49 J 20, 25.*

ments should be sent from Niagara for the completion of the fort and for protection against Clark, who was daily expected.[17] Presuming on the weakness of the garrison, the French refused to assist in the project. Spades, shovels, and other tools necessary for carrying on the work were lacking. Provisions were scarce, owing to the large quantities consumed on the expedition to Vincennes. The Indians tributary to Detroit were panic-stricken, and demanded that detachments of troops with cannon should be sent to them at once as they were not able to contend, unaided, with the enemy. " So situated," wrote General Haldimand, " it will require great judgment and temper to preserve the Indians in our interest after so glaring and recent a proof of our want of strength or want of conduct. If we lose the Indians a valuable fur-trade will be lost to Great Britain." [18]

British commanding officers in the northwest were disheartened. Even before the capture of Hamilton, the fears of the officials at Detroit were so much excited that they demanded his return.[19] " The loss of Governor Hamilton is a most feeling one to me," said Captain Lernoult in a dispatch from Detroit, " I find the burthen heavy without assistance. It requires, I confess, superior abilities, and [a] better constitution. I beg leave to repeat to you the necessity of a re-enforcement being sent as the consequences may be fatal." [20] His position was made still more trying through the burning of the *Angelica,* a boat being sent from Niagara with supplies for his relief.[21]

[17] *Draper MSS., 58 J 9.*

[18] General Haldimand to Lord George Germaine. *Ill. Hist. Coll's,* I., p. 445.

[19] Letters captured on the expedition of Lieutenant Helm, February 6.

[20] *Draper MSS., 58 J 9-12.* R. L. Lernoult to Lieutenant Bolton, March 26, 1779.

[21] *Draper MSS., 49 J 42.*

DePeyster was convinced that Mackinac, defended, as
it was, by an inadequate garrison poorly provisioned,
would be doomed the moment Detroit surrendered, although a single man should not be sent against it.[22] Mysti-
fied by the report, purposely sent out by Clark, that he
contemplated an advance on the post at Mackinac also,
effort was made to render it defensible.[23]

Clark was fully aware of the effects of his victory.
"This stroke," he said, "will nearly put an end to the
Indian war. Had I but men enough to take advantage
of the present confusion of the Indian nations, I could
silence the whole in two months."[24] "Never was a person more mortified than I was at this time," he wrote a
few months later, "to see so fair an opportunity to push a
victory; Detroit lost for want of a few men."[25] Clark's
regrets over his want of men are explained by the fact that
when the excitement incident to the capture of the fort at
Vincennes was over, many of his men succumbed to the
efforts of the campaign. Sickness among them increased,
and their recovery was retarded owing to the unusually
stormy days at the beginning of March.

Despite these conditions, Clark did not at this time
doubt the ultimate success of his plans to take Detroit,
for in addition to his own men and the French militia, he

[22] DePeyster to Haldimand, May 13, 1779. *Mich. Pioneer and Hist.
Coll's*, IX., pp. 380, 387.

[23] *Ill. Hist. Coll's*, I., p. 436. DePeyster to Haldimand, May 13, 1779.
"The Canadians who want to return to this post have leave on taking
the oaths not to serve against the United States. Clarke assures them that
he will be here nearly as soon as themselves. I don't care how soon Mr.
Clarke appears, provided he comes by Lake Michigan and the Indians
prove stanch and above all that the Canadians do not follow the example
of their brethren at the Illinois, who have joined the Rebels to a man."

[24] *Draper MSS., 58 J 4.* Clark to Colonel Harrison, speaker of the Virginia House of Delegates, March 10, 1779. This letter was captured by
a party of Hurons and carried to Detroit.

[25] Letter to Mason, November 19, 1779.

counted on from two to three hundred men from Kentucky. He was further encouraged by a messenger from Williamsburg, who arrived at Vincennes three days after the capitulation of that post with the good news that five hundred men were to be sent at once from Virginia.[26] To avail himself of these re-enforcements and collect the necessary supplies, the forward movement was deferred until June.

Meanwhile he took up the problems of the territory already secured. The Indians first claimed his attention. No man better understood how to win savage favor. He awaited the coming of the chiefs, although he had not invited them to treat with him. In attendance upon their councils, he gave due regard to Indian ceremony, strengthened the chain of friendship by smoking the sacred pipe and exchanging belts, and when treaties were renewed, provided tafia and the provisions with which the Indians were wont to make merry at such times.[27]

In dealing with the Indians who had refused the advances of the British he " extolled them to the skies for their manly behavior and fidelity." He very cleverly disabused them of the thought which had been implanted by Hamilton, that in the event of a victory by the Virginians the lands of friends and foes alike would be taken. " I made a very long speech to them in the Indian manner," said Clark, " told them that we were so far from having any design on their Lands, that I looked upon it that we were on their land where the Fort stood that we claimed no land in their Country; that the first man that offered to take their Lands by violence must strike the tomahawk in my head; that it was only necessary that I should be in their Country during the war and keep a Fort in it to drive off the English, who had design[s] against all peo-

[26] Dispatch from Governor Henry in *Draper MSS., 58 J 4.*
[27] *Clark-Mason Letter.*

ple; after that I might go to some place where I could get Land to support me." [28]

In conference with the Chippewa and other Indians who had accompanied Hamilton and came to sue for mercy, Clark was the complete master, for, he said, "Nothing destroys our interest among the Savages so soon as wavering sentiments or speeches that show the least fear. I consequently had observed one steady line of conduct among them. Mr. Hamilton, who was almost deified among them, being captured by me, was sufficient confirmation to the Indians of everything I had formerly said to them, and gave the greatest weight to the speeches I intended to send them; expecting that I should shortly be able to fulfil my threats with a body of troops sufficient to penetrate into any part of their Country; and by Reducing Detroit bring them to my feet.[29]

The messages sent the Indians tributary to Detroit were well calculated to neutralize any effort which might be made on the part of the English to stir them up for new expeditions. Whether they chose the peace-belt or the war-belt, they were told, was of little consequence for the Big Knives' greatest glory was in war, and they were in search of enemies since the English were no longer able to contend against them. Those nations which did not lay down their arms at once were threatened with extermination.[30]

Preparatory to his return to Kaskaskia with the remaining prisoners, Clark carefully arranged for a satisfactory government at Vincennes by appointing the faithful Cap-

[28] *Clark-Mason Letter.* The Indians presented Clark with a body of land two and one-half leagues square (July 16, 1779). The preceding June 9, private land grants were declared null and void by the Virginia House of Delegates. *Va. State Papers,* I., p. 320.

[29] *Clark-Mason Letter.*

[30] *Clark-Mason Letter.* Clark was thus able to secure the neutrality of between three and four thousand warriors.

tain Helm to take control of all civil matters and act as
superintendent of Indian affairs.   Moses Henry was made
Indian agent.   The garrison of forty picked men was left
in command of Lieutenant Richard Brashears, assisted by
Lieutenants Bailey and Chaplin.   Letters were sent John
Bowman, then county lieutenant in Kentucky, urging him
to begin collecting men and provisions for the proposed
march on Detroit.

No victorious army ever returned with spirits more
elated than the eighty men who, on March 20, accompanied
Clark on the trail back to Kaskaskia.   Within a year the
authority of Virginia over the region stretching from the
Ohio to the Illinois and 140 miles up the Wabash had
been established by conquest.   The danger that the
frontier settlements would be cut off by savages under the
leadership of British agents was greatly lessened.   These
results had been accomplished against odds that would
have completely overcome men not already inured to the
harsh conditions incident to life on the frontier.   No assistance had been rendered by the Virginia authorities, and
for nearly a year Clark had not even received, as he expressed it, " a scrape of a pen " from Governor Henry.[31]
The six boats pushed off down the Wabash amidst the re-
joicing of the people who had assembled to wish them a
" good and safe passage."   A few of those who lingered
to watch the boats until they were lost to view fully com-
prehended the results which had been attained.   Their
thought was expressed by one of their number as follows:

" Although a handful in comparison to other armies, they have
done themselves and the cause they were fighting for, credit and
honor, and deserve a place in History for future ages; that their
posterity may know the difficulty their forefathers had gone
through for their liberty and freedom.   Particularly the back

[31] Letter of Clark to Patrick Henry, April 29, 1779.

settlers of Virginia may bless the day they sent out such a Commander, and officers, men etc., etc., I say, to root out that nest of
Vipers, that was every day ravaging on their women and children;
which I hope will soon be at an end, as the leaders of these
murderers are taken and sent to Congress." [32]

When the boats reached Kaskaskia, " Great Joy " was
manifested by the garrison, then commanded by Captain
Robert George, who had recently returned with sixty men
from New Orleans.[33]   The villagers, too, were not less
gratified at the return of Clark, for he was the one American who had gained and continued to hold their love and
confidence.

The problems and disappointments Clark was forced
to meet with during the succeeding three months were
among the most trying of his whole career.   Upon arrival
he found the people excited over the recent conduct of a
party of Delaware warriors.   Learning also of depredations committed at Vincennes by another party, Clark, by
way of warning to the other tribes, ordered a ruthless
war against the marauders.   In the attacks on their villages which followed, no mercy was shown except to the
women and children.   The Indians soon sued for peace.

Without money for the support of his army Clark had
begun after the capture of Kaskaskia to issue bills of credit
on Virginia in exchange for provisions.   These were satisfactory to the merchants and traders, for they were received and paid at their face value in silver by Oliver Pollock, agent for the state at New Orleans.[34]   In a letter
of July 18, Clark said to Pollock: " I have succeeded
agreeable to my wishes, and am necessitated to draw bills

[32] *Bowman's Journal.*
[33] *Draper MSS., 48 J 33.*
[34] The first money Clark received from Virginia was in January, 1778,
when £1200 in state currency was sent to him. Clark, *Accounts Against
Virginia.*

on the state and have reason to believe they will be accepted by you, the answering of which will be acknowledged by his Excelly. the Governor of Virginia." Large batteaux rowed with twenty-four oars, loaded with goods sent by Pollock, under the protection of the Spanish flag, slipped past Natchez, then under the control of the British, and in from eighty-five to ninety days arrived at St. Louis or the Illinois posts. Full credit was given by Clark to Pollock for this assistance, by which he was able to hold the Illinois country. " The invoice Mr. Pollock rendered upon all occasions in paying those bills," Clark declared, " I considered at the time and now to be one of the happy circumstances that enabled me to Keep Possession of that Country." [35] During September, 1778, goods were sent by Pollock to Clark, amounting to seven thousand two hundred dollars. The following January five hundred pounds of powder and some swivels were received by Clark from the same source. By February 5, 1779, bills were drawn on Pollock by Clark amounting to forty-eight thousand dollars. Of this amount, ten thousand dollars were paid by Pollock after he had disposed of his own remaining slaves at a great disadvantage.[36]

By July, 1779, however, Pollock had so far exhausted his credit that in meeting an order from Governor Henry for goods amounting to ten thousand dollars, he was forced to mortgage a part of his lands. He had at that time paid bills drawn on the state amounting to thirty-three thousand dollars. The flour and meal which had been promised him had not been forwarded. " Being already drained of every shilling I could raise for the use of yours and the rest of the United States," he wrote, " I

[35] Certificate signed by Clark, July 2, 1785. Copy in *Calendar of Oliver Pollock Letters and Papers* in the Department of State, Bureau of Indexes and Archives, CXV., Miscellaneous Letters, January-April, 1791.
[36] *Papers of the Continental Congress, Pollock Papers*, L., I., pp. 1-14.

went first to the Governor of this place, and then to every merchant in it, but could not prevail upon any of them to supply said goods, giving for their reason the few goods they had were imported, would in all probability become double the value of what they were just now, particularly at this juncture, as war between Spain and Great Britain was daily expected, and the little probability there was of getting paid from your quarter in any reasonable time, by depending only on the Letter of Credit and Mr. Lindsay's contract. In fine finding it impracticable to obtain any by that means, and at same time being fearful of the bad consequences that might attend your being disappointed in those goods, I have voluntarily by mortgaging part of my property for the payment at the latter end of this year, purchased the greater part of them from a Mr. Salomon; you have therefore invoice and bill of loading amounting to 10,029 dollars 1 Rial." [37]

Twenty-five thousand dollars' worth of the bills drawn by Clark were under protest at New Orleans. [38] They were issued in favor of a number of the inhabitants of Illinois. These drafts had been received by the French merchants and traders in preference to the Continental money, which had recently appeared in the west in small quantities. [39]

While borrowing money on his own credit, Pollock, in order to encourage the shipment of arms, Indian goods, rum, sugar, etc., to the Illinois country, and in order to encourage down cargoes, in exchange, made up of deerskins, beaver, otter, and flour while at the same time keeping up the credit of the continental currency, continued until July, 1779, to pay " Bateauxmen and Traders

[37] *Draper MSS., 49 J 60.* Pollock to Henry, July 17, 1779.

[38] Fully one-half of these represented the expense incident to the fitting out of the expedition against St. Vincents. Clark's *Accounts Against Virginia.*

[39] Clark to Pollock, June 12, 1779. Copy in Virginia State Library, *Clark Papers,* bundle I.

silver dollars for Paper Currency Dollar for Dollar." [40]

Continental currency had been used but little in the west previous to the expedition against Vincennes. The confidence of the people in the government, together with the efforts of Pollock, sustained this money at par when it had so far depreciated in the east as to be worth only twelve cents on the dollar.[41] Traders from the east became aware of this situation, and rushed to this region, where goods might be procured with the "continentals" at their face value. They brought with them such large sums and distributed the money so liberally in trade that the inhabitants became alarmed and refused to receive it.

On returning to Kaskaskia, Clark was not surprised to learn that his credit at New Orleans was exhausted. "I am sorry to learn," he wrote Pollock, "you have not been supplied with funds as expected your protesting my late bills has not surprised me. As I expected it being surrounded by enemies Mr. Hamilton and his savages being obligated for my own safety to lay in Considerable Stores I was obliged to take every step I possibly could to procure them unwilling to use force." He was confronted also with the problems growing out of a depreciated money, of which he says in writing Governor Henry:

"There is one circumstance very distressing, that of our own moneys being discredited, to all intents and purposes, by the great numbers of traders who come here in my absence, each outbidding the other, giving prices unknown in this country by five hundred per cent., by which the people conceived it to be of no value, and both French and Spaniards refused to take a farthing of it." [42]

[40] *Papers of the Continental Congress, Letters and Papers of Oliver Pollock,* Vol. L., I., pp. 1-44.

[41] *Orderly Book of William Shannon,* February 10, 1783. Virginia State Library.

[42] Letter of Clark to Henry, April 29, 1779.

To the great joy of Clark he was informed that his friend, John Todd, had been appointed by Governor Henry to take charge of civil affairs in the Illinois country. His undivided attention might thus be given to "military reflections." [43]   December 9, 1778, a bill passed the Virginia legislature establishing the County of Illinois, which was to include the inhabitants of Virginia north of the Ohio River.[44]   This type of government had been brought into general usage by Virginia in her western expansion.[45] The act providing for the County of Illinois was to remain in force for a year, and "thence to the end of the next session of the Assembly, and no longer." [46]   The establishment of some temporary form of government was thought to be expedient, for, as stated in the act, "from their remote situation, it may at this time be difficult if not impracticable to govern them by the present laws of this commonwealth, until proper information, by intercourse with their fellow citizens, on the east side of the Ohio, shall have familiarized them to the same." The chief executive officer was the county lieutenant or commander-in-chief, who was appointed by the governor and council.   He was to appoint at his discretion, deputy commandants, militia officers, and commissaries.   The civil officers, with whom the inhabitants were familiar, and whose duties were to administer the laws already in force, were to be chosen by the citizens of the different districts. Officers with new duties were to be maintained by the state.   Pardoning power was vested in the county lieutenant in all criminal cases, murder and treason excepted.   In these cases he was empowered to stay execution until such time as the will of the governor, or, in case of treason, of

[43] *Clark-Mason Letter.*   English, *sup. cit.,* I., p. 411 ff.

[44] Hening, *Statutes,* IX., p. 553.   See discussion in *Ill. Hist. Collections,* II., pp. l., 11.

[45] *Filson Club Publications,* VI., p. 43.

[46] Act of Incorporation, in Hening, *Statutes,* IX., p. 552.

the assembly, should be ascertained.[47]   Provision was made
for the protection of the inhabitants in all their religious,
civil, and property rights.

The instructions issued by Governor Henry and the
council, December 12, 1778, to Todd and to Clark, who
was to retain the command of all Virginia troops in the
County of Illinois, showed a grasp of the situation. They
were to co-operate in using their best efforts to cultivate
and conciliate the affections of the French and Indians.
The rights of the inhabitants were to be secured against
any infractions by the troops, and any person attempting
to violate the property of the Indians, especially in their
lands, was to be punished. All Indian raids on Kentucky
were to be prevented. The friendship of the Spaniards
was to be maintained. As head of the civil department,
Todd was to have command of the militia, " who are not
to be under the command of the military until ordered out
by the civil authority and act in conjunction with them." [48]
He was directed on " all Accations (sic) to inculcate on
the people the value of liberty and the Difference between
the State of free Citizens of the Commonwealth and that
Slavery to which Illinois was destined. A free and equal
representation may be expected by them in a little Time,
together with all the improvements in Jurisprudence and
police which the other parties of the State enjoy."

Todd reached Kaskaskia early in May, 1779. His
coming was hailed with joy by the inhabitants who, having
experienced some of the harshness incident to military
control, were enthusiastic for a change, no matter what
the new form of government might be. The county lieutenant was well fitted to fill his office acceptably. Besides receiving a good general education, he had studied
and practised law for a time. Unable to resist the call

[47] Hening, *Statutes,* IX., pp. 117, 552-5; V., pp. 489, 491.
[48] *Ill. Hist. Collections,* V., p. 60.

of the frontier, he enlisted for service in Dunmore's War, and in 1775, when but twenty-five years of age, Todd went to Kentucky, where he was selected as one of the representatives to form a constitutional government for the settlement of Transylvania. In 1777 he was elected delegate to the Virginia House of Burgesses from the County of Kentucky.[49] The intimate friendship existing between Todd and Clark, and their known ability and bravery, promised a successful solution of the problems with which they were confronted.

May 12 was a notable day among the villagers of Kaskaskia, for on that day they assembled at the door of their church upon the call of Clark to hear the proclamation of the new government, and participate in the election of judges. The address prepared by Clark, who acted as presiding officer of the meeting, was well suited to the occasion.[50] " From your first declaration of attachment for the American cause," he said, " until the glorious capture of post St. Vincent, I had doubted your sincerity, but in that critical time, I proved your faithfulness, I was so touched with the zeal that you have shown that my desire is to make you happy and to prove to you the sincere affection I have for the welfare and advancement of this colony in general, and of each individual in particular. The young men of this colony have returned from Post St. Vincent covered with laurels, which I hope they will continue to wear. Although there are a few who did not have anything to do with this glorious action, I do not esteem them less, hoping they will take revenge if the occasion presents itself, who, during my absence, have with great care done their duty as guardians of this fort." He promised, as soon as it was within his power, that they

[49] *Filson Club Publications,* VI., p. 43.

[50] Translated and read by Jean Girault, who was Clark's interpreter. It is printed in *Ill. Hist. Collections.,* V., p. 80.

should become partakers in the liberty enjoyed by Americans, and that a regiment of regular troops was to be sent for their protection.   They were assured that the new government was one of such " kindliness " that they would bless the day they had chosen to favor the American cause. In presenting Colonel Todd he referred to him as his good friend, and the only person in the state whom he desired to have take charge of that post.   He spoke of the great importance of their meeting for the purpose of selecting the most capable and enlightened persons, to judge their differences, and urged that only those most worthy of the offices should be chosen.

The brief response made by Todd was likewise full of promise for the success of the new government, which was to serve as guardian of their rights as citizens of a free and independent state.   Elections of judges for the district courts at Cahokia and Vincennes took place shortly afterwards, and resulted, as at Kaskaskia, in the selection of Frenchmen.[51]   On May 21, 1779, the commission for the court at Kaskaskia was issued by Todd.   He had previously appointed a sheriff and state's attorney.   The court named its own clerk.

One week earlier (May 14) military commissions were made out.   A number of the men given officer's commissions had been elected judges, and were thus expected to assume the duties of both offices.[52]

Within a few days, Todd was called on to hear a recital of the grievances of the French inhabitants which had been formulated by the Kaskaskia justices.   He was informed that a number of the oxen, cows, and other animals belonging to the petitioners had been taken and killed

[51] The court of Kaskaskia consisted of nine members; Cahokia, seven, and Vincennes, nine. *Ill. Hist. Collections,* II., p. 56; V., p. 85 *et. seq.*

[52] Five of the judges at Cahokia were also given military commissions. Mason, *Chapters from Illinois History,* p. 260.

by the soldiers; that liquor was being sold to Indians, and trade carried on with slaves without the consent of their masters. Both kinds of traffic, they complained, were contrary to French custom.[53]

Licenses for carrying on trade were issued by Todd. Fearful lest there would be a repetition of the abuses under the Virginia land law, as practised in Kentucky, and that adventurers and speculators would get possession of the rich bottom lands, he decreed that no new settlements should be made on the flat lands " unless in manner and form as heretofore made by the French inhabitants." [54]

No problem proved more trying for Todd and Clark than the effects produced by depreciated currency. Complications were greater on account of counterfeit money. By the close of April, the price of provisions was three times what it had been two months previously, and Clark was enabled to support his soldiers only by the assistance of a number of the merchants.[55] While in Kentucky Todd learned that the issues of currency bearing the dates April 20, 1777, and April 11, 1778, had been ordered to be paid into the Continental loan offices by the first of June, 1779, otherwise they would then become worthless. He hoped that the time would be extended for the Illinois holders. Upon his arrival at Kaskaskia, Todd found that the paper money had depreciated, so that it was worth only one-fifth of its face value in specie.[56] On June 11 he addressed the court in the following letter, the evident purpose of which was his desire to sustain public credit:

" The only method that America has to support the present war is by her credit. That credit at present is her bills emitted

[53] *Ill. Hist. Collections*, II., *Virginia ser.*, I., LXVII., LXVIII., V., p. 88.
[54] *Chicago Hist. Society Collections*, IV., p. 301.
[55] Clark's letter to Patrick Henry, April 29, 1779.
[56] From five to six. *Journal of Virginia House of Delegates*, May, 1783, p. 134.

from the different Treasuries by which she engages to pay the Bearer at a certain time gold and silver in Exchange. There is no friend to American Independence who has any judgment but soon expects to see it equal to Gold and Silver. Some disaffected persons and designing speculators discredit it through Enmity or Interest; the ignorant multitude have not sagacity enough to examine into this matter, and merely from its uncommon quantity and in proportion to it arises the complaint of its want of Credit." [57]

To stay depreciation Todd proposed to retire a portion of the bills through exchanging them for land certificates. Twenty-one thousand acres of land in the vicinity of Cahokia were set aside on which it was planned to borrow thirty-three thousand dollars in Virginia and United States treasury notes. The lender might demand within two years his proportion of the land or a sum in gold or silver equal to the original loan, with five per cent annual interest. Land or money might be given at the option of the state. Large sums of money were exchanged for these certificates, but the project could not be carried further.

It was, however, the capture of Detroit which was uppermost in the minds of the two leaders, and preparations were rapidly made for the expedition, which promised complete success. [58] In this they were following the orders explicitly given by Governor Henry. " The inhabitants of Illinois," so read the instructions to Todd, " must not expect safety and settled peace while their and our enemies have footing at Detroit and can interrupt and stop the Trade of the Mississippi. If the English have not the strength or courage to come to war against us themselves, their practice has been and will be to hire the savages to commit murder and depredations. Illinois must expect to pay in these a large price for her freedom, unless the Eng-

[57] *Chicago Hist. Society Collections,* IV., p. 297.
[58] *Clark-Mason Letter.*

lish can be expelled from Detroit. The means of effecting
this will not perhaps be found in yours or Col. Clark's
power. But the French inhabiting the neighborhood of
that place, it is presumed, may be brought to see it done
with indifference or, perhaps, join in the enterprise with
pleasure. This is but conjecture. When you are on the
spot you and Col. Clark may discover its fallacy or
reality."

Captain Linctot, a trader of great influence with the Indians, who had recently joined the Americans, was sent up
the Illinois with a company of forty men to secure the
neutrality of the Indians,[59] and at the same time cover the
design of the main expedition against Detroit.[60] He reported, on his return, having gone as far as " Wea "; that
peace and quietness was general.[61]

Great enthusiasm was manifested on the part of officers, troops, and the French militia. Not only were the
villagers ready to enlist, even the old men volunteering
their services. They gave further evidence of their zeal
by proffering boat-loads of flour, cattle, and horses.[62]

The arrival of Colonel John Montgomery from Virginia with one hundred and fifty men, about one-third the
number expected, was a keen disappointment to Clark.
But he did not lose confidence, for he had been promised
three hundred Kentuckians by Colonel John Bowman, their
county lieutenant.

On July 1, 1779, Clark, with a party of horsemen,
reached Vincennes, the place of rendezvous. Here he was
joined by the remainder of the Illinois troops with the
exception of a company of mounted men dispatched under Captain Linctot to reconnoiter and to obtain permis-

[59] *Mich. Pioneer and Hist. Collections,* IX., p. 389.
[60] *Clark-Mason Letter.*
[61] *Draper MSS., 49 J 45.* Joseph Bowman to Clark, May 25, 1779.
[62] *Draper MSS., 49 J 49.* Bowman to Clark, June 3, 1779.

sion of the Wea and Miami for Clark to pass through their country on his way to Detroit.

Before leaving Kaskaskia Clark learned that Colonel John Bowman had led the Kentucky forces against Chillicothe, a Shawnee town, and was fearful of the effect on his Detroit plans. This expedition consisted of two hundred and ninety-six men.[63] The Indians fortified themselves so strongly in a few log cabins that the whites were repulsed. The greater part of the town was burned and Bowman retreated with a large amount of plunder.

Clark had now to experience some of the adverse results of his earlier success. Influenced by his victories, immigrants in large numbers had entered Kentucky during the spring.[64] Some returned to the older settlements for their families, and the others were scattered over such a large area that it seemed impossible to Bowman to secure the number of men he had promised Clark by the time appointed, and especially since the militia were so disheartened by the campaign against the Shawnee that only the most tried amongst them were ready to enter upon a new enterprise.

The arrival of only thirty Kentucky volunteers was a severe blow to Clark.[65] The capture of Detroit with his available force of about three hundred and fifty, even though its fortifications were incomplete and its garrison numbered but a hundred men, was at the time, he thought, out of the question. Most of his men were barefoot,[66] and Vincennes was able to supply scarcely enough provisions for its own inhabitants, and could not, therefore, furnish food for several hundred men on a campaign of uncertain

[63] *Draper MSS., 49 J 52.*

[64] *Draper MSS., 49 J 89, 90.*

[65] "But now came the sorest blow we had yet received." *Draper MSS., 47 J 1 ff. Clark's Memoir.*

[66] *Orderly Book of the Conductor General.* Fort Patrick Henry, July 26, 1779. Virginia State Library.

length. All commerce with Detroit had ceased, and supplies could be gotten by the way of the Mississippi only with great difficulty, owing to the attachment of the southern Indians to the British.

Although abandoned, the influence of the preparations for the expedition proved of great significance. Threatenings from Vincennes led the British officials at Detroit to give up their plans for the recapture of that post.[67] A summer campaign against Pittsburgh, with a force of regulars and Indians, was likewise abandoned. Instead of taking the field for an offensive campaign in 1779, the British at Detroit and Mackinac were engaged in considering defensive operations and in re-enforcing these posts with all possible dispatch.[68] Even after large expenditures by the British for rum and presents for the warriors, and food for the old men, women, and children, disaffection among the Indians became constantly more open.[69] They and their French neighbors were frightened over the report that an alliance between the French, Spanish, Germans, and Americans had been formed with the object of driving the English out of America.[70]

---

[67] *Draper MSS., 49 J 41,* and *ibid., 1 H 104.*

[68] *Draper MSS., 58 J 37.* Haldimand to Clinton, May 31, 1779.

[69] *Draper MSS., 58 J. 39.* Also *Mich. Pioneer and Hist. Collections,* IX., p. 411.

[70] *Mich. Pioneer and Hist. Collections,* IX., p. 417. "Fear acts stronger on them than all arguments can be made use of to convince them of enemy's ill designs against their lands." Brehm to Haldimand, May 28, 1779. *Mich. Pioneer and Hist. Collections,* IX., p. 411. In a letter of DePeyster, at Mackinac, to Haldimand, June 1, 1779, he excused the increased expenditures as follows: "As the Indians are growing very importunate since they hear that the French are assisting the Rebels. The Canadians are a great disservice to the Government, but the Indians are perfect free masons when intrusted with a secret by a Canadian, most of them being much connected by marriage." *Mich. Pioneer and Hist. Collections,* IX., p. 382. Only the Menominee and Sioux remained true to the British.

Despite their apparent demoralization the British showed signs of activity. Lieutenant Bennett was sent from Mackinac (May 29) with a force of twenty soldiers, sixty traders, and two hundred Indians for the purpose of intercepting Linctot or to " distress the Rebels " in any other way.[71] Captain Langlade was directed to levy the Indians at LaFourche and " Milwakee," and join Bennett at " Chicagou." [72] Indian scouts sent out by Bennett from St. Joseph's were frightened by reports obtained from other Indians and soon returned. Their fears quickly brought about a general panic. " We have not," wrote Bennett, " twenty Indians in our camp who are not preparing for leaving us, I believe you will join with me when I say they are a set of treacherous poltroons." [73] The return to Mackinac was begun shortly afterwards.[74]

In like manner, a force of six hundred, chiefly Indians, led by Captain McKee, was sent from Mackinac. Forgetting his boast that he would place a pair of handcuffs on every rebel officer left in the country, McKee retreated from St. Joseph's upon hearing the report that Clark was marching towards Detroit.[75]

Early in June, Captain Henry Bird collected some two hundred Indians at the Mingo town. The account brought in by runners of the attack which had been made by Colonel Bowman on the Shawnee town produced a panic among his followers. Some of the savages deserted in order to protect their villages against the American advance which was momentarily expected. Still more of them were anxious to sue for peace.[76]

---

[71] *Ibid.*, IX., p. 390.

[72] *Wis. Hist. Collections*, XVIII., pp. 375, 376.

[73] *Mich. Pioneer and Hist. Collections*, IX., pp. 392-396. *Wis. Hist. Collections*, XVIII., pp. 394-396.

[74] *Wis. Hist. Collections*, XVIII., pp. 397-401.

[75] *Draper MSS.*, 49 J 73. *Mich. Pioneer Collections*, IX., p. 417.

[76] *Mich. Pioneer Collections*, X., pp. 336, 337. Captain Bird to Captain

By August 1, all was confusion at Detroit, for the messages brought by couriers promised the coming of Clark with an army of two thousand Americans and French Creoles.[77]

"Every effort is making to strengthen and complete our new Fort," so wrote an officer who demanded that re-enforcements should be sent, " as we are not equal to oppose the passage of such numbers to this place. Our ditch and glacee will be in a very good state the end of this week. An abatis afterwards to be thrown round the barracks will be ready at the same time. I wish to God I could say the same of our well; it is now upwards of 60 feet below the level of the river, and no appearance of water. Could we only rely on the inhabitants, or had they either the inclination or the resolution to defend their town, there would be nothing to apprehend on that head as we might then take the field."

Clark, as we have seen, had now definitely abandoned his purpose of an immediate movement against Detroit, but he continued to make preparations by collecting supplies for a campaign against that post in the spring. Clark himself reached the Falls of the Ohio, August 26, and there began the establishment of his headquarters. Colonel Montgomery was left in charge of the Illinois battalion.[78]

These events ended American activity in the northwest in 1779. In contrast with Clark's bold and successful dash against Vincennes, with which the year had opened, and the larger plans of 1780, the story of the later months of 1779 has often seemed to historians tame and relatively

Lernoult, June 9, 1779. Report said that the Americans were coming with a force of 4,000.

[77] *Draper MSS., 58 J 46-49.* Letter of Captain Parke, July 30, 1779.

[78] *Draper MSS., 23 J 127.* Captain John Wiliams was appointed his aid at Fort Clark (Kaskaskia); Captain Richard McCarty at Cahokia; Captain James Shelby at Fort Patrick Henry (Vincennes); Major Joseph Bowman was given the direction of the recruiting parties.

unimportant. This study will have served its main purpose if it makes evident that in the establishment of peaceful relations with the Indians, in the founding of civil government in the Illinois country, and in the neutralization of all British activity in the northwest by the zeal and publicity with which the proposed expedition against Detroit was promoted, George Rogers Clark and his associates had successfully met the problems which confronted them. In view of these larger events Clark's judgment upon his success in spreading reports may well be given a wider content by the historian, and the summer of 1779 pronounced one that " was spent to advantage. . . ." [79]

JAMES ALTON JAMES.

[79] *Clark's Memoir.*

KANSAS

SOME years ago, in a New England college town, when I informed one of my New England friends that I was preparing to go to Kansas, he replied rather blankly, " Kansas?! Oh." The amenities of casual intercourse demanded a reply, certainly, but from the point of view of my New England friend I suppose there was really nothing more to say; and, in fact, standing there under the peaceful New England elms, Kansas did seem tolerably remote. Some months later I rode out of Kansas City and entered for the first time what I had always pictured as the land of grasshoppers, of arid drought, and barren social experimentation. In the seat just ahead were two young women, girls rather, whom I afterwards saw at the university. As we left the dreary yards behind, and entered the half-open country along the Kansas River, one of the pair, breaking abruptly away from the ceaseless chatter that had hitherto engrossed them both, began looking out of the car window. Her attention seemed fixed, for perhaps a quarter of an hour, upon something in the scene outside—the fields of corn, or it may have been the sunflowers that lined the track; but at last, turning to her companion with the contented sigh of a returning exile, she said, " Dear old Kansas! " The expression somehow recalled my New England friend. I wondered vaguely, as I was sure he would have done, why any one should feel moved to say " Dear old Kansas! " I had supposed that Kansas, even more than Italy, was only a geographical expression. But not so. Not infrequently, since then, I have heard the same expression—not always from emotional young girls. To understand why people say " Dear

old Kansas!" is to understand that Kansas is no mere
geographical expression, but a "state of mind," a religion,
and a philosophy in one.

The difference between the expression of my staid New
England friend and that of the enthusiastic young Kansan,
is perhaps symbolical, in certain respects, of the difference
between those who remain at home and those who, in successive generations, venture into the unknown "West,"—
New England or Kansas,—wherever it may be. In the
seventeenth century there was doubtless no lack of Englishmen—prelates for example, in lawn sleeves, comfortably
buttressed about by tithes and the Thirty-nine Articles—
who might have indicated their point of view quite fully by
remarking, "New England?! Oh." Whether any New
Englander of that day ever went so far as to say "Dear
old New England," I do not know. But that the sentiment was there, furnishing fuel for the inner light, is past
question. Now-a-days the superiority of New England is
taken for granted, I believe, by the people who live there;
but in the seventeenth century, when its inhabitants were
mere frontiersmen, they were given, much as Kansans are
said to be now, to boasting,—alas! even of the climate. In
1629, Mr. Higginson, a reverend gentleman, informed his
friends back in England that "The temper of the aire of
New England is one special thing that commends this
place. Experience doth manifest that there is hardly a
more healthful place to be found in the world that agreeth
better with our English bodyes. Many that have been
weake and sickly in old England, by coming hither have
been thoroughly healed and growne healthfull strong.
For here is a most extraordinarie cleere and dry aire that
is of a most healing nature to all such as are of a cold, melancholy, flegmatick, rheumatick temper of body. . . . And
therefore I think it a wise course for all cold complections
to come to take physic in New England; for a sup of New

England aire is better than a whole draft of Old England's ale." Now, we who live in Kansas know well that its climate is superior to any other in the world, and that it enables one, more readily than any other, to dispense with the use of ale.

There are those who will tell us, and have indeed often told us, with a formidable array of statistics, that Kansas is inhabited only in small part by New Englanders, and that it is therefore fanciful in the extreme to think of it as representing Puritanism transplanted. It is true, the people of Kansas came mainly from "the Middle West"— from Illinois, Indiana, Ohio, Iowa, Kentucky, and Missouri. But for our purpose the fact is of little importance, for it is the ideals of a people rather than the geography they have outgrown that determine their destiny; and in Kansas, as has been well said, "it is the ideas of the Pilgrims, not their descendants, that have had dominion in the young commonwealth." Ideas, sometimes, as well as the star of empire, move westward, and so it happens that Kansas is more Puritan than New England of to-day. It is akin to New England of early days. It is what New England, old England itself, once was—the frontier, an ever changing spot where dwell the courageous who defy fate and conquer circumstance.

For the frontier is more than a matter of location, and Puritanism is itself a kind of frontier. There is an intellectual "West" as well as a territorial "West." Both are heresies, the one as much subject to the scorn of the judicious as the other. Broad classifications of people are easily made and are usually inaccurate; but they are convenient for taking a large view, and it may be worth while to think, for the moment, of two kinds of people—those who like the sheltered life, and those who cannot endure it, those who think the world as they know it is well enough, and those who dream of something better, or, at any rate, something different. From age to age society builds its shelters of various sorts—accumulated traditions, religious creeds, political institutions, and intellectual conceptions, cultivated and well kept farms, well built and orderly cities —providing a monotonous and comfortable life that tends always to harden into conventional forms resisting change. With all this the home-keeping and timid are well content. They sit in accustomed corners, disturbed by no fortuitous circumstance. But there are those others who are forever tugging at the leashes of ordered life, eager to venture into the unknown. Forsaking beaten paths, they plunge into the wilderness. They must be always on the frontier of human endeavor, submitting what is old and accepted to conditions that are new and untried. The frontier is thus the seed plot where new forms of life, whether of institutions or types of thought, are germinated, the condition of all progress being in a sense a return to the primitive.

Now, generally speaking, the men who make the world's frontiers, whether in religion or politics, science, or geographical exploration and territorial settlement, have certain essential and distinguishing qualities. They are primarily men of faith. Having faith in themselves, they are individualists. They are idealists because they have faith in the universe, being confident that somehow everything is right at the center of things; they give hostages to the future, are ever inventing God anew, and must be always transforming the world into their ideal of it. They have faith in humanity and in the perfectibility of man, are likely, therefore, to be believers in equality, reformers, intolerant, aiming always to level others up to their own high vantage. These qualities are not only Puritan, they are American; and Kansas is not only Puritanism transplanted, but Americanism transplanted. In the individualism, the idealism, the belief in equality that prevail in Kansas, we shall therefore see nothing strangely new, but simply a new graft of familiar American traits. But as Kansas is a community with a peculiar and distinctive experience, there is something peculiar and distinctive about the individualism, the idealism, and the belief in equality of its people. If we can get at this something peculiar and distinctive, it will be possible to understand why the sight of sunflowers growing beside a railroad track may call forth the fervid expression, " Dear old Kansas."

I

Individualism is everywhere characteristic of the frontier, and in America, where the geographical frontier has hitherto played so predominant a part, a peculiarly marked type of individualism is one of the most obvious traits of the people. " To the frontier," Professor Turner has said, "the American intellect owes its striking characteristics. That coarseness and strength combined with acuteness and inquisitiveness; that practical, inventive turn of mind, quick to find expedients; that masterful grasp of material things, lacking in the artistic but powerful to effect great ends; that restless nervous energy; that dominant individualism, working for good and for evil, and withal that buoyancy and exuberance that comes from freedom." On the frontier, where everything is done by the individual and nothing by organized society, initiative, resourcefulness, quick, confident, and sure judgment are the essential qualities for success. But as the problems of the frontier are rather restricted and definite, those who succeed there have necessarily much the same kind of initiative and resourcefulness, and their judgment will be sure only in respect to the problems that are familiar to all. It thus happens that the type of individualism produced on the frontier and predominant in America, has this peculiarity, that while the sense of freedom is strong, there is nevertheless a certain uniformity in respect to ability, habit, and point of view. The frontier develops strong individuals, but it develops individuals of a particular type, all being after much the same pattern. The individualism of the frontier is one of achievement, not of eccentricity, an individualism of fact arising from a sense of power to overcome obstacles, rather than one of theory growing out of weakness in the face of oppression. It is not because he fears governmental activity, but because he has so often had to dispense with it, that the American is an individualist. Altogether averse from hesitancy, doubt, speculative or introspective tendencies, the frontiersman is a man of faith: of faith, not so much in some external power, as in himself, in his luck, his destiny; faith in the possibility of achieving whatever is necessary or he desires. It is this marked self-reliance that gives to Americans their tremendous power of initiative; but the absence of deep-seated differences gives to them an equally tremendous power of concerted social action.

The confident individualism of those who achieve through endurance is a striking trait of the people of Kansas. There, indeed, the trait has in it an element of exaggeration, arising from the fact that whatever has been achieved in Kansas has been achieved under great difficulties. Kansans have been subjected, not only to the ordinary hardships of the frontier, but to a succession of reverses and disasters that could be survived only by those for whom defeat is worse than death, who cannot fail because they cannot surrender. To the border wars succeeded hot winds, droughts, grasshoppers; and to the disasters of nature succeeded in turn the scourge of man, in the form of "mortgage fiends" and a contracting currency. Until 1895 the whole history of the state was a series of disasters, and always something new, extreme, bizarre, until the name Kansas became a byword, a synonym for the impossible and the ridiculous, inviting laughter, furnishing occasion for jest and hilarity. "In God we trusted, in Kansas we busted," became a favorite motto of emigrants, worn out with the struggle, returning to more hospitable climes; and for many years it expressed well enough the popular opinion of that fated land.

Yet there were some who never gave up. They stuck it out. They endured all that even Kansas could inflict. They kept the faith, and they are to be pardoned perhaps if they therefore feel that henceforth there is laid up for them a crown of glory. Those who remained in Kansas from 1875 to 1895 must have originally possessed staying qualities of no ordinary sort, qualities which the experience of those years could only accentuate. And as success has at last rewarded their efforts, there has come, too, a certain pride, an exuberance, a feeling of superiority that accompany a victory long delayed and hardly won. The result has been to give a peculiar flavor to the Kansas spirit of individualism. With Kansas history back of him, the true Kansan feels that nothing is *too much* for him. How shall he be afraid of any danger, or hesitate at any obstacle, having succeeded where failure was not only human, but almost honorable? Having conquered Kansas, he knows well that there are no worse worlds to conquer. The Kansas spirit is therefore one that finds something exhilarating in the challenge of an extreme difficulty. "No one," says St. Augustine, "loves what he endures, though he may love to endure." With Kansans, it is particularly a point of pride to suffer easily the stings of fortune, and if they find no pleasure in the stings themselves, the ready endurance of them gives a consciousness of merit that is its own reward. Yet it is with no solemn martyr's air that the true Kansan endures the worst that can happen. His instinct is rather to pass it off as a minor annoyance, furnishing occasion for a pleasantry, for it is the mark of a Kansan to take a reverse as a joke rather than too seriously. Indeed, the endurance of extreme adversity has developed a keen appreciation for that type of humor, everywhere prevalent in the west, which consists in ignoring a difficulty, or transforming it into a difficulty of precisely the opposite kind. There is a tradition surviving from the grasshopper time that illustrates the point. It is said that in the midst of that overwhelming disaster, when the pests were six inches deep in the streets, the editor of a certain local paper fined his comment on the situation down to a single line, which appeared among the trivial happenings of the week: "A grasshopper was seen on the court-house steps this morning." This type of humor, appreciated anywhere west of the Alleghanies, is the type *par excellence* in Kansas. Perhaps it has rained for six weeks in the spring. The wheat is seemingly ruined; no corn has been planted. A farmer, who sees his profits for the year wiped out, looks at the murky sky, sniffs the damp air, and remarks seriously, "Well, it looks like rain. We may save that crop yet." "Yes," his neighbor replies with equal seriousness, "but it will have to come soon, or it won't do any good." When misfortunes beat down upon one in rapid succession, there comes a time when it is useless to strive against them, and in the end they engender a certain detached curiosity in the victim, who finds a mournful pleasure in observing with philosophical resignation the ultimate caprices of fate. Thus Kansans, "coiners of novel phrases to express their defiance of destiny," have employed humor itself as a refuge against misfortune. They have learned not only to endure adversity, but in a very literal sense to laugh at it as well.

I have already said that the type of individualism that is characteristic of America is one of achievement, not of eccentricity. The statement will bear repeating in this connection, for it is truer of Kansas than of most communities, notwithstanding there is a notion abroad that the state is peopled by freaks and eccentrics. It was once popularly supposed in Europe, and perhaps is so yet, that Americans are all eccentric. Now, Kansans are eccentric in the same sense that Americans are: they differ somewhat from other Americans, just as Americans are distinguishable from Europeans. But a fundamental characteristic of Kansas individualism is the tendency to conform; it is an individualism of conformity, not of revolt. Having learned to endure to the end, they have learned to conform, for endurance is itself a kind of conformity. It has not infrequently been the subject of wondering comment by foreigners that in America, where every one is supposed to do as he pleases, there should nevertheless be so little danger from violence and insurrection. Certainly one reason is that while the conditions of frontier life release the individual from many of the formal restraints of ordered society, they exact a most rigid adherence to lines of conduct inevitably fixed by the stern necessities of life in a primitive community. On the frontier men soon learn to conform to what is regarded as essential, for the penalty of resistance or neglect is extinction: there the law of survival works surely and swiftly. However eccentric frontiersmen may appear to the tenderfoot, among themselves there is little variation from type in any essential matter. In the new community, individualism means the ability of the individual to succeed, not by submitting to some external formal authority, still less by following the bent of an unschooled will, but by recognizing and voluntarily adapting himself to necessary conditions. Kansas, it is true, has produced its eccentrics, but there is a saying here that freaks are raised for export only. In one sense the saying is true enough, for what strikes one particularly is that, on the whole, native Kansans are all so much alike.

It is a community of great solidarity, and to the native it is "the Easterner" who appears eccentric.

The conquest of the wilderness in Kansas has thus developed qualities of patience, of calm, stoical, good-humored endurance in the face of natural difficulties, of conformity to what is regarded as necessary. Yet the patience, the calmness, the disposition to conform, is strictly confined to what is regarded as in the natural course. If the Kansan appears stolid, it is only on the surface that he is so. The peculiar conditions of origin and history have infused into the character of the people a certain romantic and sentimental element. Beneath the placid surface there is something fermenting which is best left alone—a latent energy which trivial events or a resounding phrase may unexpectedly release. In a recent commencement address, Mr. Henry King said that conditions in early Kansas were "*hair-triggered.*" Well, Kansans are themselves hair-triggered; slight pressure, if it be of the right sort, sets them off. "Every one is on the *qui vive,* alert, vigilant, like a sentinel at an outpost." This trait finds expression in the romantic devotion of the people to the state, in a certain alert sensitiveness to criticism from outside, above all in the contagious enthusiasm with which they will without warning espouse a cause, especially when symbolized by a striking phrase, and carry it to an issue. Insurgency is native in Kansas, and the political history of the state, like its climate, is replete with surprises that have made it " alternately the reproach and the marvel of mankind." But this apparent instability is only the natural complement of the extreme and confident individualism of the people: having succeeded in overcoming so many obstacles that were unavoidable, they do not doubt their ability to destroy quickly those that seem artificially constructed. It thus happens that while no people endure the reverses of nature with greater fortitude and good humor than the

people of Kansas, misfortunes seemingly of man's making
arouse in them a veritable passion of resistance; the mere
suspicion of injustice, real or fancied exploitation by those
who fare sumptuously, the pressure of laws not self-imposed, touch something explosive in their nature that
transforms a calm and practical people into excited revolutionists. Grasshoppers elicited only a witticism, but the
"mortgage fiends" produced the Populist régime, a kind
of religious crusade against the infidel Money Power. The
same spirit was recently exhibited in the "Boss Busters"
movement, which in one summer spread over the state like
a prairie fire and overthrew an established machine supposed to be in control of the railroads. The "Higher
Law" is still a force in Kansas. The spirit which refused
to obey "bogus laws" is still easily stirred. A people
which has endured the worst of nature's tyrannies, and
cheerfully submits to tyrannies self-imposed, is in no mood
to suffer hardships that seem remediable.

II

Idealism must always prevail on the frontier, for the
frontier, whether geographical or intellectual, offers little
hope to those who see things as they are. To venture into
the wilderness, one must see it, not as it is, but as it will be.
The frontier, being the possession of those only who see
its future, is the promised land which cannot be entered
save by those who have faith. America, having been such
a promised land, is therefore inhabited by men of faith:
idealism is ingrained in the character of its people. But
as the frontier in America has hitherto been geographical
and material, American idealism has necessarily a material
basis, and Americans have often been mistakenly called
materialists. True, they seem mainly interested in
material things. Too often they represent values in terms

of money: a man is " worth " so much money; a university is a great university, having the largest endowment of any; a fine building is a building that cost a million dollars, better still, ten millions. Value is extensive rather than intensive or intrinsic. America is the best country because it is the biggest, the wealthiest, the most powerful; its people are the best because they are the freest, the most energetic, the *most* educated. But to see a materialistic temper in all this is to mistake the form for the spirit. The American cares for material things because they represent the substance of things hoped for. He cares less for money than for making money: a fortune is valued, not because it represents ease, but because it represents struggle, achievement, progress. The first skyscraper in any town is nothing in itself, but much as an evidence of growth; it is a white stone on the road to the ultimate goal.

Idealism of this sort is an essential ingredient of the Kansas spirit. In few communities is the word progress more frequently used, or its meaning less frequently detached from a material basis. It symbolizes the *summum bonum,* having become a kind of dogma. Mistakes are forgiven a man if he is progressive, but to be unprogressive is to be suspect; like Aristotle's non-political animal, the unprogressive is extra-human. This may explain why every Kansan wishes first of all to tell you that he comes from the town of X——, and then that it is the finest town in the state. He does not mean that it is strictly the finest town in the state, as will appear if you take the trouble to inquire a little about the country, its soil, its climate, its rainfall, and about the town itself. For it may chance that he is free to admit that it is hot there, that the soil is inclined to bake when there is no rain, that there is rarely any rain—all of which, however, is nothing to the point, because they are soon to have water by irrigation, which is, after all, much better than rainfall. And then he describes the town, which you have no difficulty in picturing vividly: a single street flanked by nondescript wooden shops; at one end a railroad station, at the other a post-office; side streets lined with frame houses, painted or not, as the case may be; a school house somewhere, and a church with a steeple. It is such a town, to all appearances, as you may see by the hundred anywhere in the west —a dreary place which, you think, the world would willingly let die. But your man is enthusiastic; he can talk of nothing but the town of X——. The secret of his enthusiasm you at last discover in the inevitable " but it will be a great country some day," and it dawns upon you that, after all, the man does not live in the dreary town of X——, but in the great country of *some day*. Such are Kansans. Like St. Augustine, they have their City of God, the idealized Kansas of some day: it is only necessary to have faith in order to possess it.

I cannot illustrate this aspect of Kansas idealism better than by quoting from Mrs. McCormick's little book of personal experience and observation. Having related the long years of struggle of a typical farmer, she imagines the Goddess of Justice revealing to him a picture of " the land as it shall be " when justice prevails.

" John beheld a great plain four hundred miles long and two hundred miles wide—a great agricultural state covered with farmers tilling the soil and with here and there a city or village. On every farm stood a beautiful house handsomely painted outside and elegantly furnished inside, and equipped with all modern conveniences helpful to housekeeping. Brussels carpets covered the floors, upholstered furniture and pianos ornamented the parlors, and the cheerful dining-room had elegant table linen, cut glass, and silverware. Reservoirs carried the water into the houses in the country the same as in the cities. The farmers' wives and daughters, instead of working like slaves without proper utensils or house furnishings, now had everything necessary to lighten work and make home attractive. They had the summer-kitchen, the wash-house, houses for drying clothes, arbors, etc. The door-yards consisted of nicely fenced green lawns, wherein not a pig rooted nor mule browsed on the shrubbery nor hen wallowed in the flower-beds. Shade trees, hammocks, and rustic chairs were scattered about, and everything bespoke comfort. Great barns sheltered the stock. The farms were fenced and subdivided into fields of waving grain and pastures green."

This is what John is supposed to have seen on a summer's day when, at the close of a life of toil, he had just been sold up for debt. What John really saw had perhaps a less feminine coloring; but the picture represents the ideal, if not of an actual Kansas farmer, at least of an actual Kansas woman.

This aspect of American idealism is, however, not peculiar to Kansas: it is more or less characteristic of all western communities. But there is an element in Kansas idealism that marks it off as a state apart. The origin of Kansas must ever be associated with the struggle against slavery. Of this fact, Kansans are well aware. Kansas is not a community of which it can be said, " happy is the people without annals." It is a state with a past. It has a history of which its people are proud, and which they insist, as a matter of course, upon having taught in the public schools. There are Old Families in Kansas who know their place and keep it—sacred bearers of the traditions of the Kansas Struggle. The Kansas Struggle is for Kansas what the American Revolution is for New England; and while there is as yet no " Society of the Daughters of the Kansas Struggle," there doubtless will be some day. For the Kansas Struggle is regarded as the crucial point in the achievement of human liberty, very much as Macaulay is said to have regarded the Reform Bill as the end for which all history was only a preparation. For all true Kansans, the border wars of the early years have a perennial interest: they mark the spot where Jones shot Smith, direct the at-

tention of the traveler to the little village of Lecompton,
or point with pride to some venerable tree bearing honorable scars dating from the Quantrill raid. Whether John
Brown was an assassin or a martyr is a question which only
a native can safely venture to answer with confidence. Recently, in a list of questions prepared for the examination of
teachers in the schools, there appeared the following:
" What was the Andover Band? " It seems that very few
teachers knew what the Andover Band was; some thought
it was an iron band, and some a band of Indians. The
newspapers took it up, and it was found that, aside from
some of the old families, ignorance of the Andover Band
was quite general. When it transpired that the Andover
Band had to do with the Kansas Struggle, the humiliation
of the people was profound.

The belief that Kansas was founded for a cause distinguishes it, in the eyes of its inhabitants, as pre-eminently the
home of freedom. It lifts the history of the state out of
the commonplace of ordinary westward migration, and
gives to the temper of the people a certain elevated and
martial quality. The people of Iowa or Nebraska are well
enough, but their history has never brought them in touch
with cosmic processes. The Pilgrims themselves are felt
to have been actuated by less noble and altruistic motives.
The Pilgrims, says Thayer, " fled from oppression, and
sought in the new world ' freedom to worship God.' " But
the Kansas emigrants migrated " to meet, to resist, and to
destroy oppression, in vindication of their principles. These
were self-sacrificing emigrants, the others were self-seeking.
Justice, though tardy in its work, will yet load with the
highest honors, the memory of the Kansas pioneers who
gave themselves and all they had to the sacred cause of
human rights."

This may smack of prejudice, but it is no heresy in
Kansas. The trained and disinterested physiocratic his-

torian will tell us that such statements are unsupported by
the documents.   The documents show, he will say, that
the Kansas emigrants, like other emigrants, came for cheap
land and in the hope of bettering their condition; the real
motive was economic, as all historic motives are; the Kansas
emigrant may have thought he was going to Kansas to
resist oppression, but in reality he went to take up a farm.
At least, that many emigrants thought they came to resist
oppression is indisputable.   Their descendants still think
so.   And, after all, perhaps it is important to distinguish
those who seek better farms and know they seek nothing
else, from those who seek better farms and imagine they
are fighting a holy war.   When the people of Newtown
wished to remove to Connecticut we are told that they advanced three reasons: first, " their want of accommodation
for their cattle; " second, " the fruitfulness and commo-
diousness of Connecticut;" and finally, *" the strong bent of
their spirits to remove thither."*   In explaining human history perhaps something should be conceded to " the strong
bent of their spirits."   Unquestionably cattle must be ac-
commodated, but a belief, even if founded on error, is a
fact that may sometimes change the current of history.   At
all events, the people of Kansas believe that their ancestors
were engaged in a struggle for noble ends, and the belief,
whether true or false, has left its impress upon their character.   In Kansas the idealism of the geographical frontier
has been strongly flavored with the notion that liberty is
something more than a by-product of economic processes.

If Kansas idealism is colored by the humanitarian liberalism of the first half of the last century, it has nevertheless
been but slightly influenced by the vague, emotional, Jean
Paul romanticism of that time.   Of all despondent and
mystic elements, the Kansas spirit is singularly free.   There
are few Byrons in Kansas, and no Don Juans.   There is
plenty of light there, but little of the " light that never was

on land or sea." Kansas idealism is not a force that expends itself in academic contemplation of the unattainable. It is an idealism that is immensely concrete and practical, requiring always some definite object upon which to expend itself, but once having such an object expending itself with a restless, nervous energy that is appalling: whatever the object, it is pursued with the enthusiasm, the profound conviction given only to those who have communed with the Absolute. It would seem that preoccupation with the concrete and the practical should develop a keen appreciation of relative values; but in new countries problems of material transformation are so insistent that immediate means acquire the value of ultimate ends. Kansas is a new state, and its inhabitants are so preoccupied with the present, so resolutely detached from the experience of the centuries, that they can compare themselves of to-day only with themselves of yesterday. The idea embodied in the phrase, " *Weltgeschichte ist das Weltgericht,*" has slight significance in a community in which twenty years of rapid material improvement has engendered an unquestioning faith in indefinite progress towards perfectibility. In such a community, past and future appear foreshortened, and the latest new mechanical device brings us an appreciable step nearer the millennium, which seems always to be just over the next hill. By some odd mental alchemy it thus happens that the concrete and the practical have taken on the dignity of the absolute, and the pursuit of a convenience assumes the character of a crusade. Whether it be religion or paving, education or the disposal of garbage that occupies for the moment the focus of attention, the same stirring activity, the same zeal and emotional glow are enlisted: all alike are legitimate objects of conquest, to be measured in terms of their visual and transferable assets, and won by concerted and organized attack. I recall reading in a local Kansas newspaper some

time ago a brief comment on the neighboring village of
X—— (in which was located a small college mistakenly
caHed a university), which ran somewhat as follows:
" The University of X—— has established a music festival
on the same plan as the one at the State University, and
with most gratifying results.   The first festival was altogether a success.   X—— is a fine town, one of the best in
the state.   It has a fine university, and a fine class of people, who have made it a center of culture.   X—— lacks
only one thing; it has no sewers."   Perhaps there are people who would find the juxtaposition of culture and sewers
somewhat bizarre.   But to us in Kansas it does not seem
so.   Culture and sewers are admittedly good things to possess.   Well, then, let us pursue them actively and with
absolute conviction.   Thus may an idealized sewer become
an object worthy to stir the moral depths of any right-
minded community.

An insistent, practical idealism of this sort, always busily
occupied with concrete problems, is likely to prefer ideas
cast in formal mold, will be a little at a loss in the midst
of flexible play of mind, and look with suspicion upon the
emancipated, the critical, and the speculative spirit.   It
is too sure of itself to be at home with ideas of uncertain
pressure.   Knowing that it is right, it wishes only to go
ahead.   Satisfied with certain conventional premises, it
hastens on to the obvious conclusion.   It thus happens that
Americans, for the most part, are complaisantly satisfied
with a purely formal interpretation of those resounding
words that symbolize for them the ideas upon which their
institutions are supposed to rest.   In this respect Kansas
is truly American.   Nowhere is there more loyal devotion to such words as liberty, democracy, equality, education.   But preoccupation with the concrete fixes the attention upon the word itself, and upon what is traditionally
associated with it.   Democracy, for example, is tradition-

ally associated with elections, and many of them. Should
you maintain that democracy is not necessarily bound up
with any particular institution, that it is in the way of being smothered by the complicated blanket ballot, you will
not be understood, or, rather, you will be understood only
too well as advocating something aristocratic. Democracy
is somehow bound up with a concrete thing, and the move
for the shorter ballot is therefore undemocratic and un-
American. Or, take the word socialism. Your avowed
socialist is received politely, and allowed to depart silently
and without regret. But if you tell us of the movement
for the governmental control of corporate wealth, we grow
enthusiastic. The word socialism has a bad odor in
Kansas, but the thing itself, by some other name, smells
sweet enough.

If one is interested in getting the essential features of
socialism adopted in Kansas, or in America itself, the
name to conjure with is indeed not socialism, but equality.

III

In a country like America, where there is such confident
faith in the individual, one might naturally expect to find
the completest toleration, and no disposition to use the government for the purpose of enforcing uniform conditions:
logically, it would seem, so much emphasis on liberty should
be incompatible with much emphasis on equality. Yet it is
precisely in America, and nowhere in America more than
in the west, that liberty and equality always go coupled
and inseparable in popular speech; where the sense of liberty is especially strong, there also the devotion to equality
is a cardinal doctrine. Throughout our history, the west
has been a dominant factor in urging the extension of the
powers of the national government, and western states
have taken the lead in radical legislation of an equalizing

character. This apparent inconsistency strikes one as especially pronounced in Kansas. The doctrine of equality is unquestioned there, and that governments exist for the purpose of securing it is the common belief. " A law against it " is the specific for every malady. The welfare of society is thought to be always superior to that of the individual, and yet no one doubts that perfect liberty is the birthright of every man.

Perhaps the truth is that real toleration is a sentiment foreign to the American temper. Toleration is for the skeptical, being the product of much thought or of great indifference, sometimes, to be sure, a mere *modus vivendi* forced upon a heterogeneous society. In America we imagine ourselves liberal-minded because we tolerate what we have ceased to regard as important. We tolerate religions but not irreligion, and diverse political opinion, but not unpolitical opinion, customs, but not the negation of custom. The Puritans fought for toleration—for themselves. But having won it for themselves, straightway denied it to others. No small part of American history has been a repetition of the Puritan struggle; it has been a fight, not for toleration as a general principle, but for recognition of a civilization resting upon particular principles: in exterior relations, a struggle for recognition of America by Europe; in interior relations, a struggle for recognition of " the West " by " the East." The principle of toleration is written in our constitutions, but not in our minds, for the motive back of the famous guarantees of individual liberty has been recognition of particular opinion rather than toleration of every opinion. And in the nature of the case it must be so. Those who create frontiers and establish new civilizations have too much faith to be tolerant, and are too thoroughgoing idealists to be indifferent. On the frontier conditions are too hazardous for the speculative and the academic to flourish readily: only those who are right and are sure of it can succeed. Certainly it is characteristic of Americans to know that they are right. Certainly they are conscious of having a mission in the world and of having been faithful to it. They have solved great problems hitherto unsolved, have realized utopias dreamed of but never realized by Europe. They are therefore in the van of civilization, quite sure of the direction, triumphantly leading the march towards the ultimate goal. That every one should do as he likes is part of the American creed only in a very limited sense. That it is possible to know what is right, and that what is right should be recognized and adhered to is the more vital belief.

That liberty and equality are compatible terms is, at all events, an unquestioned faith in Kansas. The belief in equality, however, is not so much the belief that all men are equal as the conviction that it is the business of society to establish conditions that will make them so. And this notion, so far from being inconsistent with the pronounced individualism that prevails there, is the natural result of it. In Kansas at least, no one holds to the right of the individual to do as he likes, irrespective of what it is that he likes. Faith in the individual is faith in the particular individual, the true Kansan, who has learned through adversity voluntarily to conform to what is necessary. Human nature, or, at all events, Kansas nature, is essentially good, and if the environment is right all men can measure up to that high level. That the right environment can be created is not doubted. It is not possible for men so aggressive and self-reliant, who have overcome so many obstacles, to doubt their ability to accomplish this also. Having conquered nature, they cheerfully confront the task of transforming human nature. It is precisely because Kansans are such thoroughgoing individualists, so resourceful, so profoundly confident in their own judg-

ments, so emancipated from the past, so accustomed to de-
vising expedients for every new difficulty, that they are un-
impressed by the record of the world's failures. They
have always thrived on the impossible, and the field of
many failures offers a challenge not to be resisted.

To effect these beneficent ends, the people of Kansas turn
naturally to the government because they have a very
simple and practical idea of what the government is and
what it is for. The government, in Kansas, is no abstract
concept. It is nothing German, nothing metaphysical. In
this frontier community no one has yet thought of the government as a power not ourselves that makes for evil.
Kansans think of the government, as they think of everything else, in terms of the concrete. And why, indeed,
should they not? Within the memory of man there was
no government in Kansas. They, Kansans, made the government themselves for their own purposes. The government is therefore simply certain men employed by themselves to do certain things; it is the sum of the energy, the
good judgment, the resourcefulness of the individuals who
originally created it, and who periodically renew it. The
government is the individual writ large; in it every Kansan
sees himself drawn to larger scale. The passion for controlling all things by law is thus not the turning of the
hopeless and discouraged individual to some power other
and higher than himself for protection; it is only the instinct to use effectively one of the many resources always at
his command for achieving desired ends. Of a government hostile to the individual, they cannot conceive; such a
government is a bogus government, and its laws are bogus
laws; to resist and overthrow such a government, all the
initiative and resourcefulness is enlisted that is devoted to
supporting one regarded as legitimate. There is a higher
law than the statute book; the law of the state is no law if
it does not represent the will of the individual.

To identify the will of the individual with the will of society in this easy fashion, presupposes a certain solidarity in the community: an identity of race, custom, habits, needs; a consensus of opinion in respect to morals and politics. Kansas is such a community. Its people are principally American born, descended from settlers who came mainly from the middle west. It is an agricultural state, and the conditions of life are, or have been until recently, much the same for all. " Within these pastoral boundaries," says ex-Senator Ingalls, in his best Kansas manner, " there are no millionaires nor any paupers, except such as have been deprived by age, disease, and calamity of the ability to labor. No great fortunes have been brought to the state and none have been accumulated by commerce, manufactures or speculation. No sumptuous mansions nor glittering equipages nor ostentatious display exasperates or allures." And the feeling of solidarity resulting from identity of race and uniformity of custom has been accentuated by the peculiar history of the state. Kansans love each other for the dangers they have passed; a unique experience has created a strong *esprit de corps*—a feeling that while Kansans are different from others, one Kansan is not only as good as any other, but very like any other. The philosophy of numbers, the doctrine of the majority, is therefore ingrained, and little sympathy is wasted on minorities. Rousseau's notion that minorities are only mistaken finds ready acceptance, and the will of the individual is easily identified with the will of society.

And in a sense the doctrine is true enough, for there is little difference of opinion on fundamental questions. In religion there are many creeds and many churches, but the difference between them is regarded as unimportant. There is, however, a quite absolute dogmatism of morality. Baptism is for those who enjoy it, but the moral life is for all. And what constitutes the moral life is well understood: to be honest and pay your debts; to be friendly and charitable, good-humored but not cynical, slow to take offense, but regarding life as profoundly serious; to respect sentiments and harmless prejudices; to revere the conventional great ideas and traditions; to live a sober life and a chaste one,—to these they lay hold without questioning. Likewise in politics. One may be democrat or republican, stalwart or square-dealer, insurgent or stand-patter: it is no vital matter. But no one dreams of denying democracy, the will of the people, the greatest good to the greatest number, equal justice and equal opportunity to all. Whether in respect to politics or economics, education or morals, the consensus of opinion is very nearly perfect: it is an opinion that unites in the deification of the average, that centers in the dogmatism of the general level.

It goes without saying that the general level in Kansas is thought to be exceptionally high. Kansans do not regard themselves as mere westerners, like Iowans or Nebraskans. Having passed through a superior heat, they are westerners seven times refined. "It is the quality of piety in Kansas," says Mr. E. H. Abbott, "to thank God that you are not as other men are, beer-drinkers, shiftless, habitual lynchers, or even as these Missourians." The pride is natural enough, perhaps, in men whose judgment has been vindicated at last in the face of general skepticism. Having for many years contributed to the gaiety of nations, Kansas has ceased to be the pariah of the states. Kansans have endured Job's comforters too long not to feel a little complaisant when their solemn predictions come to naught. "While envious rivals were jeering, . . . pointing with scorn's slow unmoving finger at the droughts, grasshoppers, hot winds, crop failures, and other calamities of Kansas, the world was suddenly startled and dazzled by her collective display of . . . products at the Centennial at Philadelphia, which received the highest awards." It is inevitable that those who think they have fashioned a corner-stone out of the stone rejected by the builders should regard themselves as superior workmen.

To test others by this high standard is an instinctive procedure. There is an alert attention to the quality of those who enter the state from outside. The crucial question is, are they " our kind of men? " Do they speak " the Kansas language? " Yet the Kansas language is less a form of speech, or the expression of particular ideas, than a certain personal quality. Some time since a distinguished visitor from the east came to the state to deliver a public address. He was most hospitably received, as all visitors are, whether distinguished or otherwise, and his address—permeated with the idealistic liberalism of a half century ago—was attentively listened to and highly praised. But to no purpose all these fine ideas. The great man was found wanting, for there was discovered, among his other impedimenta, a valet. It was a fatal mischance. The poor valet was more commented upon than the address, more observed than his master. The circumstance stamped the misguided man as clearly not our kind of man. Obviously, no man who carries a valet can speak the Kansas language. Needless to say, there are no valets in Kansas.

The feeling of superiority naturally attaching to a chosen people, equally inclines Kansans to dispense readily with the advice or experience of others. They feel that those who have worn the hair shirt cannot be instructed in asceticism by those who wear silk. In discussing the university and its problems with a member of the state legislature, I once hazarded some comparative statistics showing that a number of other states made rather more liberal appropriations for their universities than the state of Kansas did for hers. I thought the comparison might be enlightening, that the man's pride of state might be touched. Not at all. " I know all about that," he replied. "That argument is used by every man who is interested in larger appropriations for any of the state institutions. But it doesn't go with a Kansas legislature. In Kansas, we don't care much what other states are doing. Kansas always leads, but never follows." And, in fact, the disregard of precedent is almost an article of faith; that a thing has been done before is an indication that it is time to improve upon it. History may teach that men cannot be legislated into the kingdom of heaven. Kansans are not ignorant of the fact, but it is no concern of theirs. The experience of history is not for men with a mission and faith to perform it. Let the uncertain and the timid profit by history; those who have at all times the courage of their emotions will make history, not repeat it. Kansans set their own standards, and the state becomes, as it were, an experiment station in the field of social science.

The passion for equality in Kansas is thus the complement of the individualism and the idealism of its people. It has at the basis of it an altruistic motive, aiming not so much to level all men down as to level all men up. The Kansan's sense of individual worth enables him to believe that no one can be better than he is, while his confident idealism encourages him to hope that none need be worse.

IV

The Kansas spirit is the American spirit double distilled. It is a new grafted product of American individualism, American idealism, American intolerance. Kansas is America in microcosm: as America conceives itself in respect to Europe, so Kansas conceives itself in respect to America. Within its borders, Americanism, pure and undefiled, has a new lease of life. It is the mission of this self-selected people to see to it that it does not perish from off the earth. The light on the altar, however neglected elsewhere, must ever be replenished in Kansas. If this is provincialism, it is the provincialism of faith rather than of the province. The devotion to the state is devotion to an ideal, not to a territory, and men can say " Dear old Kansas! " because the name symbolizes for them what the motto of the state so well expresses, *ad astra per aspera.*

CARL BECKER.

FEDERALISM AND THE WEST

THE fate of the Federalist party has been a puzzle of long standing. The narrow margin by which the Republicans won the election of 1800 was not prophetic of invariable success, and at first sight it appears anomalous that the Federalist party which carried the ratification of the constitution and successfully established the government under it should have been condemned to successive defeats and lingering death. To say that the party was not in accord with the political tendencies of the country is rather a conclusion than an explanation; yet if we assert that Federalism was non-expansive, while the growth of the west accrued to the benefit of Republicanism, we rise to the dignity of a working hypothesis which, if established, affords at least a partial solution.

The first parties of the constitutional period were the results of two sets of contending forces. In the areas of earliest colonization, where constant intercourse with England had been the condition of existence, social evolution inevitably followed old-world lines. From the beginning political privilege was limited in these communities by property and religious qualifications which followed English precedents. However much in advance of English practice, the colonies at the outbreak of the Revolution still betrayed the aristocratic temper of the mother-country in their political arrangements. But American conditions had given birth to a new ideal. In the interior, where nothing was known of the back-to-nature call of French political philosophy, a primitive society had come into being which actualized in a measure the ideal of Rousseau. The self-reliant backwoodsmen owed slight allegiance to any master, and held the divine right of kings and the traditional right of aristocrats in equal contempt. When the coastwise oligarchies, firm in adherence to the right of blood and wealth to rule, attempted to exercise control over the back country, maintaining their dominance against popular majorities by suffrage qualifications and inequitable apportionment of representation, the ideals of the interior democracies and of the ruling classes clashed. The contest was a long one, and was still in progress when the Revolution came. Each stage of the contest with England had its effect upon this intestine conflict, and it was presently transferred to the national arena. The philosophy of natural rights, advanced to justify the revolt of the colonies, spread the democratic leaven and strengthened the popular cause against the aristocrats, and the success of the colonies in destroying British authority over them weakened the respect in which all authority was held. To this cause was due in part the confusion of the Confederation period. The movement for the new constitution was a reaction against the prevalent excess of democracy. This reaction enabled men of the essentially conservative class to regain control and frame an instrument more adequate for the ends of government as they conceived them. The issue of ratification gathered the commercial and professional classes into one camp, leaving the agricultural interest, with the exception of the large planters, in the other. The line of division thus separated the propertied from the unpropertied, the Atlantic coast from the interior.

These divisions corresponded closely, on a national scale, to the old local groupings of aristocrats and democrats, and perpetuated the antagonism between east and west. The new issues of the Federalist administrations produced only a partial realignment: the Federalist party continued to include those who believed social order to be the chief purpose of government, and who, distrusting the political capacity of the masses, favored the vigorous rule of the well-born.[1] To the extent to which it was the party of aristocratic tradition, and the representative of the commercial against the agricultural interest, it was a party of inherent antagonism to the interests and ideals of the west. Let us now test this *a priori* conclusion by studying the attitude of the party and its leaders towards the west, and tracing its fortunes in western regions.

The idea that property interests are the main concern of society was prominent in the debates in the constitutional convention, and affected the provision for the admission of new states. Men who were prominent later in the ranks of the Federal party insisted upon some scheme of apportionment which would safeguard the interests and power of the original states. They feared the crudity of the frontier and the military burdens which it might impose upon the maritime states. Said Gouverneur Morris: "The busy haunts of men, not the remote wilderness, is the proper school of political talents. If the western people get the power into their hands, they will ruin the Atlantic interest."[2] The efforts of this conservative

[1] Broad construction was not a fundamental tenet of the Federalists, so much as a means by which they sought to secure the ends of government as they conceived them. When their opponents secured control, strict construction became the natural defense for the same interests.

[2] *Madison's Notes of the Debates* (Scott's edition), p. 327. On another occasion Morris said: "Property was the main object of society. . . . The rule of representation ought to be so fixed, as to secure to the Atlantic States a prevalence in the national councils. The new States will know less of the public interest than these, will have an interest in many respects different; in particular will be little scrupulous of involving the community in wars the burdens and operations of which would fall chiefly on the maritime States." *Ibid.*, p. 298. Similar views were advanced by Rufus King (p. 300), Rutledge (p. 298), Butler (p. 301), Gerry (p. 345), and Williamson (p. 313). All of these men were Federalists except Gerry, although Butler presently ceased to act with that party and Rutledge did not become an active partisan until the late

group to render the western communities permanently dependent failed; they succeeded only in securing to Congress an uncertain measure of discretion in the admission of new states, in the provision that " new states may be admitted by the Congress."[3]   The ambiguous phrase did not close the gate of statehood against the territories, nor did it shut the door against future controversies.

The discussions of the convention betray the natural bias of men of the type which gave tone to Federalism.   And certainly the western communities then in existence gave little promise of such development as these men would have wished.   The middle-state and southern emigrants to the Kentucky and Tennessee frontiers came chiefly of that stock which had given birth to the American ideal of democracy. When the ratifying conventions of North Carolina and Virginia met, the delegates from these western counties voted almost solidly against ratification,[4] and ratification once an accomplished fact, even the Federal party there tended rapidly towards Republicanism.   The excise and direct tax powerfully alienated western sentiment.   In Tennessee there were a few admirers of Hamilton's policies;[5] in Kentucky the excesses of the French Revolution and the violence of Genet's partisans tended for awhile to maintain an administration party.[6]   But in a great outburst of indignation over Jay's treaty, Senator Marshall was denounced for his favorable vote,[7] and within a few years the Federal party was destroyed so completely

nineties.   The champions of equal rights for the west were Madison, Mason, and Wilson.   *Ibid.*, pp. 322, 329, 344.

[3] See Farrand: "Compromises of the Constitution," in *American Historical Review*, IX., pp. 483-4.

[4] Libby, O. G., *Geographical Distribution of the Vote on the Ratification of the Constitution, University of Wisconsin Bulletin*, I., No. 1, pp. 35, 39.

[5] Phelan, J., *Tennessee*, pp. 241-2.

[6] Shaler, N., *Kentucky*, p. 129.

[7] *Ibid.*, p. 131.

that the legislature of that commonwealth was chosen as
an organ for the Republican pronunciamento against the
Alien and Sedition laws. The test of Federalist policy,
culminating in these acts, proved the real affinity of the
pseudo-Federalism of Kentucky and Tennessee to be the
Jeffersonian party.

Nevertheless, the nascent Federalism of 1792 offered
no protest against the admission of the first of these western states. Never a territory of the Union, Kentucky
came quietly into the sisterhood of states in pursuance of
an agreement between Virginia and Congress. But the application of Tennessee in 1796 was the signal for Federalist opposition. The people of the "Territory South of
the Ohio River," as it was officially designated, acting under an ordinance of the territorial legislature, without
authorization of Congress, had held a convention and
adopted a constitution under which they now claimed
recognition. By the terms of North Carolina's cession,
Congress was pledged to grant eventual statehood on terms
defined by the Ordinance of 1787 for the Northwest Territory. Not venturing to impugn this pledge, the Federalists professed friendship for the statehood aspirations
of the people of the territory, and confined their objections
to insistence upon safe precedent, since "in a few years,
other States would be rising up in the Western wilderness,
and claiming their right to admission," and "it was of
considerable moment to the United States, that a proposi-
tion which admitted a new State to the equal rights in one
important branch of Government in the affairs of the nation should be seriously considered and grounded on clear
constitutional right."[8] They maintained that action by
Congress must precede the organization of a state govern-

[8] Speech of William Smith of South Carolina, May 5. *Annals of Congress, Fourth Congress, I sess.*, 1300-1304. Smith's leadership is significant of the non-sectional character of the Federalist opposition.

ment, and pointed out that it was quite within the power of Congress, by dividing the territory into two states, to " leave less than sixty thousand inhabitants in either, and consequently deprive them of any claim whatever to admission into the Union at this time." [9] The Federalists had no desire, however, to increase the ultimate number of Republican states, as such a division would have done; they considered the eagerness of their opponents to grant recognition as due to the hope of electing Jefferson,[10] and wished to delay recognition long enough to deprive the Republicans of three electoral votes in the presidential campaign then in progress. By a vote of 43 to 30, however, the House took action in favor of immediate recognition, and so far as the alignment of parties has been ascertained, it stood: Republicans 17 to 1 in favor, Federalists 2 to 12 against.[11]

In the Senate, Rufus King presented a committee report which declared the inhabitants of Tennessee, in the absence of action of Congress, not yet entitled to admission as a state.[12] This report the Senate adopted, and by a vote of 15 to 8 passed a bill reported later from King's committee for "laying out into one State the territory ceded by the State of North Carolina."[13] In the end the Senate passed the House bill by the casting vote of acting-president Livermore, whose action gave his Federalist friends chagrin.[14] On the whole, the Federalist attitude in the Tennessee

[9] *Ibid.*

[10] " No doubt this is but one twig of the electioneering cabal for Mr. Jefferson."—Chauncey Goodrich to Oliver Wolcott, Sr., quoted by Phelan, *Tennessee,* p. 188.

[11] To ascertain the party politics of obscure congressmen is very difficult. I have relied upon the *Congressional Biographical Directory,* correcting and supplementing it where possible. Notwithstanding the incomplete figures the party alignment is evident.

[12] *Annals of Congress, Fourth Cong., I sess.,* 91-94.

[13] *Ibid.,* pp. 97, 109.

[14] Goodrich to Wolcott, *loc. cit.*

episode is what one would expect in the light of the speeches
in the convention of 1787.   They displayed a willingness
to prolong the territorial status, which is in marked contrast with the Republican view of it as " a degraded situation," lacking " a right essential to freemen—the right of
being represented in Congress." [15]

" There is no question," asserts one historian, " that the
rapid growth of the new settlements, whether in the old
States or in the West, from 1790 on, was a material cause
of the final complete annihilation of the Federal party." [16]
" The decision between Federalism and the so-called Republican party," writes another, " depended on the two
great and growing states of Pennsylvania and New York;
and from the very fact that they were growing, that both
of them had an extensive backwoods frontier. . . ." [17]   But
it must not be hastily concluded that the frontier was in-
variably Republican.   If the Kentucky and Tennessee area
was a natural region for Republican expansion, Federalism
also showed a marked tendency to spread westward with
the migrating New England stock, and did not yield to the
forces of democracy without a struggle.   The expansion
of Federalism and its gradual approximation to Republicanism are excellently illustrated in the history of New
York, and the study has especial interest because of the
unique part played by that state in the election of Jefferson.
In the struggle over ratification of the constitution, the
Federalist vote came from the commercial regions of the
lower Hudson; the patroon aristocracy and their tenants
on the upper Hudson, and the German population of the
Mohawk Valley were strongly opposed to ratification.   If
the New York convention had been among the earliest to

[15] The words are Madison's. *Annals, Fourth Cong., I sess.*, 1308-9.
See note 2, p. 115.
[16] Hinsdale, B. A., *Old Northwest*, p. 295.
[17] Hildreth, K., *History of the United States*, V., p. 416.

meet, there is little doubt it would have refused to ratify;
but the geographical position of the state made rejection
impracticable in the face of the action of the other states.
But while the Federalists were strengthened by this initial
victory, and aided by the influence of federal patronage
in the state, they could hardly have shaken the dominance
of the democracy led by George Clinton without the augmentation of their voting strength by immigrants from
New England.   To this immigration chiefly must be at-
tributed the revolution which gave the state into the hands
of the Federalists from 1794 to 1800.   The influx of New
Englanders in these years affected most the very regions
which had been anti-federal, and the frontiers.   The
opening of cheap lands drew swarms of farmers from Connecticut and Massachusetts, while the establishment of new
counties attracted to the county towns young lawyers and
merchants of Federalist principles, whose political talents
provided leadership for the rural electorate.[18]   In the apportionment of 1791, the population of the Western District entitled it to five of the twenty-four state senators.[19]
The rapid increase of freeholders, due chiefly to the immigration from New England, necessitated a reapportion-
ment four years later, when, of the twenty additional senators for the entire state, twelve fell to the Western District.[20]   During the nineties, this district was the most
certainly Federalist area in the state, electing candidates
of that party almost without opposition.   By 1798, however, Republican gains gave warning of the early passing
of Federalist control in the state at large, and in the election of 1800, which restored the Republicans to power,
the Federalists were defeated even in the Western District,

[18] Benton, Nathaniel S., *A History of Herkimer County, Including the Upper Mohawk Valley*, p. 259.
[19] Hammond, J. D., *History of Political Parties in the State of New York*, p. 52.
[20] *Ibid.*, p. 99.

which now became as regularly Republican as it had been Federalist.

These facts point to the actual conversion of Federalist voters to Republicanism, and suggest that the Federalism of the New England-New York frontiersman was traditional rather than vital. Naturally, the appeal of the wilderness was strongest with the younger and less prosperous men—the very class least steeped in the orthodox Federalism of their native communities. Transplanted from its original environment, Federalism of this type easily conformed to its new surroundings and presently merged into Republicanism. The actual process may, indeed, be traced. During the two or three years preceding 1800, there were in the assembly eight or ten members who had been chosen as Federalists, but who were beginning to question the doctrines of that party, and to act with the Republicans.[21] Among these was Jedediah Peck, an uneducated immigrant from Connecticut, who plied the trade of surveyor in behalf of his fellows who, during the nineties, redeemed Otsego County from the wilderness. " He would survey your farm in the daytime, exhort and pray in your family at night, and talk on politics the rest part of the time." [22] Such was the character of the man chosen by the Otsego settlers to represent them in the councils of the state, and from the representative may be inferred the character of the constituents. The latent aristocracy of Federalism, which showed its hand in the Alien and Sedition acts, was too much for these people, and Peck circulated a petition for the repeal of the Sedition law. For this Judge Cooper, the novelist's father, an ardent Federalist, caused Peck to be arrested and carried two hundred miles to New York for trial. The effect of such a spectacle upon a population already disaffected, on the eve of a state and national election, is easily imagined.

[21] *Ibid.,* p. 123.   [22] *Ibid.,* p. 124.

" A hundred missionaries in the cause of democracy, stationed between New York and Cooperstown, could not have done so much for the Republican cause as this journey of Jedediah Peck from Otsego to the capital of the State." [23]   Meantime other influences had been working in the same direction.   Of a type similar to Peck was Obadiah German, member from the neighboring county of Chenango.   To these waverers Aaron Burr had been paying court, conscious that their espousal of democracy would be an important factor in the winning of the west.   Falling in as it did with the events narrated, Burr's plan was completely successful, and in the decisive campaign of 1800 these counties followed their converted leaders into the ranks of Republicanism.[24]   Herkimer, another of this group of western counties, was won by similar means, disaffection caused by the policies of the Adams administration coinciding with the coming of a Republican lawyer sent to organize the local democracy.[25]

In its new garb the Western District speedily became dominant in state politics.   By 1805, German was the recognized leader of the Republicans in the assembly;[26] in 1809, western New York demanded the choice of a citizen of that section for United States senator, and secured the election of German over several prominent competitors.[27] In the gubernatorial campaign of 1810 the issue was admitted to rest with the same section.   In the hope of carrying this stronghold of Republicanism, the Federalists nominated Jones Platt, a pioneer of Whitesborough, who, notwithstanding the revolution of sentiment which had taken place around him and his own steadfast Federalism, had retained his popularity in the part of the state with

[23] *Ibid.*, p. 132.
[24] *Ibid.*, pp. 124, 134.
[25] Benton, *History of Herkimer County*, p. 262.
[26] Hammond, *History of Political Parties*, p. 213.
[27] *Ibid.*, p. 276.

which he had so long been identified.[28]   But the device failed.

The conversion of the west to Republicanism sealed the doom of the Federalist party in New York; and the Republican victory in the state in 1800 swung twelve electoral votes from the Federalist column, which, in view of the balance of parties in the rest of the country, may fairly be said to have decided the presidential election.   Never after 1796 did New York cast a Federalist electoral vote, and that party gradually sank to the position of a faction acting with one or the other of the Republican groups as interest seemed to dictate.[29]

In that portion of the Northwest Territory which became the state of Ohio, Federalism had its severest test in direct competition with the democratic stock which had already captured Kentucky and Tennessee.   The Federalists were first on the ground; the veterans who followed Putnam to Marietta found themselves, in the period of nascent parties, in sympathy with their eastern relatives. In the settlements around Cincinnati, also, were many easterners whose leanings were towards Federalism, and Arthur St. Clair, the territorial governor, was a staunch adherent of that party.   The governor himself entered the lists as a pamphleteer in defense of the Adams administration,[30] and the legislature of 1799 voted a complimentary address to the president with but five dissenting voices.[31]   These five votes, however, were ominous of approaching discord.   Into the Cincinnati region and the

[28] *Ibid.*, p. 279.

[29] Hammond's explanation of the fall of the Federalists is: " They did not properly appreciate the intelligence and good sense of the mass of the community. . . . It was this unjust estimate . . . which carried them into a course of reasoning and action which resulted in . . . utter overthrow." P. 162.   Hammond's work was published in 1842.

[30] Smith, W. H., *St. Clair Papers,* II., p. 442.

[31] *Ibid.,* I., p. 213; II., p. 484.

Virginia military reservation was pouring a flood of southern immigrants imbued with a dislike of the dependent territorial status; with characteristic impatience at arbitrary
power, the leaders of this element had clashed with St.
Clair in the interpretation of his powers. The result was a
firm conviction on their part that they should never get fair
play under the territorial régime. The rapid increase of
population promised them relief through early statehood,
but St. Clair, true to his Federalist instincts, mistrusted the
classes to whom he foresaw power would fall. To him
they seemed an indigent and ignorant people, ill qualified
to form a constitution and government for themselves, and
too remote from the seat of government to feel a wholesome respect for the power of the United States. " Fixed
political principles they have none. . . . Their government would most probably be democratic in form and
oligarchic in its execution, and more troublesome and more
opposed to the measures of the United States than even
Kentucky." [32]   To Timothy Pickering, the Federalist secretary of state, St. Clair therefore proposed a departure
from the plan of division of the Northwest Territory laid
down in the Ordinance of 1787, and a division of the " inhabitants in such a manner as to make the upper or Eastern
division surely Federal, and form a counterpoise . . . to
those who are unfriendly to the General Government." [33]
Upon reflection, however, he abandoned this project on
the ground that " the eastern division is too thinly inhabited, and the design would be too evident," and, as suggested in the Tennessee debate, proposed a division which,
while leaving each portion " a sufficient number of inhabitants to continue in the present [second territorial] stage
of government," would keep " them in the colonial state

[32] St. Clair to James Ross, December, 1799. *Ibid.*, II., pp. 481-3.
[33] This letter has been lost. St. Clair gives a summary in his communication to Ross, cited above.

for a good many years to come." Instead of lending
himself to St. Clair's scheme, Pickering submitted the letter to William Henry Harrison, delegate of the Territory
in Congress, on whose recommendation a division was
made (May, 1800) in accordance with the Ordinance.
Hoping to secure a reconsideration by Congress, St. Clair's
partisans next (November, 1801) carried through the
legislature a bill assenting to a departure from the bounds
of the prospective state, as defined by the Ordinance, which
Fearing, Harrison's successor as territorial delegate, was
instructed to submit for the approval of Congress. Meantime, the Jeffersonian régime had been inaugurated at
Washington, and St. Clair's opponents met the issue by
appealing to their friends at the capital, not only to reject
the boundary act, but to take steps favorable to the admission of the state.

The quarrel of Ohio Federalists and Republicans over
statehood now transferred to the larger arena of the national Congress, bade fair to become a national party issue. It was predicted that Federalists would oppose admission, because the increase of western and southern
states accrued to the advantage of their opponents.[34]   On
the other hand, the Republicans were eager to add to their
party strength three electoral votes which might prove
decisive in the contest of 1804. The boundary act was
decisively rejected on January 27, 1802, only five votes
being recorded in its favor; and the next day the first steps
towards a statehood bill were taken under a motion by
Giles, a zealous Republican from Virginia.[35]   In the debate
which ensued the expected Federalist opposition failed to
break cover. Roger Griswold of Connecticut was allowed, almost unsupported, to voice the protest of the opposition. In the Tennessee debate, the Federalists held

[34] *Ibid.,* I., p. 238.
[35] *Annals of Congress, Seventh Cong., I sess.,* pp. 465-6, 469.

that an act of Congress must precede the formation of a state government by the people of a territory; now Griswold maintained that the passage of an act giving the assent of Congress to such action, upon the petition of individuals, and contrary to the wish of the legislature as implied in the boundary act, was an unwarranted interference with the concerns of the people of the territory.[36] The Republicans maintained, as in 1796, that territorial governments " were arbitrary at best, and ought not to exist longer than they could with propriety be dispensed with. They were opposed to the genius of the people of this country. . . . The people resident in the Territory had emigrated from the different States in the Union, where they had been in the habit of enjoying the benefits of a free form of government; they no doubt looked forward to a very short period, at which they might again enjoy the same as pointed out by the Ordinance . . . but if the doctrine now contended for in opposition, shall prevail in this House, all their hopes are blasted," for, answering Griswold, it was urged that it was " not to be supposed that men who have power to nullify every act of the people, will ever sanction one to put an end to their own political existence." In support of this contention the boundary act was cited.[37]

It is interesting to note the bearing of these early party contests upon the evolution of our practice in admitting states. In these two instances, the Federalist objections tended to correct extreme action by the Republicans. The Federalists were nevertheless opportunists, and Griswold's plea was not entirely consistent with the Federalist contention in 1796. Then it was asserted that the action of the territorial legislature should not be taken as conclusive of

[36] *Ibid.,* 1104-5.
[37] Extract from the speech of R. Williams of North Carolina. *Annals, sup. cit.,* pp. 1107-10.

the wish of the people of Tennessee, since many were known to oppose statehood; while Griswold maintained that the action of the legislature was the only evidence of the attitude of the inhabitants of a territory cognizable by Congress.

The final vote on the Ohio statehood bill shows more clearly than the debate the partisan nature of the issue. The vote of those whose politics have been ascertained shows the Republicans 14 to 1 in favor of it, with seven Federalists opposed. The bill as passed offended the Federalists by separating what is now eastern Michigan from the proposed state. This they believed to have been done from the fear that that district, which Federalism seems to have dominated, would give a majority against statehood, or, if favorable, would carry the state into the Federalist column.[38] It is significant of the extent to which Federalism had invaded the west, that a gerrymander was necessary to insure Republican ascendency.

The passage of the enabling act was only the beginning of disaster for the Ohio Federalists. Their delegates in the constitutional convention were outnumbered nearly three to one; St. Clair was dismissed by Jefferson, with scant courtesy, before the expiration of his term as territorial governor, for criticising the action of Congress in a speech before the convention.[39] The convention, true to the current creed of democracy, and mindful of the conflicts with the late governor, framed a constitution which trusted large powers to the legislature, but reduced the governor to a figurehead. In the first election the Republicans carried even Marietta by a large majority, the disheartened Federalists casting blank ballots, in view of the certainty of defeat.[40] The rout of the party by these events was so com-

[38] Burnet, Jacob, *Notes on the Early Settlement of the North-Western Territory*, p. 337.

[39] *St. Clair Papers*, I., pp. 244-6; II., pp. 592-601.

[40] *Ibid.*, I., p. 247.

plete that it practically disappeared from the state.   Virginian, New Yorker, Yankee, Scotch-Irishman, Irishman, and Englishman were drawn alike into the all-embracing democracy.   All of these stocks were represented in the governor's chair within a quarter-century,[41] but no man who before the party title of Federalist attained important office until about 1820, by which time that designation was fast losing its significance.   Among the politicians of these early days, however, were many men from New England, and especially Connecticut, who had imbibed the principles of democracy in their earlier home, or who found their Federalism no longer tenable in the changed social and political conditions of the West.[42]

[41] Tiffin, English; Kirker, Irish; Morrow, Scotch-Irish.   Huntington was born in Connecticut, Looker in New York, and Worthington in Virginia.

[42] Congressmen of Connecticut birth:

RETURN JONATHAN MEIGS, Jr., Middletown.   A graduate of Yale, originally a Federalist; went over to the Republicans during the statehood contest.   When a candidate for governor in 1810, his opponents sought to defeat him by calling him a Federalist.

JOHN S. EDWARDS, New Haven.   First congressman from the Western Reserve counties, under apportionment of 1812.   An "extreme Jeffersonian Republican."

LEVI BARBER, Litchfield.

PHILEMON BEECHER, Kent.   Sent to the Fifteenth Congress by the fifth Ohio district.   "Originally a Federalist with broadened ideas." The first of that party name elected to Congress by an Ohio constituency.

PETER HITCHCOCK, Cheshire.

JOHN C. WRIGHT, Weathersfield.

ELISHA WHITTLESEY, Washington.

STANLEY GRISWOLD, Torringford.

JAMES KILBOURNE, New Britain.

BENJAMIN RUGGLES, Woodstock.

ETHAN ALLEN BROWN, Darien.   A law student and protégé of Alexander Hamilton, but none the less an "uncompromising Democrat."

In connection with these should be mentioned Samuel Huntington, who became governor in 1808.   He was the namesake and adopted heir of an uncle, a governor of his native state.   In Ohio he ranked with the moderate Republicans, respected and trusted by men of both parties.

In contrast with all of the above is the record of William A. Trimble, of Virginia stock and Kentucky birth.   Trimble studied law at Litchfield,

The approach of the election of 1804 found the Federalists, as a national party, in desperate straits. The general moderation of Jefferson's administration won popular approval, at the same time that such measures as the attack on the judiciary confirmed the apprehensions of Federalist leaders. There appeared little hope of staying the tide of evil. By means of the twelfth amendment, the vice presidency, which, under the original provision, the Federalists might expect to fall as a consolation prize to their minority party, had been seized by the majority. Through this amendment, the constitutional provision for slave representation, and the growth of the west, the Federalists saw their opponents becoming more and more firmly entrenched in the executive and legislative departments of the general government. During the nineties, Kentucky had sent two members to Congress; under the apportionment following the census of 1800, she sent six, and enjoyed a double allotment of presidential electors. The admission of Ohio added three more electors to the Republican column, destined to swell to eight on the next apportionment. " In thirty years," wailed Pickering, " the white population on the Western waters will equal that of the thirteen States when they declared themselves independent of Great Britain." [43] The expansion of democracy seemed likely to find no limit, for, worst of all, the Louisiana Purchase had added a vast new world, which in time would swell the number of Republican states. The ruin of the Atlantic interest, predicted by Morris in 1787, seemed drawing near: the friends of commerce, of con-

Conn., and became a " liberal Federalist." He was elected United States Senator in 1819, enjoying the distinction of being the first non-democratic senator chosen by Ohio.

For these personal notes I am indebted to many sources, especially to Taylor, *Ohio in Congress.*

[43] Letter to Rufus King, March 4, 1804: Adams, Henry, *New England Federalism*, p. 352.

servative government and good order, seemed destined to permanent subjection to the party of " incongruous materials, all tending to mischief." [44]

Under these circumstances the ultra Federalists began to feel that the Union had failed to secure their dearest interests, and to consider the feasibility of a northern confederation.[45] " The people of the East," wrote Pickering to Cabot, " cannot reconcile their habits, views, and interests with those of the South and West. The latter are beginning to rule with a rod of iron. . . . I do not believe in the practicability of a long-continued union. A northern confederacy would unite congenial characters." [46] In the end conservative counsels prevailed; the " disease " of democracy was preying on the vitals of New England herself, and was not to be cured by separation from the south and west.[47] But the secession project only slum-

---

[44] Hamilton's characterization of the Republican party in letter to Jay, 1800: Lodge, *Works of Alexander Hamilton*, VIII., p. 550. Space forbids review of the Louisiana debates. In the discussion of the treaty of purchase, the Federalists admitted the right of the United States to acquire foreign territory, but denied the constitutionality as well as the policy of admitting such territory to statehood. See, *e.g.*, Pickering's speech: " He had never doubted the right to the United States to acquire new territory, either by purchase or by conquest, and to *govern the territory so acquired as a dependent province.*" *Annals, Eighth Cong., I sess.*, p. 45. See also Morris's opinion, quoted by Farrand in *American Historical Review*, IX., p. 484. The above italics are mine. Compare the arguments on previous occasions. It is interesting to speculate on the course our territorial system would have taken under unhampered Federalist control.

[45] " They saw in Louisiana the question of life or death. . . . They were fully aware that the popular will throughout the length and breadth of the country was arrayed against them, and they knew of but one method of relief—a dissolution of the Union. . . . They did not fear the measure of acquiring Louisiana *per se,* but the supremacy of Democracy, which was its meaning to them. They saw in it the assurance of a perpetuation of Jefferson's power and of his maxims." Lodge, H. C., *Life of George Cabot,* pp. 435-6.

[46] January 29, 1804: Adams, Henry, *New England Federalism,* p. 339.

[47] Cabot to Pickering, February 14, 1804: " I greatly fear that a separation would be no remedy, because the source of [the evils] is in the

bered, and was awakened by Jefferson's policy of commercial restriction, and the War of 1812.   Then, indeed, was Morris's prophecy fulfilled, that, if admitted to full political rights, the west would join the south in forcing war upon the maritime states.[48]   In all the clamor of disaffected New England in this period, from Quincy's declamation against the admission of Louisiana [49] to the de-

political theories of our country and in ourselves. . . . Even in New England . . . we are full of errors. . . . *We are democratic altogether;* and I hold democracy, in its natural operation, to be *the government of the worst.* . . . If no man in New England could vote for legislators who was not possessed in his own right of two thousand dollars' value in land, we could do something better." Adams, *sup. cit.,* pp. 346-9. *Cf.* the advice of Hamilton: " Dismemberment of our empire will be a clear sacrifice of great positive advantages, without any counterbalancing good; administering no relief to our real disease, which is *Democracy:* the poison of which by a subdivision will only be the more concentrated in each part, and consequently the more virulent." *Ibid.,* p. 365.

[48] Morris thought the west and south would join in a war with Spain for the Mississippi. *Madison's Notes* (Scott's edition), p. 343.   The interesting point is the perception that in the alignment of sections west and south would stand together against the east.

[49] " The debates of the convention period will show that the effect of the slave votes, upon the political influence of this part of the country, and the anticipated variation of the weight of power to the West, were subjects of great jealousy to some of the best patriots in the Northern and Eastern States.   Suppose, then, that it had been distinctly foreseen, that, in addition to the effect of this weight, the whole population of a world beyond the Mississippi was to be brought into this and the other branch of the Legislature, to form our laws, control our rights, and decide our destiny.   Sir, can it be pretended that the patriots of that day would for one moment have listened to it?   They were not madmen." *Annals of Cong., Eleventh Cong., 3 sess.,* p. 537.

Such views were not confined to New England Federalists. *Cf.* speech of Sheffey, a Federalist from Virginia, *ibid.,* p. 484.   Analysis of the vote on the admission of Louisiana shows the following:

	Ayes	Noes		
Republicans	56	2	Federalist Noes in South	5
Federalists	1	26	Other " " "	3
Politics unknown	20	8		
	77	36		

The Republican attitude was the old one of friendship for the west.

mand of the Hartford Convention for a limitation on the
power of Congress to admit new states,[50] there sounds the
old Federalist antipathy to the west. Even the project
of secession, in the thought of Pickering, was not designed to rid the east of southern influence, so much as to
free it from the pernicious connection with the west,
which had led the south astray. "I believe," he wrote in
1813, "an immediate separation would be a real blessing
to the ' good old thirteen states,' as John Randolph once
called them."[51]   The British attack on New Orleans
aroused the hope that such a separation might be the for-
tunate outcome of the war. In January, 1815, Pickering wrote:

> "By taking and holding New Orleans, and consequently com-
> manding the whole Western country, she will break the Union.
> . . . The Atlantic States remaining united will in due time
> acquire a force sufficient to guard them from insult and injury,
> but short of that which would tempt ambition to involve them in
> destructive wars with children of our common ancestors. This
> view of things presents an additional reason to repress solicitude,
> where it exists, among any Atlantic citizens to recover New
> Orleans, should it fall into the hands of the British. Domestic
> or internal motives have excited in many a willingness, and in some
> a wish, that the Western States might go off and leave the At-
> lantic States free from their mischievous control,—a control every
> day becoming more powerful and dangerous."[52]

Said Macon: "He would treat these people as he would the people of every
other Territory. . . . He was as willing now to make Orleans a State as he
had been to make Ohio a State." *Ibid.*, p. 485.

[50] "No new State shall be admitted into the union by Congress in virtue
of the power granted by the Constitution, without the concurrence of two-
thirds of both Houses." Second constitutional amendment recommended
in the Report of the Hartford Convention.

[51] To George Logan, in Adams, H., *New England Federalism*, p. 391.
Cf. Letter to Edward Pennington, July 12, 1812, *ibid.*, p. 388, in which he
says: "The only permanent severance will be of the Western from the
Atlantic States."

[52] To Lowell. *Ibid.*, pp. 425-6.

But at the date of this letter the war was over: the British had been repulsed at New Orleans, and the treaty of peace was a month old. The control of the United States over the Mississippi Valley had been threatened for the last time, and the expansion of the Republic was secure. An unprecedented westward movement of population followed the return of peace, and within as many years a half-dozen new states had entered the Union. A trace of the old hostility may be discernible in the Federalist votes against the admission of some of these;[53] but during these years that party ceased to maintain a national organization and gradually disintegrated. Even in its old strongholds it was making its last fight against the reflex influence of the tide of democracy which had swept the west; and the adoption by the northeastern states of new constitutions or amendments granting practically universal suffrage drove it from its last entrenchments.[54] Its passing seemed likely, however, to be memorable for one signal victory. In the contest over the admission of Missouri, Rufus King, the old Federalist champion of eastern rights, led the demand for the abolition of slavery in the new state. King's chief argument was the old Federalist contention that slave representation was politically unjust, but

[53] Vote on admission of Mississippi:

	Ayes	Noes
Republicans	46	12
Federalists	1	32
Politics unknown	23	9
	70	53

Three members of the House voted against the admission of Indiana: Goldsborough, a Maryland Federalist, J. Lewis, Jr., a Virginia Federalist, and John Randolph. There was neither debate nor division on the Illinois and Alabama bills, but when a resolution declaring Illinois admitted was before the House, Tallmadge attacked the constitution of the new state on the ground that it did not sufficiently guarantee the exclusion of slavery. The vote shows the obliteration of the old party lines.

[54] Connecticut, 1818; Massachusetts, 1820; New York, 1821.

coinciding with the growing anti-slavery sentiment of the north, at a time when the old party lines were nearly obliterated, it gathered Federalists and northern Republicans into a united body which for a time successfully withstood the demand of the south that Missouri be allowed to determine her own domestic institutions. In the sequel, however, the prominence of Federalist leadership made against the cause, and a number of northern democrats, in the belief that the whole movement was a stratagem of the Federalists for the resuscitation of that party, forsook their colleagues, and by voting with the south, carried the compromise which admitted Missouri with slavery.[55]

Such is the story of the old Federalist party in its relations with the west. Its conservative and aristocratic temper, as the heir of old-world tradition, and its peculiarly commercial basis, unfitted it for expansion into regions where only society of a primitive agricultural type flourished. But the Federalists erred in believing the societies of east and west to be permanently dissimilar. They were so only during the immaturity of the west. By the mid-twenties, the older section had been tempered by the spirit of democracy, and an industrial revolution had shifted its dominant interest from commerce to manufactures, while "the old Northwest" was reaching a maturer stage marked by the growth of towns as centers of trade and manufactures. At the same time a stream of New Englanders was flowing into this part of the west, swamping the southern stock, and assimilating the section in traditions and social heritage to New England and New York. Under the pull of these economic and social forces, the states north of the Ohio River slowly swung away from the old-time alliance with the south and by 1860 had cast in their political fortunes with the east. The Whig and Republican parties,

[55] See an article by the present writer, "Rufus King and the Missouri Compromise," in *Missouri Historical Review* of April, 1908.

which mark this transition in its political aspects, were in some measure the liberalized heirs of Federalism.

But the old Federalism did not live to profit by this change; it had feared western influence because it was itself essentially aristocratic and exclusive; its creed was too harsh to spread, and the growth of the west involved its downfall.

HOMER C. HOCKETT.

INDEPENDENT PARTIES IN THE WESTERN
STATES, 1873-1876

It has been a peculiarity of American politics since the Civil War that the two principal parties have been controlled, in the main, either by men of a conservative type who are naturally opposed to taking up any new or radical issues, or by professional politicians who find it to their interests to keep in the foreground the old familiar questions on which parties have divided in the past, and thus draw away attention from new issues which are likely to disrupt party lines.[1]   Consequently almost the only method by which the advocates of new measures have been able to get them before the public has been the formation of third parties.   Though these parties have seldom had any considerable or lasting success as parties, they have frequently accomplished their purpose by forcing the adoption of their platforms on one or the other of the old parties, and this it is which gives to third parties their importance in American political history.

The close of the Civil War in 1865 left the Republican party[2] in control in every state of the northwest from Ohio to the Pacific coast.   In Ohio and Indiana on the east, in Missouri on the south, and in California and Oregon on the west, the Democratic party remained a factor to be reckoned with, but in the rest of this section—in

[1] *Cf.* Bryce, *American Commonwealth,* II., chaps. liii.-lvi., and Ostrogorski, *Democracy and the Organization of Political Parties,* II.

[2] The party called itself "Union" at that time, but in 1868 it adopted the name of "National Republican."   In an article in the *American Historical Review* for October, 1910, Professor W. A. Dunning points out that this party was distinct in purpose, in personnel, and in name, from the Republican party which elected Lincoln to the presidency in 1860.

Illinois, Michigan, Wisconsin, Minnesota, Iowa, Kansas,
and Nebraska—the great majority of the voters looked
upon the term " Democrat " as practically synonymous
with " rebel " or " Copperhead," and the party which was
thus handicapped could not be expected to make much
headway for many years to come.   There was, however,
considerable opposition to the dominant Republicans in this
section during the decade of the seventies, and almost of
necessity much of this opposition took the form of third
parties.   The first movement in this direction was the organization of the Liberal Republican party, which won
some victories in Missouri, but the presidential election
of 1872 demonstrated that this was a party of leaders
rather than of the people.   Following closely on the heels
of the failure of this movement, there appeared a series
of " Independent " parties which were, on the other hand,
distinctly popular in their origin, and were able to make
a considerable showing in the elections, though receiving
little support from prominent politicians of the old school.[3]

These " Independent " parties have received very little
consideration from historical writers, and there has been a
tendency to look upon them as merely preliminaries leading up to the organization of the National Greenback
party.   This tendency is a natural one in view of the fact
that in one or two states the " Independent " organization
did affiliate with the Greenback party.   In other states,
however, the platforms of the " Independent " parties
specifically rejected the Greenback policy, and an examination of the movement in all of the states in which it ap-

[3] That this movement attracted considerable attention among the politicians of the country is evident from President Grant's fifth annual message
to Congress, dated December 1, 1873, which contains the statement that
" political partisanship has almost ceased to exist, especially in the agricultural regions."   Just what meaning the president intended to convey by
these words and whether or no he looked upon the situation as one to be
deplored, is difficult to determine.

peared makes it clear that its causes are to be sought primarily, not in the desire for a fiat currency, but in two other factors which have no connection with the old issues of war time. The first of these factors is the growing demand for the regulation of railway charges by the state, and closely related to this is the second—the rapid organization of the agricultural population of the west into clubs and granges.

Prior to about 1870 there was little thought of public control of railroads; they were looked upon as blessings to the country, the extension of which should be encouraged rather than checked by subjecting them to any interference. It was generally supposed that competition would prove an efficient regulator, and so the demand was for more railroads, and hence for more competition, rather than for control by the state. During the period of rapid railway expansion which followed the war, however, it began to be evident that the regulating force of competition could easily be nullified by consolidations and agreements, and that serious evils were developing in the management of railroads—evils which were injurious to large groups of people, and which could be checked only by the interposition of the state. In particular were there complaints that freight rates on agricultural products were too high to leave the farmer a fair return for his labor, and that invidious discriminations in rates were made between shippers and between places.[4] The result was a growing de-

---

[4] The nature and causes of these evils in railway construction and management, and the way in which they affected the farmers, are more fully developed in a forthcoming monograph by the writer on *The Granger Movement*. Of the many works which cover the railroad problem in this period, the following are perhaps the most useful: Adams, C. F., Jr., *Railroads, Their Origins and Problems*; Cook, W. W., *The Corporation Problem*; Hudson, J. F., *The Railways and the Republic*; Johnson, E. R., *American Railway Transportation*; Larrabee, W., *The Railroad Question*; Ringwalt, J. L., *Development of Transportation Systems in the United*

mand, especially on the part of the farmers, for legislation to regulate the charges of railroads, a demand which the dominant Republican party was not inclined to heed.

Partly as a result of the railway situation, a movement for agricultural organization was spreading like a prairie fire over the states of the west. In 1867 the National Grange of the Patrons of Husbandry was established in Washington by a number of government clerks who were interested in improving the social and intellectual conditions of the farmers of the country.[5] The first state grange was established in Minnesota in 1869, but the order did not make much headway until about 1872, when it began to advocate government regulation of railroad rates, and to establish co-operative enterprises for the purpose of eliminating the profits of the middlemen. From that time on, however, the growth of the Grange, as it was generally called, was phenomenal: by May, 1873, there were almost three thousand local granges in the North Central states, about half of which were in the state of Iowa; and by September, 1874, there were twelve thousand local granges in these states and twenty thousand in the country at large. Indiana, Iowa, and Missouri had each about two thousand granges, while Ohio, Illinois, and Kansas had over a thousand apiece, and as the average membership of a grange was from fifty to seventy-five, it will be seen that a large proportion of the western farmers were connected with the order.

The Patrons of Husbandry was an organization professedly non-political in character, but that did not prevent

States; Stickney, A. B., The Railroad Problem; and the report of the Windom Committee of the United States Senate (43 Cong., 1 sess., Senate Reports, No. 307).

[5] The idea of the order originated in the brain of one Oliver H. Kelley, a clerk in the agricultural bureau, and later in the post-office department. Kelley's book, Origin and Progress of the Patrons of Husbandry, gives the early history of the order.

it from taking a decided stand on questions of public policy, and especially upon the railroad question, while in some states the local granges took part in the organization of new political parties.[6] On the whole, however, the leaders of the order were able to keep it from participating directly in partisan politics, but there were also a large number of non-secret and more or less independent farmers' clubs which grew up side by side with the granges, and the union of these local clubs into state farmers' associations paved the way for the establishment of the " Independent " parties in a number of states.[7] This was particularly the case in Illinois, in which state the movement for a new political party, with railroad regulation as its principal plank, first came to a head. There the agitation for restrictive railroad laws had been going on with more or less intensity ever since 1865, and finally in 1870 its advocates succeeded in incorporating mandatory provisions in the new constitution which directed the legislature to enact laws to prevent extortion and unjust discrimination in railway charges. The general assembly of 1871 responded with a series of so-called " Granger laws," one of which was declared contrary to the constitution by the state supreme court in January, 1873, because it prohibited not merely unjust discrimination, but all discrimination in railway charges.[8]

In the same month in which this decision was handed

[6] The " Declaration of Principles " adopted by the National Grange in February, 1874, asserted " that the Grange . . . is not a political or party organization. No Grange, if true to its obligations, can discuss political or religious questions, nor call political conventions, nor nominate candidates, nor even discuss their merits in its meetings." National Grange, *Proceedings of the Seventh Session*, p. 58.

[7] The files of the *Chicago Tribune* and the *Prairie Farmer* for 1873 and 1874 contain a large amount of information about these organizations.

[8] Gordon, J. H., *Illinois Railway Legislation and Commission Control since 1870* (Univ. of Ill., *Studies*, I., No. 6), pp. 25-40; Paine, A. E., *The Granger Movement in Illinois* (*ibid.*, No. 7), pp. 20-24; Moses, John,

down by Chief Justice Lawrence, the State Farmers' Association of Illinois was organized. It immediately adopted a series of radical resolutions on the transportation question, and asserted " that the power of this and all local organizations should be wielded at the ballot-box, by the election of such and only such, persons as sympathize with us in this movement." [9]   The legislature was in session at this time, and was considering a revision of the railroad laws to overcome the objections of the supreme court.[10] In order to insure the enactment of effective laws on this subject, the executive committee of the newly organized State Farmers' Association issued a call for a " State Farmers' Convention," to be held at Springfield, the capital city, April 2, 1873, " for the purpose of attending to our interests in the Legislature, and of giving that body and the Governor to understand that we *mean business* and are no longer to be trifled with; and that while we have no disposition to infringe upon the rights of others, we demand that protection at their hands from the intolerable wrongs now inflicted upon us by the railroads which they have a constitutional right to give us." [11]

The principal work of this convention, which was opened with speeches by Governor Beveridge and ex-Governor Palmer, was the adoption of a series of resolutions setting forth its ideas concerning railroad legislation, but these

Illinois, Historical and Statistical, II., pp. 801, 1059-1061. The decision of the supreme court is in 67 *Illinois,* p. 11.

[9] *Prairie Farmer,* XLIII., pp. 316, 364; XLIV., pp. 9, 12, 25 (October, 1872-January, 1873); *Chicago Tribune,* 1873, January 16, p. 4, January 17, p. 8, January 18, p. 2; Perriam, Jonathan, *The Groundswell,* pp. 232-262.

[10] Illinois, *Senate* and *House Journals,* 1873. The pages of the *Chicago Tribune* and the *Prairie Farmer* at this time are filled with resolutions of farmers' meetings on the railroad question. For a sample, see resolutions of a Livingston county convention of farmers, in *Chicago Tribune,* January 10, 1873, p. 5.

[11] *Prairie Farmer,* XLIV., p. 100 (March 29, 1873); *Chicago Tribune,* March 21, 1873, p. 2.

were followed by other resolutions relating to navigation
on the inland lakes and the protective tariff, which furnish
the first important indication that the movement was to
spread out from an agitation for railroad regulation into a
full-fledged political party, with views to express on a
variety of questions.   These resolutions, which were said
to be the result of efforts of Democratic politicians to capture the movement and of railroad men to nullify it by
throwing the blame for high charges upon the policy of
protection, met with considerable opposition in the convention on the ground that the farmers should concentrate
their efforts upon the question of railroad regulation; and
the next day a rump composed of about one hundred of the
delegates to the convention held a meeting, at which the
resolutions in question were reconsidered and laid on the
table.[12]   Despite this split in the ranks, the work of this
convention on the railroad problem and the sustained agitation on the part of the farmers finally bore fruit in the
passage by the legislature, May 2, 1873, of a new act for
the regulation of railroads, more radical and more effective
than the laws of 1871.

The first attempt of the farmers of Illinois to take part
as an organized body in the election of public officers appears to have been a result of the decision of Chief Justice
Lawrence on the constitutionality of the railroad law of
1871.   The idea was gaining ground that the farmers
must control the courts as well as the legislature if they
were to secure any solid results, and the judicial elections
of June, 1873, seemed to them a good opportunity for
making a beginning in that direction.   Particularly was
that the case in the fifth district, where the term of the
chief justice himself was about to expire.   Lawrence was

---

[12] *Prairie Farmer*, XLIV., pp. 114, 123 (April, 1873); *Chicago Tribune*,
1873, April 2, p. 8, April 4, p. 8; *American Annual Cyclopedia*, 1873, p.
367; Perriam, J., *The Groundswell*, pp. 280-291.

renominated by means of a petition widely signed by the lawyers of the district, but the farmers, who felt that he was not in sympathy with their interests, held a convention at Princeton in April and nominated Honorable Alfred M. Craig for the position.   No pledges were exacted of the nominee, but he had shown himself favorable to the regulation of corporations by his action in the constitutional convention of 1869-1870.   The convention which nominated him also adopted a series of resolutions demanding such action by the legislature and the courts as would make effective the railroad provisions of the constitution, declaring an intention to support no one whose sentiments were not in accord with those of the farmers in these matters, and recommending to the " anti-monopolists " of the state the nomination of candidates for the judicial positions in the various districts.[13]

This advice was followed by the farmers of the second district, the only other one in which a supreme court vacancy occurred at this time, and in eight or nine of the twenty-six circuits of the state, in each of which a judge was to be elected; while in many of the other districts one or more of the candidates openly declared themselves in sympathy with the farmers' views.[14]   The election which followed first displayed to the astonished politicians of the country the political possibilities of the movement; for in nearly every instance the candidate nominated or favored by the farmers was elected, even Chief Justice Lawrence being defeated by a large majority in spite of a vigorous campaign waged in his behalf.   These victories provoked

[13] *Prairie Farmer*, XLIV., p. 153 (May 17, 1873) ; Perriam, *The Groundswell*, pp. 312-316.   Many of the local clubs and granges ratified the nomination of Craig, but in one or two cases they indorsed Lawrence.   See *Prairie Farmer*, XLIV., p. 266 (May 31, 1873) ; *Chicago Tribune*, May 15, 1873, p. 1; Paine, *Granger Movement in Illinois*, p. 35, note.

[14] *Prairie Farmer*, XLIV., p. 153 (May 17, 1873) ; *Chicago Tribune*, May, 1873, *passim*; Perriam, *The Groundswell*, pp. 312-316.

a storm of criticism from the conservative press, especially in the east, and the movement was denounced as an attempt to pack the judiciary in the interests of a class.[15] Given an elective judiciary, however, it is difficult to see how the voters can justly be blamed for casting their ballots for candidates who were expected to uphold what they believed to be their rights.[16]

Greatly encouraged by the success which had been won and nothing daunted by the adverse criticism incurred, the farmers of Illinois threw themselves with vigor into the campaign for the election of county officers in the fall. Even before the judicial elections had taken place, a movement was started in Livingston county to put a farmers' ticket in the field for the fall elections. May 31, 1873, the committee-men representing the different townships in the county farmers' association, adopted a platform or declaration of principles which so well expressed the sentiments of farmers throughout the state that it was adopted or indorsed by farmers' meetings in many other counties. The preamble to this document asserted the failure of the old parties, declared in favor of a new political organization, and invited the co-operation of all other classes in carrying out the declaration of principles. The platform which followed expressed opposition to " railroad steals, tariff steals, salary-grab steals," approved the control by law of railway corporations, denounced taxation for the benefit of special classes, favored equal privileges for all in the banking system, " so that supply and demand shall regulate our money market," opposed further grants of public lands to corporations, and favored " a true system

[15] *Nation,* XVI., pp. 393, 397 (June 12, 1873); *Prairie Farmer,* XLIV., p. 185 (June 14, 1873); *Chicago Tribune,* 1873, June 6, p. 4, June 21, p. 8; Perriam, *sup. cit.,* pp. 312-316.

[16] Lawrence was later attorney for the Chicago and Northwestern Railroad in litigation over the Granger law of Wisconsin. *Industrial Age* (Chicago), June 6, 1875, p. 4.

of civil service reform" and the application of the principle " that the office should seek the man and not the man the office." [17]

The adoption of this declaration was followed by the appointment of a committee to call a convention of farmers and all others in sympathy with them to nominate candidates for county officers. This action received the approval of Secretary Smith of the State Farmers' Association and similar steps were taken in other counties.[18] A great impetus was given to the movement by the celebrations on Independence Day, of what was widely known as the " Farmers' Fourth of July." At the suggestion of the executive committee of the State Farmers' Association this day was made the occasion of numerous and well attended gatherings of farmers in nearly every county in the state. At the most of these meetings an important part of the program was the reading of the new " Farmers' Declaration of Independence," which was circulated by the association. This document was a skillful parody on the original Declaration of Independence, and set forth at great length the conditions which had led to the uprising of the agricultural class. It concluded by declaring the farmers absolutely independent of all past political connections, and by pledging them to give their suffrage to such men only as would use their best endeavors to promote the desired ends.[19] This declaration was solemnly read at hundreds

[17] *Prairie Farmer*, XLIV., p. 187 (June 14, 1873); *Chicago Tribune*, June 3, 1873, pp. 2, 4; *Industrial Age*, August 20, 1873, p. 7. For indorsements of the declaration, see *Chicago Tribune*, June-August, 1873, *passim*.

[18] *Chicago Tribune*, June, 1873, *passim; Industrial Age*, August 20, 1873, pp. 4, 7.

[19] *Prairie Farmer*, XLIV., p. 196 (June 21, 1873); *Chicago Tribune*, June 16, 1873, p. 1. The declaration is printed in full in *Prairie Farmer*, XLIV., p. 217 (July 12, 1873), and in *Chicago Tribune*, June 17, 1873, p. 2. Some extracts from this curious document may not be out of place:

of gatherings in Illinois and in some of the neighboring
states, and the customary spread-eagle oratory by local politicians gave way to earnest discussions of political topics
by the farmers themselves, and fiery addresses by leaders
of the movement, such as that by the Honorable S. M.
Smith, the secretary of the State Farmers' Association, at
Pontiac in Livingston county.[20]

Thus the enthusiasm of the farmers for their cause was
wrought up, and numerous picnics and harvest festivals,[21]
together with the many regular meetings of local clubs and
granges, kept it at a fever heat throughout the summer;
the political results being seen when county after county
fell into line, held conventions, and nominated farmers'

"When in the course of human events it becomes necessary for a class
of the people, suffering from long continued systems of oppression and
abuse, to rouse themselves from an apathetic indifference to their own interests, which has become habitual . . . a decent respect for the opinions of
mankind requires that they should declare the causes that impel them to a
course so necessary to their own protection."

Then follows a statement of "self-evident truths" and a catalogue of
the sins committed by the railroads, together with a denunciation of railroads and congresses for not having redressed these evils. The document
concludes:

"We, therefore, the producers of the state in our several counties assembled . . . do solemnly declare that we will use all lawful and peaceable means to free ourselves from the tyranny of monopoly, and that we
will never cease our efforts for reform until every department of our government gives token that the reign of licentious extravagance is over, and
something of the purity, honesty, and frugality with which our fathers inaugurated it, has taken its place.

"That to this end we hereby declare ourselves absolutely free and independent of all past political connections, and that we will give our
suffrage only to such men for office, as we have good reason to believe
will use their best endeavors to the promotion of these ends; and for the
support of this declaration, with a firm reliance on Divine Providence, we
mutually pledge to each other our lives, our fortunes, and our sacred
honor."

[20] *Prairie Farmer*, XLIV., pp. 217, 220, 225 (July 12, 19, 1873) ; *Chicago
Tribune*, July, 1873, *passim.*

[21] *Prairie Farmer*, XLIV., p. 244 (August 2, 1873); *Chicago Tribune*,
1873, August 7, pp. 1, 2, 4, August 22, p. 1.

tickets for the fall elections.   The procedure in organizing
the new party in most of the counties was similar to that
in Livingston, already described,[22] and the platforms
adopted were generally similar to the Livingston county
declaration of principles, though in some instances they
contained more outspoken denunciation of the protective
tariff.   The completeness with which old party lines were
broken up by this movement is seen in the fact that in some
counties one party and in others the opposite party, either
openly joined the " Reformers " or refrained from making
separate nominations.[23]

Of the one hundred and two counties of the state, independent nominations were made by the new party in sixty-
six, while in many of the other counties the candidates of
one or the other of the old parties were acceptable to the
farmers.   The returns of the elections, which took place
early in November, showed the farmers' or " Anti-Monopoly " tickets victorious in fifty-three of the sixty-six counties
in which they were in the field, while Republican candidates
were elected in sixteen, Democratic in twenty, and independents in thirteen of the remaining counties of the
state.[24]   The total vote in the sixty-six counties contested
by the new party was 176,263, of which the " Reform "
candidates received 94,188, leaving 82,075 to all the other
candidates; and it was calculated that the same ratio carried throughout the state would have given the party a
majority in a state election of twenty-two thousand over
all.[25]   In estimating this election, the results of which were

[22] For examples, see *Chicago Tribune,* 1873, June 25, p. 1, August 2, p. 1.
[23] This was generally, but not always, the party which had previously
been in a minority in the county. See *Chicago Tribune,* August, 1873,
passim.
[24] These figures are based on votes for county treasurers, who appear
to have been the most important officials elected in the several counties.
[25] For returns and classification of counties, see: *Industrial Age,* 1873,
November 8, pp. 4, 5, November 15, pp. 3, 6; *Chicago Tribune,* 1873, Octo-

more favorable to the new party than any other in which it took part, the fact must be taken into consideration that it was for local officers; and that, in general, party politics play a less important part in local than in state elections. The " Reformers " were to find their party unable to retain these handsome majorities when it entered the broader field of state politics, because many voters, while willing to cast their ballots for neighbors running on an " Anti-Monopoly " ticket, were likely, when it was a question of unknown candidates for state offices, to return to their old party allegiance.

Meanwhile similar movements were getting under way in Iowa, Minnesota, and Wisconsin, which resulted in state "Anti-Monopoly" or " Reform " parties in the general elections in the fall of 1873. The political situations in these three states were strikingly similar. In each the Republican party was in complete control; in each a growing demand for railroad regulation was being reflected in messages and addresses of the governor, and in numerous bills before the legislature; and in each the farmers were being rapidly organized into granges of the Patrons of Husbandry. The outcome was the organization of new parties which took the name of "Reform" in Wisconsin, and " Anti-Monopoly " in Iowa and Minnesota; and in each case the Democratic party either fused with or accepted the candidates of the new party. The method of getting the movement under way was about the same in the three states: the farmers and Grangers in the different counties got together during the summer in meetings " outside the gate " and nominated candidates for county and legislative offices; after which calls were issued, either by one of these local meetings, or by self-constituted leaders of the move-

ber 20, p. 4, November 6, p. 1, November 10, p. 5, November 19, p. 4; *Prairie Farmer,* XLIV., pp. 361, 363, 371, 379 (November, 1873); *Amer. Annual Cyclo.,* 1873, p. 368; *World Almanac,* 1874, p. 23.

ment, for state conventions, which were held in Iowa at
Des Moines, August 13, in Minnesota at Owatonna, September 2, and in Wisconsin at Milwaukee, September
23.[26]

In Iowa the state central committee of the Democratic
party decided to hold no convention, and issued an address
advising Democrats to support the Anti-Monopoly ticket.[27]
In Minnesota the Democratic convention was held and
adopted a platform, but indorsed the nominees of the new
party.[28]   In Wisconsin the Democratic convention met in
Milwaukee the day after the Reformers came together,
and the two conventions agreed upon a fusion ticket and
adopted a joint platform.[29]   All three of the platforms
adopted by these new parties declared for the regulation of
railroads or, putting it more generally, for the subjection of corporations to the authority of the state.   Reduction of the tariff to a revenue basis, lower salaries for
public officials, and a more economical administration of
the government, were also demanded by each platform.
In no case did these platforms contain planks favorable to
the Greenback idea, while the Wisconsin platform contained a declaration that the public debt should be honestly
paid, and in Minnesota the platform adopted by the Democratic convention, which indorsed the Anti-Monopoly nom-

[26] The summary in this and the following paragraphs is based on a
study of legislative journals, governors' messages, party platforms, and the
files of the *Chicago Tribune, Prairie Farmer,* and local papers. Information concerning parties and elections, including the platforms in full, can
usually be found in the *American* (after 1874, *Appleton's*) *Annual Cyclopedia* under the name of the state.   The Owatonna platform of the Minnesota Anti-Monopolists, which is not given in the *Cyclopedia,* is in Martin,
E. W. (pseudonym for J. D. McCabe), *History of the Grange Movement,*
pp. 510-513.

[27] *Chicago Tribune,* September 2, 1873, p. 1.

[28] *Amer. Annual Cyclo.,* 1873, p. 511.

[29] *Chicago Tribune,* August-September, 1873, *passim; Industrial Age,*
September 6, 1873, p. 5.

inees, declared for a speedy return to specie payment. It
early became evident that large numbers of Republicans
were going into the new party movement in these states,
and the Republican politicians made frantic efforts to coun-
teract it. Fortunately for them, the Republican governors
in each state had advocated railroad regulation, and these
governors were all renominated on platforms which expressed great concern for the welfare of the farmers, and
which contained planks favoring the regulation of railroads by the state.

The campaigns which followed were spirited, and the
new parties achieved some surprising results. In Iowa the
Anti-Monopoly committee suffered from a lack of campaign funds, and the Republican state ticket was elected,
but its majority, which had been sixty thousand the year
before, was cut down to about twenty thousand, and it was
claimed that the fact of Governor Carpenter being himself a prominent Patron, and his pledge to favor the
farmers' policy, were all that prevented an Anti-Monopoly
victory. The district elections resulted in a legislature
composed of thirty-four Republican and sixteen opposition
senators, with fifty of each party in the lower house.[30]   As
a result of this tie, a long struggle ensued over the organization of the House of Representatives, in the course of
which, the seventy members who were also Patrons held a
meeting and tried to unite on a Grange candidate for
speaker, but found that they too were equally divided into
Republicans and opposition. This shows clearly that a
large proportion of the Grange element had not gone
definitely into the Anti-Monopoly party. The deadlock
was finally broken after 140 ballots by a compromise, according to which the Republicans got the speakership and

[30] *Chicago Tribune,* November 8, 1873, p. 2; *Industrial Age,* 1873, October 18, p. 4, November 8, p. 6, November 15, p. 5; *American Agricul-
turist,* (N. Y.), XXXII., p. 439 (November, 1873).

the opposition the other officers, and the control of a number of committees.[31]

In Minnesota the outcome was somewhat the same. The Republican majority for the head of the ticket was reduced from the usual fifteen or twenty thousand, to about five thousand, and the Anti-Monopoly candidates for secretary of state and treasurer were elected, while the Republican majority in the lower house of the legislature was reduced to two. Moreover, a considerable number of the members of the legislature elected as Republicans were also Grangers, and in favor of state regulation of railroads.[32]

It was in Wisconsin, however, that the most startling results were achieved. The campaign in that state developed a peculiar alignment of interests. Governor Washburn, who was renominated by the Republicans, had frequently recommended legislation for the regulation of railroads, and in other ways incurred the enmity of the railroad interests. As a consequence much of the railroad influence was exerted in favor of Taylor, the Reform candidate, whose principles were not so well known as those of Washburn, apparently with the idea of putting him under obligation to these interests. Another factor in the election was the Graham liquor law, passed by a Republican legislature, which imposed serious restrictions on the liquor traffic, and resulted in turning the powerful brewery interests of the state, as well as a large part of the foreign vote, to the new Reform party. Then, of course, the order of

[31] Iowa, *House Journal*, 1874, pp. 3-48; *Chicago Tribune,* January, 1874, *passim; Industrial* Age, 1874, January 24, p. 3, February 7, p. 6.

[32] *Chicago Tribune*, May, 1873-January, 1874, *passim; Industrial Age,* September 6, 1873, p. 4; *Prairie Farmer*, XLIV., p. 291 (September 13, 1873); Martin, E. W., *Grange Movement*, pp. 510-513; Smith, Stephe, *Grains for the Grangers*, pp. 233-236; Neill, E. D., *History of Minnesota,* 4th ed., pp. 760-763; *Amer. Annual Cyclo.*, 1873, pp. 510-513.

For the attitude of the Patrons of Husbandry toward this political movement in Minnesota, see the *Farmers' Union* (Minneapolis), 1873, pp. 172, 194, 197, 218, 243, 261, 269, 276, 279, 285, 356 (May-November, 1873).

Patrons of Husbandry was a factor in the election, and it seems probable that the major part, though by no means all, of the " Granger vote " was cast for the Democratic-Reform ticket.   Although Wisconsin was normally Republican by large majorities, this " unholy alliance " of the railroad interests and the liquor interests with the Granger movement was sufficient to turn the scale and bring about the election of Taylor and the whole fusion ticket of state officers.   The Democrats and Reformers also secured a majority of twenty in the lower house of the legislature, though the Republicans retained a majority of one in the Senate.[33]

In Kansas and Nebraska there were no state elections in 1873, but Independent or farmers' tickets were put in the field in a number of counties; and in Kansas the result was the election of a sufficient number of Independents or Reformers to give the opposition to the Republican party a majority of about twenty in the lower house of the legislature.   This was sufficient to over-balance the strongly Republican hold-over Senate, and made possible the election of ex-Governor Harvey, a farmer and a Reformer, to the United States Senate.[34]   In California also, the new party movement first made its appearance in a struggle to control the legislature elected in 1873.   The Republican party here was believed by many to be under the influence of the Central Pacific Railroad, and a large number of Republicans led by Governor Newton Booth, broke

---

[33] *Prairie Farmer,* XLIV., p. 379 (November 29, 1873) ; *Chicago Tribune,* October, 1873-January, 1874, *passim; Industrial Age,* November, 1873, *passim;* Wisconsin, *Legislative Manual,* 1874, pp. 325, 348 ; *Amer. Annual Cyclo.,* 1873, pp. 774-776; Lea, C. W., *Granger Movement in Wisconsin* (Univ. of Wis., MS. thesis, 1895), p. 20; Tuttle, C. R., *Illustrated History of the State of Wisconsin,* p. 642; Peck, G. W., ed., *Wisconsin in Cyclopedic Form,* p. 183.

[34] *Chicago Tribune,* June, 1873-February, 1874, *passim; Industrial Age,* 1873, November 8, p. 4, November 15, p. 5; Andreas, *Illustrated History of the State of Kansas,* p. 264.

away from the party organization and supported Anti-
Monopoly or Reform tickets in the various districts. The
result of the election was a legislature composed of thirty-
seven Republicans, forty-two Democrats, and forty-oné
Reformers, but many members elected as Republicans or
Democrats were opposed to the railroad monopoly. The
principal business of this legislature was the election of two
United States senators, and a long struggle finally terminated in the election of Governor Booth for the long
term, and of John S. Hager, an " anti-railroad Democrat,"
for the short term.[35]

During the year 1874 state Reform or Anti-Monopoly
parties were organized in all these states, and in some
other states as well. Even in Ohio there were a few local
efforts in the fall of 1873 looking toward the organization of farmers' or workingmen's parties,[36] but these came
to naught, probably owing to a vigorous revival, which
took place in the Democratic party in the state at this
time. In Indiana, on the other hand, similar local meetings in the fall of 1873, at which former party bonds were
declared to be severed, finally led up to the calling of a
state convention of Independents, which met at Indianapolis, June 10, 1874, and nominated candidates for state
offices. The platform here adopted differed from those
of the Reform parties in the other states in that its principal plank was a demand, not for railroad regulation, but
for the issue of greenbacks interchangeable with government bonds and the payment of the government debt in
legal tender. Two of the nominees of this convention re-

[35] *Chicago Tribune,* December 22, 1873, p. 4, January 23, 1874, p. 3;
Industrial Age, 1873, October 18, p. 4, December 27, p. 4; California State
Grange, *Proceedings at Organization* (July, 1873); Carr, E. S., *Patrons
of Husbandry on the Pacific Coast,* pp. 75-103, 131-153; *Amer. Annual
Cyclo.,* 1873, p. 83.
[36] *Chicago Tribune,* 1873, June 9, p. 1, June 18, p. 5.

fused the honor and another convention, held in August, not only filled their places, but also nominated new candidates in the places of two others who had accepted Democratic nominations for the same offices.   In the election the new party cast about sixteen thousand votes, the Democratic candidates for state offices being victorious.   The Independents secured five senators and eight representatives in the legislature, which gave them the balance of power in the Senate, but the Democrats controlled the House.[37]

In Michigan an attempt was made to break the Republican dominance by the organization of a " National Reform " party, which held conventions in August and September, 1874.   The principal planks in its platform were civil service reform, states' rights, tariff for revenue only, and a speedy return to " hard money."   Some of the Reform nominees were accepted by the Democratic convention, but the Republicans were victorious, though by greatly reduced majorities.   The vote for Reform candidates on which there was no fusion ran from two to seven thousand.[38]

In Illinois the movement which had been so successful in local elections in 1873 speedily developed into a state party in 1874.   The resolutions adopted at the meeting of the State Farmers' Association in December, 1873, furnished the basis for the organization of the new party. These declared that the old parties had forfeited the respect and confidence of the people and demanded a reduction of the salaries of public officials, civil service reform,

[37] On the Independent party movement in Indiana, see: *Chicago Tribune,* 1873, June 18, p. 5, August 23, p. 1, 1874, June 11, pp. 1, 12, August 13, p. 7; *Industrial Age,* 1874, April 18, p. 4, June 13, p. 5, June 27, p. 4, September 5, p. 5, October 17, p. 4; *Amer. Annual Cyclo.,* 1874, pp. 412-415.

[38] *Chicago Tribune,* 1874, February 12, p. 8, June 18, p. 3, August 7, p. 1; *Industrial Age,* February 28, 1874, p. 4; *Amer. Annual Cyclo.,* 1874, pp. 557-559.

and the enforcement of the railroad laws. The resolutions
on tariff and currency were somewhat ambiguous, but the
latter seems to have definitely committed the association to
the Greenback policy.[39]   In May, 1874, the advisory board
of the State Farmers' Association issued a call to " the
farmers, mechanics, and other laboring men, as well as all
other citizens of Illinois who believe as declared by this
Association at Decatur, December 18, 1873," to send delegates to a state convention at Springfield, June 10.[40]   This
convention chose " Independent Reform " as a name for
the new party; nominated candidates for treasurer and superintendent of public instruction—the only state officers
to be elected—and adopted the resolutions of the State
Farmers' Association as a platform with almost no changes,
although a vigorous minority, led by the Honorable Wil-
lard C. Flagg, president of the association, strove for the
adoption of a resolution " uncompromisingly opposing any
further inflation." [41]

The Democratic convention, which met in August, took
issue with the Independents by demanding the resumption
of specie payments as soon as practicable and nominated
a separate candidate for treasurer, but accepted the Inde-

[39] Ill. State Farmers' Assn., *Proceedings of the Second Annual Meeting*,
pp. 98-109.   The resolutions and reports of this meeting are also to be
found in *Prairie Farmer*, XLIV., p. 409, XLV., p. 1 (December 27, 1873,
January 3, 1874) ; *Industrial Age*, December, 1873-January, 1874, *passim;*
Amer. Annual Cyclo., 1873, p. 368.

[40] *Prairie Farmer*, XLV., p. 155 (May 16, 1874) ; *Chicago Tribune*,
1874, May 6, pp. 1, 5, May 11, p. 2.

[41] For the platform and reports of this convention, see: *Prairie Farmer*,
XLV., p. 195 (June 20, 1874) ; *Chicago Tribune*, June 11, 1874, p. 1 ; *Industrial Age*, June 13, 1874, p. 5 ; *Amer. Annual Cyclo.*, 1874, p. 402 ;
Moses, *Illinois, Historical and Statistical*, II., pp. 824-826.   On the campaign and local conventions, see: *Industrial Age*, 1874, September 19, p. 4,
October 10, p. 4 ; *Prairie Farmer*, XLV., p. 275 (August 29, 1874).   Thirty-
three papers which supported the Independent party in the campaign are
listed in the *Chicago Tribune*, June 22, 1874, p. 7.

pendent nominee for superintendent.[42]   In the election
which ensued, the fusion candidate for superintendent of
public instruction received a majority of about thirty thousand votes, but the Republican candidate for treasurer was
elected with a plurality of thirty-five thousand, while the
Independent nominee received about seventy-five thousand
votes out of a total of nearly three hundred and seventy
thousand.   In the congressional elections the opposition
fared somewhat better, regular Republican candidates being elected in but seven of the nineteen districts, while the
remainder were classified: eight as Democrats, three as
Independent Reformers, and one as an independent Republican.   In the state legislature also, the Republicans lost
their majority through this election, while the Independents secured the balance between the two other parties with
three senators and twenty-seven representatives.[43]

In Wisconsin, Iowa, and Minnesota there were enough
representatives of the new party in the legislatures of 1874
to secure the enactment, with some assistance from anti-
railroad Republicans, of the Granger railroad laws of
those states.[44]   Although the railroad companies denied the
validity of these laws and endeavored to have them set
aside by the courts, they entered at the same time upon a
campaign to secure their repeal.   In the legislative elections of 1874 the railroad forces generally supported the
Republican candidates, and the Republicans secured a majority over the combined Democratic and Reform opposi-

[42] *Amer. Annual Cyclo.*, 1874, p. 403; Moses, *Illinois, Historical and Statistical*, II., p. 827; Koerner, Gustav, *Memoirs*, II., p. 583.

[43] Election returns can be found in: *Industrial Age*, 1874, November 7, p. 4, November 14, p. 5; *Amer. Annual Cyclo.*, 1874, p. 404; *Tribune Almanac*, 1875, pp. 47, 80-82; *World Almanac*, 1875, p. 24; Moses, J., *sup. cit.*, II., p. 827.

[44] The history of this legislation and of the struggle over its enforcement is dealt with in the writer's forthcoming monograph on *The Granger Movement.*

tion in both houses of all three of the legislatures.[45]　In Minnesota, the result was the immediate repeal of the Granger railroad law enacted the year before, but in Wisconsin and Iowa enough of the Republican legislators were " anti-railroad " to prevent the repeal of the Granger laws in those states at this time.

The various local farmers' and Reform parties were also drawn together into state parties in Missouri, Kansas, and Nebraska in 1874.　In Missouri the new party was one of opposition to the Democrats who were then in control and received the support of the Republicans;[46] in Kansas, on the other hand, all the elements of opposition to the dominant Republican party were joined under the " Independent Reform " banner;[47] and in Nebraska candidates were put in the field by all three of the parties.[48]　The new party movement does not seem to have made much of an impression upon the political situation in these states, for the Democrats won in Missouri with nearly forty thousand majority, and the Republicans in Kansas with about

[45] On the campaigns of 1874 in these states, see: *Chicago Tribune,* January-July, 1874, *passim; Industrial Age,* February-November, 1874, *passim; Amer. Annual Cyclo.,* 1874, pp. 418, 564, 810; Tuttle, *Wisconsin,* p. 649.

In Wisconsin the officers of the State Grange took part in this campaign, first by calling upon all Patrons to vote for candidates who would support the Granger railroad law, and then by circulating a list of questions calculated to be submitted to candidates and to force them to declare their positions on the question of railroad regulation. Wis. State Grange, *Proceedings at the Second Session* (1874), especially the appendix, pp. 3-12; Maynard, M. E., *Patrons of Husbandry in Wisconsin* (Univ. of Wis., MS. thesis, 1895), p. 57.

[46] *Chicago Tribune,* 1874, January 10, p. 2, January 12, p. 8, February 21, p. 8, June 11, p. 1; *Industrial Age,* 1874, May 16, p. 5, May 30, p. 5, June 13, p. 4, July 25, p. 6, September 5, p. 4; *Prairie Farmer,* XLV., p. 75 (March 7, 1874) ; *Amer. Annual Cyclo.,* 1874, pp. 576-579.

[47] *Chicago Tribune,* February 21, 1874, p. 8; *Industrial Age,* 1874, July 25, p. 5, September 26, p. 4; *Amer. Annual Cyclo.,* 1874, pp. 435-437; Wilder, D. W., *Annals of Kansas,* pp. 643-646, 655, 658; Andreas, *Kansas,* pp. 218, 264.

[48] *Amer. Annual Cyclo.,* 1874, p. 586.

twenty thousand, while in Nebraska the vote cast by the third party was inconsiderable.

In Oregon an Independent party made its appearance in the spring of 1874 with candidates for the June election and an anti-monopoly platform. The two old parties were very closely balanced in this state, and are said to have formed a coalition in some districts to defeat the new movement. The Independents had the support of a considerable portion of the press and probably of most of the Grangers, who at this time numbered nearly all the farmers of the state in their ranks, and they displayed considerable strength in the election, the votes on state officers and congressman being about ninety-seven hundred for the Democrats, ninety-two hundred for the Republicans, and sixty-five hundred for the Independents. In the legislative elections the new party fared even better, securing twenty-nine members of the lower house to twenty-eight Republicans and twenty Democrats, while in the Senate six Independents held the balance of power between the two old parties. Two supreme court judges and many county officials were also elected by the Independents.[49]

The " People's Independent " party of California, which had been fairly successful in the legislative elections of 1873, did not have an opportunity to take part in a state election until 1875. In that year candidates were put in the field by all three of the parties, the outcome being the election of the Democratic ticket with about sixty-two thousand votes, the Republican vote being thirty-one thousand and the Independent, thirty thousand.[50]

[49] *Chicago Tribune*, 1874, April 16, p. 8, April 17, p. 5, May 6, p. 4, June 3, p. 5, June 4, p. 5, June 26, p. 2; *Amer. Annual Cyclo.*, 1874, pp. 671-674.

[50] Davis, W. J., *History of Political Conventions in California*, pp. 331-333; Bancroft, H. H., *History of California*, VII., pp. 65-67; Hittell, T. H., *History of California*, IV.; *Appleton's Annual Cyclo.*, 1875, pp. 98-101.

S. J. Buck

Although some striking results were achieved by these Independent parties in 1873 and 1874, and in a few states in 1875, their careers were all very brief. In Michigan, Missouri, Kansas, and Nebraska, where the movement met with little success, nothing further was heard of it after 1874. The Independent Reform parties of Indiana and Illinois took part in the formation of and became component parts of the National Greenback party in 1875 and 1876,[51] and as such cast considerably smaller votes than they had in 1874, although enough Independents and Greenbackers were elected to the legislature in Illinois to hold the balance between the two old parties and bring about the election of Judge David Davis as an Independent to the United States Senate.[52] In Wisconsin and Iowa, the fusion of Democrats and Reformers or Anti-Monopolists was tried again in 1875, and with some success in Wisconsin, where the fusion candidates for state officers, with the exception of governor, were elected, though by very small

[51] The State Farmers' Association of Illinois was represented by delegates in the conventions at Cleveland and Philadelphia in 1875, which made arrangements for the national "Independent" or Greenback convention in Indianapolis, May 17, 1876. See the proceedings at the third annual session of the association in *Prairie Farmer*, XLV., p. 403, XLVI., pp. 35, 38 (December 19, 1874, January 30, 1875). On the last stages of the Independent Reform party in Illinois and its transition to the Greenback party, see: *ibid.*, XLVI., pp. 163, 196 (May 22, June 19, 1875); *Western Rural* (Chicago), XIII., p. 196 (June 19, 1875); *Appleton's Annual Cyclo.*, 1875; p. 393, 1876, p. 392; Moses, *Illinois, Historical and Statistical*, II., pp. 834, 839, 848-850. The fourth and fifth, which were probably the last, annual sessions of the State Farmers' Association, were held in January, 1876, and January, 1877. *Industrial Age*, 1876, February 5, March 25; Ill. State Farmers' Assn., *Proceedings of the Fifth Annual Meeting*.

[52] Judge Davis had been agreed upon as the independent member of the electoral commission to decide the Hayes-Tilden contest, but his election to the Senate at this time necessitated the choice of another. If the Independents had not held the balance of power in this Illinois legislature, it is possible, if not probable, that Tilden instead of Hayes would have become president of the United States.

majorities. The Republicans regained complete control of the legislature, however, in both states and repealed the Granger railroad law of Wisconsin in 1876, the Iowa Granger law meeting the same fate two years later. The presidential campaign of 1876 put an end to the Independent movement in both of these states.[53] In Minnesota a " Reform " party, which seems to had no direct connection with the Anti-Monopoly party of 1873, although probably composed of about the same men, put a ticket in the field in 1875 against both Republicans and Democrats, but secured less than two thousand votes, and did not appear again.[54]

There was an election for congressman in Oregon in 1875 and the Independent party again had a candidate in the field, but he received only about eight thousand votes. In the legislature which was elected in June, 1876, there were also a few Independents in both houses, but the presidential election in the fall probably put an end to the movement here also.[55] Nor does the People's Reform party of California appear to have kept up its organization after 1875, although many of the Grangers and others who belonged to it cast in their lot with the " Workingmen's party," which was organized by the followers of Dennis Kearney in 1877 and played a considerable part in California politics until 1880.[56]

As a result of this survey of western state and local politics from 1873 to 1876, it appears that Independent, Reform, or Anti-Monopoly parties were organized in

[53] *Wisconsin Statesman* (Madison), 1875, September 18, p. 3, November 13, p. 2, 1876, March 11, p. 1, March 25, p. 1; *Appleton's Annual Cyclo.*, 1875, pp. 402, 763, 1876, pp. 413-415, 806-808.

[54] *Appleton's Annual Cyclo.*, 1875, pp. 509-511.

[55] *Ibid.*, 1875, p. 609; *Wisconsin Statesman*, July 10, 1875, p. 3.

[56] Bryce, *American Commonwealth*, II., chap. xc.; Andrews, E. Benj., *The Last Quarter Century*, I., chap. xiii.; Bancroft, H. H., *California*, VII., pp. 335-412.

eleven states—Indiana, Illinois, Michigan, Wisconsin, Minnesota, Iowa, Missouri, Kansas, Nebraska, California, and Oregon. In some of these states, as in Wisconsin and Iowa, the new parties secured victories, including the election of the state ticket in Wisconsin, by coalescing with the Democrats and forming a new party of opposition to the dominant Republicans. In other states, as in Oregon and in part in Illinois, they maintained their independence of the old parties and secured local victories over both of them, and in three states—Illinois, Kansas, and California —they secured the election of " Reformers " to the United States Senate.[57]

The purpose and character of this Independent movement can best be determined by an examination of the platforms adopted. In all of the states, except Indiana and Michigan, these contained planks demanding the subjection of corporations and especially railroad corporations to the control of the state, and in several states regulation of all monopolies was demanded. It was thus an " anti-monopoly " movement, and in this direction the Granger laws were its principal achievement. Though most of these laws were subsequently repealed, still they definitely established the right of a state to regulate railroad charges and pointed the way for all future legislation on this important subject. But it was more than an " anti-monopoly " movement—it was also a " reform " movement. Every platform adopted by the new parties in all of the states denounced corruption in government and demanded reform, economy, and reduction of taxation, and several of the platforms contained specific demands for " civil service reform." In this direction the movement seems to have been

[57] The *Biographical Congressional Directory* lists Harvey of Kansas as a Republican, but Booth of California is described as an " Antimonopolist " and Hager of the same state as an " Antimonopoly Democrat," while Davis of Illinois is listed as " elected . . . by the votes of Independents and Democrats."

a result of the unusually large amount of corruption which
prevailed in both national and state governments during
the first half of the decade of the seventies.[58]

These, then, were the two principal and distinguishing
characteristics of the new parties—they were anti-monopoly
(or anti-railroad) and reform movements. Their platforms contained many other planks, but some had reference to local matters only, while others, such as a demand
for the reduction of the tariff to a revenue basis,[59] were bor-
rowed from the Democrats. On the currency question the
platforms varied somewhat, but the majority took a definite stand in favor of a return to specie payment as soon
as practicable. In some cases the currency planks appear
to have been attempts to straddle the issue, but in only
two states—Indiana and Illinois—is it possible to trace
a direct connection between the Independent movement and
the Greenback parties which followed it.

There are a number of reasons which help to explain the
shortness of the lives of these Independent parties. While
the issue of reform is a good one upon which to arouse
temporary enthusiasm, it is hardly a satisfactory basis for
the organization of a new party—if the reform is accomplished the *raison d'être* of the party is gone, and if it is
not accomplished the party is a failure. It might seem
that the issue of railroad regulation would furnish a basis
upon which a more permanent political party might be
built up, but in this direction the movement suffered from
the fact that the Granger laws for which it was held responsible did not work well, partly because of their crude-
ness, partly because of the determination of the railroads

[58] *Cf.* Dunning, W. A., *Reconstruction Political and Economic,* chaps.
xiv., xviii.

[59] The objection to the protective tariff seems to have been based upon
the feeling that it was class legislation—that it taxed the farmer for the
benefit of the manufacturer—rather than upon the more recent argument
that it fosters monopolies.

to make them appear injurious to everybody, but most of all because of the financial depression which followed the panic of 1873. Moreover, in many parts of the west the people still desired the construction of more railroad lines and there was a feeling that this would be checked by restrictive legislation.[60]

Again, it seems to be true, on the whole, that no political party can survive a presidential campaign without a national organization. The appearance of the National Greenback party and its absorption of the Independent Reform organization in Illinois, where the movement had been the most promising, practically barred the way to the organization of a National Reform party for the campaign of 1876. Large numbers of the Independents, not only in the states where the parties had declared for sound money but in Illinois and Indiana as well, could not reconcile themselves to the Greenback doctrine and as a result most of the wandering sheep returned to the Democratic or Republican folds. The fundamental cause for the failure of the movement, however, seems to have been the same as that which has caused the failure of every third-party movement in the United States since the Civil War— the innate political conservatism of the bulk of the American people. Although recognizing that the issues which originally divided the old parties have largely passed away, they prefer, even though it may be a somewhat slower process, to bring forward the new issues and to work out the desired reforms in the established parties rather than to attempt to displace them with new organizations.

Solon Justus Buck.

[60] The unsatisfactory operation of the Granger laws was also a factor in bringing about the co-incident decline of the Patrons of Husbandry and the other agricultural organizations. The Grange was also discredited by the failure of most of its co-operative enterprises, and during the years 1875-1877 it declined almost to extinction in the western states.

VIRGINIA AND THE PRESIDENTIAL SUCCESSION, 1840-1844

For the spirit with which it was conducted, the surprises which it developed, and the importance of its results, the campaign in Virginia to name John Tyler's successor to the presidency has scarcely a parallel. It lasted four years and was, during the greater part of the time, a four-cornered contest waged by the respective friends of Henry Clay, John Tyler, Martin Van Buren, and John C. Calhoun. It resulted in the repudiation of two native sons, Tyler and Clay, in a temporary breach in the political alliance between Virginia and New York, in making continental expansion a great national issue, and last but not least, it was largely instrumental in effectively blighting the long-cherished presidential hopes of John C. Calhoun.

Before the results of the election of 1840 were fully known, except to warrant the claims of an overwhelming victory for the Whigs, Thomas Ritchie [1] of the *Richmond*

---

[1] Thomas Ritchie was born at Tappahannock, Essex County, Virginia, November 5, 1778, and died July 12, 1854. He was the son of Archibald Ritchie, a Scotch merchant. By application of his fine natural abilities young Ritchie acquired a good education. His tastes ran to literature and to subjects pertaining to politics and economics. In 1804 he became editor of the *Richmond Enquirer,* formerly the *Examiner,* in which position he remained until 1845, when he went to Washington to become editor of the *Union,* the mouthpiece of Polk's administration. After Polk retired from the presidency Ritchie continued to edit the *Union* until 1852, when he was practically forced to retire to restore accord in the Democratic party. In Virginia Ritchie was known as the "Napoleon of the press," and he there exercised a power in politics surpassed only by that of such leaders as Jefferson and Madison. After 1830 he had scarcely a peer among the Democratic leaders of his native state. Although a state-rights politician of the most uncompromising character,

Enquirer set himself to the task of allaying sectional and personal jealousies, in order to make possible subsequent victory for the Democrats in the state and in the nation. To these ends he desired a return to fundamental principles.[2] Despite the fact that the Whigs of Virginia had urged the election of General Harrison on the ground that he was a true Whig, intent only upon a desire to check executive usurpations and abuses,[3] Ritchie looked upon their success as a triumph for old-time Federalism.[4] He and his political friends felt that Henry Clay, the real leader of the Whig party, interpreted the victory of 1840 as a repudiation of Jackson and of Van Buren and as a popular demand for the re-charter of a United States bank and the enactment of a protective tariff law.[5] They insisted that, as an opposition, the Whig party had ceased to exist and that it had, by a return to the principles and leaders of 1832, become the Federalist party of the elder and younger Adams.[6] Accordingly the *Richmond Enquirer* raised the " beacon flag of Virginia," the resolutions of 1798, and invited the states

he was rarely found on the side of John C. Calhoun. He was devoted to the Union of the fathers, which he maintained could be preserved only by adhering to the letter of the federal constitution. As a last resort he believed that a state had the right to secede, but he thought that such a course would never be necessary. One of his favorite expressions was, "I shall never despair of the republic." His devotion to the Union, opposition to negro slavery, liberal attitude on constitutional reforms, internal improvements, and education, and his consequent popularity in the western counties made him a political power in his own day and did much to keep western Virginia loyal to the Union in 1861.

[2] *Richmond Enquirer*, November 10, 13, 20, 1840.

[3] *Ibid.*, December 1, 1843. This number of the *Enquirer* contains an excellent article by Thomas W. Gilmer, a former Whig, on the origin and history of the Whig party.

[4] *Ibid.*, January 7, 1841.

[5] Thomas Ritchie to Martin Van Buren, May 19, 1841. *Van Buren MSS.*, in the Library of Congress.

[6] *Richmond Enquirer*, December 1, 1843.

to rally in an effort to save the constitution and to return to the party of Jefferson and of Jackson.[7]

To relieve her favorite son of the odium cast upon him by nullification and to place his candidacy for the presidency in a more favorable light in the other states of the Union, South Carolina, at the same time, practically repudiated her doctrines of 1832 and proclaimed the resolutions of 1798 to be the true principles of the Democratic party.[8] This feigned surrender was joyfully received in Virginia, where it was looked upon as the peaceful preliminary to a bitter contest between the friends of Calhoun and of Van Buren for the presidential nomination. But it was too soon to begin the fray, and Ritchie, who had done more than any other one person except Andrew Jackson to thwart the ambitions of Calhoun, now proclaimed that " the Democrats of Virginia will stand by the side of South Carolina and Alabama [9] and maintain the institutions of the South and the great principles of '98-'99." [10]

The first phase of the contest over the succession was fought out within the Whig party. As soon as Tyler had taken the oath of office, the state-rights Whigs of the " Virginia lowlands " led by Henry A. Wise, Abel P. Upshur, L. W. Tazewell, and Judge N. Beverly Tucker [11] began to lay plans to thwart the ambitions of Clay, to restore the fallen prestige of Virginia, and to make it possible for Tyler to be his own successor. Tyler's conscien-

---

[7] *Ibid.*, November 13, 1840.

[8] *Ibid.*, January 7, 1841.

[9] These states had given their electoral vote to Van Buren.

[10] *Richmond Enquirer,* January 2, 1841.

[11] A writer from Accomac County, the home of Mr. Wise, said that Tyler wrote to Wise " to come immediately." He added, " Webster will have a tough colt to manage, and Wise will defeat him in his federal plans." *Ibid.,* May 14, 1841. T. W. Gilmer and W. C. Rives of the Piedmont section were also friendly to Tyler.

tious desire to interpret the constitution strictly, his sensitive vanity, and his inordinate jealousy of Clay made it possible for this " corporal's guard " [12] to lead him whithersoever it would. It is difficult to determine the extent of the influence exercised by Calhoun upon these leaders and their plans.[13] With Tyler they were his ardent admirers. They had followed him into the Whig party in 1834, but had not yet, like their hero, retraced their steps, when the untimely death of General Harrison threw the executive branch of the government into their hands.

It is evident in any case, that a breach between the state-rights Whigs and the national Whigs of Virginia was inevitable. In the presidential election of 1840, Hunter had refused to attend the polls.[14]   Later Wise strenuously objected to the proposed extra session of Congress decided upon by Harrison.[15]   In the congressional elections, which came immediately after Tyler's elevation to the presidency, Wise, of the Accomac district, and Francis Mallory, of the Norfolk district, were re-elected as state-rights Whigs; [16] Thomas W. Gilmer resigned the office of governor and, as a state-rights Whig, successfully contested the re-election of the regular Whig nominee in the Albemarle district, James Garland; [17] and Hunter secured a re-election as an " independent." [18]   Of these developments and the prospects for the future Thomas Ritchie wrote to Martin Van Buren as follows: " The Whig dynasty must soon tumble

[12] This was a name applied by Clay to Tyler's advisers.
[13] Both Wise and Upshur were devoted to Calhoun. " Calhoun Correspondence," *Am. Hist. Assn. Rept.* (1899), II., pp. 549, 555.
[14] *Richmond Enquirer,* February 13, 1841.
[15] *Ibid.,* February 1, 6, 1841; Tyler, *Letters and Times of the Tylers,* II., p. 7.
[16] *Richmond Enquirer,* April 20, 1841.
[17] *Ibid.,* April 30, 1844.
[18] *Ibid.*

to pieces: Hunter, Gilmer, and Mallory will not vote for a bank." [19]

The extra session of Congress, which met in May, 1841, witnessed a battle royal between Clay and Tyler to drive each other from the coveted leadership of the Whig party. With an incredible presumption Tyler and his friends sought to crush Clay, as Jackson had done. If unsuccessful in this attempt, they hoped, at least, to divide the party and to place Tyler in a position of influence as the leader of the state-rights faction.[20]   Clay ignored them completely and used the Whig majorities in Congress to pass bank bills, which, it was known, Tyler would veto. Alleged compromise measures were met by other vetoes, and the session adjourned, leaving Tyler in the hands of unscrupulous advisers—without a party among the masses and without a cabinet.[21]

Before the session adjourned the national Whigs of Virginia had proclaimed the " Boy Orator of Slashes," Henry Clay, to be their unalterable choice for the presidency.[22] With this declaration they ceased, until Texas became an issue, to be a mere opposition party, and became a party of principles, favoring a recharter of a United States bank, an increase in the customs duties, and the distribution of the proceeds from the sales of the public lands.[23]   The old state-rights leaders were cast off, and John Minor Botts, Wm. L. Goggin, Alex. H. H. Stuart, and Geo. W. Summers, representatives in Congress, and John Hampden

[19] Thomas Ritchie to Martin Van Buren, March 19, 1841. *Van Buren MSS.* This was twelve days before the special session of Congress of 1841.

[20] Tyler, *Letters and Times of the Tylers,* II., pp. 37, 46, 707; *Richmond Enquirer,* May 14, 1841; *Ibid.,* July 13, 1841, contains a letter from Beverly Tucker; Schouler, *History of the United States,* IV., p. 395.

[21] *Richmond Whig,* November 9, 1841; *Richmond Enquirer,* November 12, 1841.

[22] *Richmond Enquirer,* August 10, 1841.

[23] *Ibid.,* February 23, 1843, December 1, 1843.

Pleasants, editor of the *Richmond Whig,* now became the
leaders of the party. Following the cue of the unscrupulous Botts,[24] the *Whig* now read Tyler out of the
party, characterizing him as a " fifteen shilling lawyer "
and a " Tittlebat Titmouse " in the seat of " the refined
Aubreys." [25]   Indignation meetings were held in all parts
of the state, and Tyler was generally condemned as a
" political traitor." [26]   So popular did Henry Clay become with the masses, that the Whig legislature of
1841-'42 thought it politic to give a newly formed county
his surname.[27]

Webster's refusal to leave the cabinet, when the other
members resigned, gave credence to the rumor that he and
Tyler had, like James Monroe and John Q. Adams, united
their fortunes with a view to the presidential succession.[28]
The administration was still young, and it was thought that
Tyler could, with the aid of his friends in Virginia, rally a
southern party which could be united with Webster's following in the north in such a way as to determine the succession for at least eight years.   Francis P. Blair, editor
of the *Washington Globe,* considered Tyler " quite as well
qualified " as Monroe to carry out such an agreement, but
he added: " The times are changed.   Old Adams still
lives, a comment on the honesty of the first coalition, and
Webster has enough of the odor of nationality to give the

[24] While the compromise bank bill was pending an ill-advised letter
written by J. M. Botts came to light. *Niles Register,* LXI., p. 35.

[25] *Richmond Whig,* November 9, 1841; *Richmond Enquirer,* November
12, 1841. About this time J. H. Pleasants became an associate editor of
the *Independent,* the spokesman of Clay in Washington. *Richmond Enquirer,* November 12, 1841. Later Joseph Segar, also a Virginian, became
an associate editor on the staff of the same paper. *Ibid.,* March 3, 1842.

[26] *Ibid.,* September 24, 1841.

[27] *Ibid.,* January 8, 1842.

[28] Francis P. Blair to Martin Van Buren, September 27, 1841. *Van
Buren MSS.*

scent to the present administration through all its departments." [29]   Whatever may have been the attitude of Tyler toward his secretary of state, it is certain that Wise and Upshur were determined to drive him from the cabinet, and to tolerate no alliance with Federalism.[30]

On the other hand, Tyler and his friends sought a popular following in the Democratic party.   They had successfully combated all efforts to recharter a United States bank and to promote the ambitions of its patron, Clay. It therefore seemed reasonable to them that the Democrats of Virginia might look upon Tyler as playing the part of Jackson.[31]   Besides, they had other reasons to hope for a popular following among the Democrats in Virginia. In an effort to regain that following and influence in his party, which his opposition to the Independent Treasury scheme had caused him to lose temporarily, Richie in his paper, the *Richmond Enquirer,* had coquetted with the administration powers by playing upon their " vanity " and by praising their " sagacity." [32]   He even sent one of his " strictly confidential " letters to one of the leaders in which he praised Mr. Tyler's bold and patriotic stand against the bank and assured him that the " Republicans [33] of the unterrified Commonwealth " were with him.[34]   So noticeable did the favor in which Ritchie held Tyler become, that the *Richmond Whig* denominated the *Richmond Enquirer* " the organ for the Whig president in the Commonwealth of Virginia." [35]   Thus it was that the *Madisonian,* Tyler's

[29] *Ibid.*

[30] Tyler, *Letters and Times of the Tylers,* II., pp. 85, 120, 704. *Richmond Enquirer,* May 28, 1841; *Ibid.,* May 26, 1843.

[31] *Richmond Enquirer,* October 22, 1841.

[32] *Richmond Enquirer,* September 14, 1841; *Ibid.,* February 10, 1842.

[33] Locally the name " Republican " was applied to the party of Jackson and of Van Buren.

[34] Letter of Thomas Ritchie, owned by the author of this paper, date August 30, 1841.

[35] *Richmond Whig,* February 22, 1842.

organ at Washington, disavowed at this time any intention to establish a third party.[36]   Wise, Mallory, and Gilmer, former Whigs, each sought re-election upon the
Democratic ticket; [37] and Tyler sent M. M. Noah, of the
Philadelphia Weekly Messenger, to Richmond to ascertain the strength of the administration in Virginia, and to
arrange, if possible, an understanding whereby the *Enquirer* would sustain his candidacy for the presidency.[38]

But the Richmond politicians desired only the votes and
influence of the administration party, and to this end
sought to drive them farther and farther from the Whigs.
Mr. Ritchie gave no promises to Mr. Noah, but assured
him that it would be his duty as well as his pleasure to
support Mr. Tyler for an election, should he get the nomination of the Democratic party.[39]   At the same time he
continued his efforts to drive Webster from the cabinet; [40]
he warned the administration of the difficulties, if not im-
possibilities, in the way of forming a third party; [41] he held
out dreams of immortality to Tyler in case he adhered to
the principles of '98 [42]—yet he consistently refused to commit himself regarding the presidency.[43]   An overwhelming
victory in the local elections of 1842, due to gains made
largely in the eastern counties,[44] attested the wisdom of

[36] *Richmond Enquirer,* February 26, 1842.

[37] *Richmond Enquirer,* September 3, 28, 1841; *Ibid.,* October 19, 1841.

[38] *Ibid.,* August 4, 1843. For a different impression see Tyler, *Letters
and Times of the Tylers,* II., pp. 101-105.

[39] *Ibid.,* August 4, 1843.

[40] *Ibid.,* February 17, 1842; *Ibid.,* May 26, 1843. This number of the
Enquirer contains an estimate of Webster as a man and a statesman.

[41] *Richmond Enquirer,* February 26, 1842; *Ibid.,* March 3, 1842.

[42] *Ibid.,* June 8, 25, 1841; *Ibid.,* July 20, 1841; *Ibid.,* August 10, 20,
1841.

[43] *Richmond Enquirer,* March 10, 1842.

[44] The Democrats gained 38 members in the House of Delegates, con-
verting a Whig majority of 2 into a Democratic majority of 36. *Ibid.,*
May 6, 1842.

Ritchie's policies and restored him to his former place of influence in his party.

Although he had retired from public life in disgust, Clay continued to gain in popular favor in those parts of eastern Virginia where the state-rights Whigs had been strongest. Except for the mistakes made by Botts, the work of the national Whig leaders was effective. The continuation of financial embarrassments, the growing desire for manufacturing industries, and the impetus given to internal improvements by the building of railroads and the application of steam to navigation, made Henry Clay and the *principles* of the Whig party popular with the artisan, commercial, and manufacturing interests.[45] In both Petersburg and Richmond hundreds of persons signed petitions to Congress praying for the enactment of a protective tariff law.[46] Many pronounced the financial " experiments " of Jackson and of Van Buren failures, and insisted that a national bank was necessary to regulate the currency and to produce the return of desirable business conditions.[47] As to its constitutionality they were unwilling to go beyond the opinion of James Madison, who had sustained the national bank in 1816 and at other times.[48] Thus the Whigs continued to be formidable until the contest was ended.

Inability to gain a popular following among the Democrats of Virginia, Clay's retirement from active participation in politics, and the demonstrations in favor of a protective tariff, caused Tyler to think of appealing to the " moderates of both parties " and doubtless

---

[45] *House Journal*, 27 Cong. 2d sess., pp. 532, 611, 617, 680, 793, 810, 854; *Niles Register*, LXII., pp. 288, 302. De Bow, *Review*, X., p. 542.

[46] *Richmond Enquirer*, June 17, 24, 1842.

[47] Wise favored the recharter of a national bank. Wise, *Seven Decades of the Union*, p. 187.

[48] *Richmond Enquirer*, September 6, 1844; Hunt, *Writings of James Madison*, IX., pp. 365, 442.

influenced his decision to sign the tariff bill of 1842.[49]   But
it was too late to conciliate the Whigs.   They laid their
defeats in the local elections at Tyler's door;[50] J. M. Botts
was insisting upon his impeachment;[51] and the *Richmond
Whig* continued to comment upon his incompetency.   At
the same time the Democrats completely deserted him.
They had received all the available spoils and were dis-
gusted with his recent concessions to the Whigs and his
approval of the tariff bill of 1842.[52]   With the Democrats went some of his former state-rights Whig advisers,
who now drew closer to Calhoun.   But Tyler was obstinate
and continued to pursue the presidency and duty, when
guided by no other light than that "reflected from burning
effigies."[53]

Meanwhile the contest within the Democratic party
had commenced in earnest.   The strength of the Van
Buren faction lay chiefly in the western counties and was
composed largely of friends of General Jackson.   The
leaders were James McDowell of Rockbridge County,
Thomas Jefferson Randolph of Albemarle County, and
George C. Dromgoole of Brunswick County.   McDowell
was a brother-in-law of Thomas H. Benton, and the ablest
politician west of the Blue Ridge.   Randolph was a grandson of Thomas Jefferson, and was intensely jealous of
W. C. Rives, who laid claim to the political legacies of
both Jefferson and Madison.   As Rives had drifted
farther from Van Buren in his opposition to the Independent Treasury scheme, Randolph had drawn closer to him.
Dromgoole was the ablest leader on the "southside" of
the James, but he was given to habits of intemperance

[49] Tyler, *Letters and Times of the Tylers*, II., p. 182.
[50] *Richmond Whig*, May 20, 1842; *Richmond Enquirer*, May 24, 1842.
[51] *Ibid.*, September 9, 1842.
[52] *Richmond Enquirer*, August 26, 1842.
[53] *Niles Register*, LXI., p. 177.

which greatly impaired his usefulness.[54]   To these leaders should be added the names of Dr. John Brockenbrough, president of the bank of Virginia, Judge Henry St. George Tucker, president of the court of appeals, Judge Peter V. Daniel of the United States district court, and W. H. Roane, late senator in Congress.   Each one of the last named group had been prominent in the " Richmond Junta."

Because of its importance in this and other contests, " the Junta " requires more than passing mention.   It was the name given to a number of relatives [55] and political associates, who rendezvoused at Richmond [56] and exercised a power in party organization and in the distribution of patronage, equaled only by its prototype, the Albany Regency.   It was held together, not merely as an organization to secure the spoils and joyful triumphs of political victories—it was the heart of that great party, then confined largely to western Virginia, where the theories of Thomas Jefferson and of Patrick Henry [57] regarding the rights of majorities in government, continued to live.   Before this time it had engaged in many a gallant and successful fight against " Calhounism." [58]

Two other tried and trusted members of the Junta,

[54] W. H. Roane to Martin Van Buren, September 11, 1843. *Van Buren MSS.*

[55] Ritchie, Roane, and Brockenbrough were cousins. Judge Richard E. Parker of the Virginia Court of Appeals, who died in 1840, was also a member of the Junta, and a relative of Ritchie and Roane. He was possibly the ablest leader in it. On more than one occasion Van Buren offered him a place in his cabinet. See *Van Buren MSS.*

[56] The public prints for this period contain many references to the Richmond Junta.

[57] W. H. Roane, a moving spirit in the Junta, was a grandson of Patrick Henry. " Jeffersonian principles " was the slogan of the Richmond leaders.

[58] Some of its leaders had committed themselves to Van Buren in letters written to him. See *Van Buren MSS.*

Thomas Ritchie, of the *Richmond Enquirer,* and Andrew
Stevenson, ex-speaker of the national House of Representatives, were friendly to the candidacy of Van Buren, but
were not, for obvious reasons, enthusiastic in his support.
As has already been seen, the Democrats and former
state-rights Whigs of eastern Virginia, many of whom were
friends of Calhoun, had just restored Ritchie to his place
of influence in his party.   Only base ingratitude or extreme narrowness of political vision, neither of which were
characteristic of him, could have induced Ritchie to turn
abruptly against these friends.   Until late in the contest
his peculiar relations with each faction and the extreme
necessity for discretion influenced the columns of the *Enquirer.*   More than once W. H. Roane wrote to Silas
Wright of the "narrow place" in which Mr. Ritchie
found himself, and of the handicap which his necessitated
inactivity placed upon their plans in Virginia.[59]   His desire
to be either governor of Virginia or vice-president of the
United States, and his willingness to make political alliances which would promote one or the other of these ambitions, kept Stevenson from taking sides.   It is not im-
probable that his ambition was a factor with Ritchie. They
were "old cronies," and Ritchie thought that the party
should vindicate Stevenson against the recent attacks made
upon his conduct as minister of the United States at the
court of St. James.[60]

Calhoun's party was confined almost entirely to eastern
Virginia.   A very large number of his friends were former
Whigs, who had either followed their leader into the
Democratic party in 1837, or deserted the Whig party
in 1841.   Of Calhoun's party W. H. Roane wrote:

[59] W. H. Roane to Martin Van Buren, February 14, 1843. *Van
Buren MSS.*

[60] The *Stevenson MSS.* in the Library of Congress contains some interesting letters from Ritchie to Stevenson.

" There is quite a stiff party in this state, calling themselves State Rights Republicans, many of whom were a few years ago State Rights Whigs." [61]   The leaders of this party were: R. M. T. Hunter of Essex County, who had long been Calhoun's right-hand man in Virginia, although he had not followed closely the political affiliations of his leader; James A. Seddon of Richmond, whose chief political duty was to watch and report the movements of the Junta; Wm. O. Goode of Mecklenberg county, the rival of Geo. C. Dromgoole; Wm. F. Gordon of Albemarle county, who, as a Whig member of Congress, had, in 1834, proposed the Independent Treasury system; and Wm. P. Taylor of Caroline county, a worthy son of the illustrious John Taylor of Caroline.

With all that aggressiveness and impatience which characterized the followers of Calhoun, his friends led off in this contest.   In the early part of 1842 they circulated a pamphlet to set forth the claims and qualifications of their favorite for the presidency.   About the same time the *Lynchburg Republican* and the *Norfolk Chronicle and Old Dominion* nominated him and Silas Wright for the presidency and vice-presidency, respectively. [62]   But Calhoun could not hope for success in Virginia without the support of Ritchie and the *Enquirer*.   He complained of Mr. Ritchie's policy of keeping Virginia attached to New York and Pennsylvania, when she (Virginia) should " be at the head of the South." [63]   For reasons already shown, the time was now thought opportune for effecting a long coveted alliance with the Richmond Junta.   The *Richmond*

[61] W. H. Roane to Martin Van Buren, February 9 and 14, 1843. *Van Buren MSS.*

[62] Thomas H. Benton to Martin Van Buren, April 17, 1842. *Van Buren MSS.*

[63] " Calhoun Correspondence," *Am. Hist. Assn. Rept.* (1899), II., pp. 517, 527, 538, 544, 546, 562, etc.

Whig became the tool of its enemies and was used with other prints already committed, to sound Ritchie and to drive him to declare for Calhoun. He was alternately accused of being both a friend and an enemy.[64] After the enactment of the tariff law of 1842 Calhoun's friends, in keeping with their disposition to rule or to ruin, sought to intimidate by insisting that Calhoun would be a candidate for the presidency, whoever might be the choice of the Democratic national convention.[65]

To all these "prods" Ritchie was evasive. He expressed the profoundest respect and admiration for the genius and ability of Mr. Calhoun, as demonstrated in his early public service, and since his return to the Republican principles of '98; [66] he denied the alleged existence, on his part, of a feeling of uncompromising hostility toward Calhoun; and he assured the public that he would joyfully support him for the presidency, should he be the nominee of the Democratic party.[67] But he consistently refused to commit himself to the candidacy of any man, preferring "the success of principles to the aggrandizement of any individual." [68]

The attitude of Ritchie and the temporary apathy of the friends of Van Buren were encouraging. Accordingly Barnwell H. Rhett, of South Carolina, came to Richmond in the autumn of 1842 and tried to ally Ritchie and the Junta actively in the interest of Calhoun.[69] He told them of Calhoun's intention to resign his seat in the federal

[64] *Richmond Enquirer,* August 12, 1842.
[65] *Richmond Enquirer,* October 18, 28, 1842; *Ibid.,* November 1, 4, 8, 1842; see also "Calhoun Correspondence," *Am. Hist. Assn. Report* (1899), II., pp. 516, 517.
[66] *Richmond Enquirer,* August 12, 1842.
[67] *Ibid.,* August 12, 1842; *Ibid.,* November 1, 4, 8, 1842.
[68] *Ibid.,* November 4, 8, 1842.
[69] W. H. Roane to Martin Van Buren, September 11, 1843. *Van Buren MSS.*

Senate, and of his resolution to rest his claims to future political preferment on a book on the principles of government, which he was then writing.   He also raised objections to the practice of electing delegates to the Democratic national conventions by state conventions, and of permitting a majority of the delegates thus selected to cast the entire vote of a state.   Moreover, he declared it to be the purpose of Calhoun's friends to remedy the alleged defects in the national nominating body, and to postpone the nomination to the latest possible date.   The echoes from Rhett's visit had not ceased, when Calhoun took advantage of an opportunity to visit Richmond while on his way to Congress.[70]   He confirmed what Rhett had said and made overtures to the political leaders.

The efforts of Calhoun were in vain, but they were treated with the greatest courtesy and with apparent consideration.   Roane advised against his contemplated retirement from the Senate and his determination to risk his chances for the presidency upon the results of the contest then pending.[71]   Meanwhile Ritchie assured the public that it would not be entirely deprived of Mr. Calhoun's services, because " he is now writing a book on the principles of government." [72]   At the same time he was careful to deny the statement of the *New York Herald* to the effect that the *Charleston* (S. C.) *Mercury* and the *Richmond Enquirer* had come out openly in support of Mr. Calhoun.[73]   Of this and other attempts to win Ritchie, Wm. Selden, one of his closest political friends, said in a letter to Van Buren: " Every device had

[70] W. H. Roane to Martin Van Buren, September 11, 1843. *Van Buren MSS.*

[71] *Ibid.*

[72] *Richmond Enquirer*, December 8, 1842.

[73] *New York Herald*, December 5, 1842.   See also *Richmond Enquirer*, December 8, 1842.

been freely exhausted to detract Mr. Ritchie from your support." [74]

With characteristic impatience, the friends of Calhoun could not wait for developments and sought to force the issue. Accordingly, they refused to vote for Stevenson in the gubernatorial contest then pending and either gave their support to James McDowell, or to an independent candidate.[75] Chagrined at the tactics of his new friends and alarmed at the demands of the west for an investigation of the state banks located in Richmond,[76] Ritchie dropped Stevenson and aided in making his rival, James McDowell, governor. At the same time he expressed, in a confidential way, to the friends of McDowell, his intention to support Van Buren for the presidency.[77] The desire to continue to be the spokesman of his party, which was now passing to the leadership of the west, and to aid Stevenson in his candidacy for the vice-presidency doubtless influenced him in this decision. The following extract from a letter by John Letcher, later governor of Virginia, to Thomas H. Benton, throws light upon the inner workings of these transactions:

" I can well imagine your surprise when I inform you that Ritchie is himself friendly to the election of Mr. Van Buren, indeed takes him as his first choice over all who are spoken of in connection with the presidency. He regards his election as essential to the purity of Republican principles—as the only fitting and

[74] Wm. Selden to Martin Van Buren, March 5, 6, 1843. *Van Buren MSS.;* also R. B. Gooch to Augusta Devezac, December, 1842. *Van Buren MSS.*

[75] John Letcher to Thomas H. Benton, December 15, 1842. *Van Buren MSS.*

[76] Ritchie owed a large sum to the State Bank of Virginia, of which his cousin, Dr. Brockenbough, was president. *Richmond Enquirer,* July 15, 1842; *Ibid.,* November 18, 1842; *Ibid.,* January 12, 14, 19, 1843.

[77] John Letcher to T. H. Benton, December 15, 1842. *Van Buren MSS.* Letcher was the spokesman for his fellow townsman, McDowell, in his campaign for governor.

proper rebuke to the log-cabin and coon-skin fooleries of 1840. He told me in making these declarations that he had spoken more fully to me, than he had done to any one else and that he did not desire that it should be made public until after our next spring elections for fear that it might be the means of creating such a division among our friends here, as had taken place in North Carolina in the Senatorial Election.[78] As soon as these elections were over he assured me that he would take the same position in his paper.

"The conversation led me to conclude that Stevenson seeks an alliance with Mr. Van Buren, on the Ticket, and that he will struggle for the nomination for the Vice-presidency. The Calhounites at Richmond are evidently taking up this idea, and the more indiscrete amongst them avow it openly. Hence they are dissatisfied with Stevenson and avow their determination to vote against him in the Gubernatorial Election, which takes place to-day. They also speak in harsh terms of Ritchie, and charge a collusion between the two, having for its sole object Stevenson's promotion. Knowing that such an opinion would result to Mr. McDowell's advantage, I was perfectly willing that they should entertain it, and use it to their heart's content." [79]

Two days later the *Richmond Whig,* in an editorial on the election of McDowell, said: " The Richmond Junta and the *Richmond Enquirer* have been defeated by the mountains," and the *Enquirer* is " therefore defunct." [80]

Alarmed at the concerted efforts of Calhoun's friends, Benton had, early in 1842, caused his followers in Missouri to nominate Van Buren for the presidency.[81] This done, he had hastened at once to the Hermitage to apprise the " Old Hero " of the movements in the political world and to secure his indorsement of Van Buren for a third

---

[78] The factional fight between the friends of Van Buren and Calhoun was also on in North Carolina. *Richmond Enquirer,* January 7, 1843.

[79] December 15, 1842. *Van Buren MSS.*

[80] *Richmond Enquirer,* December 17, 1842.

[81] Thomas H. Benton to Martin Van Buren, April 17, 1842. *Van Buren MSS.*

nomination. Jackson's approval was cheerfully given and at once conveyed to his political henchmen, but it did not arouse much enthusiasm in Virginia. Occasionally a prominent leader committed himself; [82] but it was not until Congress and the state Assembly met in December, 1842, that the friends of Van Buren began to rally. In the Assembly they outnumbered their opponents four to one,[83] and they administered stinging defeats to aspirants who sought office as the friends of Mr. Calhoun.[84]

The first spirited contest to be fought at close range between these rival factions took place in the Democratic state convention, which met in Richmond, March 2, 1843. It was waged over the method of organization and the time for holding the proposed Democratic national convention. Led by James A. Seddon, the friends of Calhoun favored May or June, 1844, and insisted that the delegates thereto should be elected by congressional districts, and that each delegate should have one vote on the floor of the convention. Following the command of Wright and Benton,[85] the friends of Van Buren, led by Geo. C. Dromgoole, favored an earlier date, October or November, 1843, for holding the convention, and adhered to the old method of appointing delegates thereto by state conventions and of letting the majority of a state's delegates cast the vote of that state.[86] They insisted upon an early nomination to prevent sectional and personal jealousies, which they feared would arise at the next Congress

[82] P. V. Daniel to Martin Van Buren, December 16, 1841. *Van Buren MSS.* See also J. R. Poinsett to Martin Van Buren, October 7, 1842, on conditions in Virginia. *Van Buren MSS.*

[83] G. W. Hopkins to Martin Van Buren, February 20, 1843. *Van Buren MSS.*

[84] *Richmond Enquirer,* February 28, 1843.

[85] F. P. Blair to M. Van Buren, January 17, 1843. *Van Buren MSS.*

[86] *Richmond Enquirer,* March 7, 1843. G. W. Hopkins to M. Van Buren, February 20, 1843. *Van Buren MSS.*

and prevent their ultimate success. On the other hand, their opponents desired a late nomination so far as the choice of a candidate was concerned, for directly opposite reasons. They expected sectional issues to arise, which would make Van Buren an unavailable candidate. If they were not already looking to Texas,[87] they expected that the agitation of the tariff would unite the south in support of their favorite, Calhoun.[88] So skillfully had the organization been manipulated that Seddon's plan carried in the select committee on address, but it was voted down on the floor of the convention.[89] Then the friends of Van Buren passed resolutions which recommended that the national convention be held on the fourth Monday in November, 1843, and that the delegates thereto be chosen by congressional districts and instructed to vote by states, each state having as many votes as it had members in Congress, and the majority of the state's delegation casting the whole vote.[90]

As the followers of Calhoun had hoped, by their plan, to control a large part of the delegation to the national convention, the decision of the Democratic state convention in Virginia came as a stinging defeat. The *Charleston* (S. C.) *Mercury* raised strenuous objections to the whole proceedings.[91] It insisted that Ritchie "had everything cut and dried for Van Buren." Ritchie replied in a long editorial article in which he denied the charge that he had called and organized the convention, but admitted taking a deep interest in it. He in-

---

[87] A. Stevenson to Van Buren, October 8, 1843. *Van Buren MSS.;* John Letcher to Thomas Ritchie, September 23, 1843. *Ibid.*

[88] *Richmond Enquirer,* March 7, 1843; "Calhoun Correspondence," *Am. Hist. Assn. Rept.* (1899), II., p. 516.

[89] *Richmond Enquirer,* March 7, 11, 1843.

[90] *Ibid.,* March 11, 1843.

[91] *Ibid.,* March 11, 1843; Silas Wright to Martin Van Buren, April 10, 1843. *Van Buren MSS.*

sisted, however, that his interest had always been directed to promote accord, and to that end he had presided at conferences of the rival factions.[92]   The *Mercury* would not be appeased, and defiantly placed at the head of its editorial column, "JOHN C. CALHOUN, FOR PRESIDENT OF THE UNITED STATES, subject to the decision of a national convention to be held in May, 1844." [93]

The next tilt between the rival factions came in the elections held in April, 1843.   It was alleged that the majority in the Assembly had gerrymandered the state to prevent the election of representatives to Congress or of delegates to a national convention, who would be friendly to Mr. Calhoun.[94]   But the consequent apathy, on the part of the friends of Calhoun, injured only themselves and in a way they could ill afford.   Wm. O. Goode was defeated by Geo. C. Dromgoole for a renomination for election to Congress;[95] Hunter failed in his contest for a re-election;[96] and Wm. Smith (Extra Billy), an avowed friend of Calhoun, went down to defeat at the polls before a Whig, Samuel Chilton.[97]   As a result of these contests Calhoun did not have a friend in Virginia's delegation in Congress, except those who were also friendly to Tyler.[98]

True to his former promises,[99] and to comply with the earnest solicitations of those who did not understand the reasons for his prolonged silence,[100] Ritchie now declared

[92] *Richmond Enquirer,* March 18, 1843.

[93] *Ibid.,* April 4, 1844.

[94] *Richmond Enquirer,* May 9, 12, 19, 1843.

[95] *Ibid.,* April 7, 1843.

[96] *Ibid.,* June 13, 1843; *New Orleans Republican,* May 31, 1843.

[97] *Richmond Enquirer,* May 16, 19, 1843.

[98] *Richmond Enquirer,* August 8, 1843.

[99] See letter of John Letcher to T. H. Benton, December 15, 1842. *Van Buren MSS.*

[100] P. V. Daniel to M. Van Buren, July 6, 1843. *Van Buren MSS.*

through the columns of the *Enquirer* his intention to support Martin Van Buren for the presidency.[101]   In so doing he desired to have it clearly understood, " that it is not ' the boys ' who make the declaration, but ' Father Ritchie.' "[102]   To prevent the establishment of a rival paper in Richmond he took the precaution, however, to make it understood that the columns of the *Enquirer* would be open to the friends of Mr. Calhoun.[103]

The open declaration of Ritchie was felt immediately in all directions.   Other prints favorable to Calhoun's candidacy, the *Petersburg Republican* and the *Wytheville Republican and Virginia Constitutionalist,* made their appearance,[104] and the *Charleston Mercury* and *Mobile Tribune* attacked the *Richmond Enquirer* without mercy.[105] Except the four papers, which had already declared for Calhoun, the press of the Democratic party followed the course of the *Enquirer*.[106]   The prints of western Virginia became enthusiastic.   The *Abingdon Banner* thought that Calhoun had not yet lived down the odium of nullification and added that " it would indeed be ' carrying coals to New Castle ' to offer reasons and considerations to the voters of Little Tennessee why they should support Martin Van Buren,"[107] " and the *Woodstock Sentinel* went for Martin Van Buren and short Dutch cabbage against the world."[108]

[101] *Richmond Enquirer,* July 18, 1843.

[102] Ritchie had recently associated with himself as editors of the *Enquirer* his two sons, Wm. F. and Thomas, Jr.   *Richmond Enquirer,* March 2, 1843.

[103] *Richmond Enquirer,* June 6, 1843.   Calhoun thought there should be a rival press in Richmond.   See " Correspondence," *Am. Hist. Assn. Report* (1899), II., pp. 529, 536.

[104] *Richmond Enquirer,* June 27, 1843.

[105] *Ibid.,* September 15, 19, 1843.

[106] See *ibid.,* August 1, 15, September 5, 12, 1843.

[107] August 12, 1843 ; see also *Richmond Enquirer,* August 22, 1843.

[108] July 27, 1843 ; see also *Richmond Enquirer,* August 1, 1843.

The friends of Calhoun became alarmed. They scattered broadcast the selected and revised speeches of their leader.[109]   The *Spectator*, a mouthpiece for their party, was established in Washington;[110] " Calhoun's Plenipotentiary," Rhett, made another visit to Richmond to see Van Buren's " Secretary of the Southern Department," Ritchie;[111] a sigh went up for " the proud old Dominion under " the feet of the Empire State;[112] and talk of throwing the election into the House of Representatives and of Calhoun's refusing to abide by the decision of a national convention was abundant.[113]   Publicly the leaders friendly to Calhoun professed to desire most of all a reduction of the tariff,[114] but their chief interest and hope lay in the " reannexation of Texas," [115] an asset which they had stolen from the political capital with which Tyler had attempted to form a third party.[116]   This issue was to be kept a profound secret and was to be used to effect a *coup d'état*, if an opportunity presented itself.[117]

But the friends of Van Buren were on the alert, as the following extract from a letter of John Letcher to Thomas Ritchie shows:

[109] *Ibid.*, September 15, 1843.
[110] J. L. Martin to M. Van Buren, September 19, 1843. *Van Buren MSS.*
[111] *Richmond Enquirer*, September 15, 1843.
[112] " Calhoun Correspondence," *Am. Hist. Assn. Rept.* (1899), II., pp. 527, 536.
[113] *Richmond Enquirer*, October 13, 1843; *Ibid.*, December 1, 5, 1843; *Alexandria Gazette*, November 30, 1843.
[114] *Richmond Enquirer*, February 1, 1844; Thomas Ritchie to H. A. Garland, January 8, 1844. *Van Buren MSS.*
[115] Andrew Stevenson to Martin Van Buren, October 8, 1843. *Van Buren MSS.;* W. H. Roane to Martin Van Buren, October 17, 1843. *Van Buren MSS.; Richmond Enquirer*, December 12, 14, 1843.
[116] *Richmond Enquirer*, July 4, 1843; *Ibid.*, December 12, 14, 16, 1843; " Calhoun Correspondence," *Am. Hist. Assn. Rept.* (1899), II., p. 556.
[117] A. Stevenson to M. Van Buren, October 8, 1843. *Van Buren MSS.* Little credit was given to the rumor that Van Buren and Clay had made an agreement to keep the question of Texas out of the campaign.

" Unless I am greatly deceived," said Letcher, " in information lately obtained they [the followers of Calhoun] are preparing to stack the cards upon us. You will recollect a letter on the annexation of Texas, written by Gilmer, and which made its appearance last winter. That letter was sent to General Jackson in manuscript, and in reply to the request which accompanied it, the Old Hero wrote out his views at large, showing particularly the advantages [of Texas] in a military point of view to the United States. This letter I understand is in the possession of the Calhounites, and is to be used at the Baltimore Convention. Mr. Van Buren is to be interrogated about the time of the meeting of that body, and it is expected that he will answer in opposition to the scheme. Mr. Calhoun is to approve the annexation and his answer is to be at the Convention ready for use." [118]

By a comparison of this letter with the writings of various historians,[119] it will be seen that it contains almost the same language as that used by them to describe an alleged plan on the part of his supposed friends in the south to deprive Martin Van Buren of the nomination of the Democratic party in 1844. The disposition made of this letter and their frank disavowal of its suggestions should free Van Buren's " friends " in Virginia from even a suspicion of double-dealing. After passing the rounds of the Junta, this letter was sent by W. H. Roane to Mr. Van Buren.[120]

Calhoun's friends were not deceived. The tone of the *Enquirer* and the caution of their rivals let it be known that their secret was out. Accordingly they were not surprised or disappointed, when, at a public dinner in King William county, Henry A. Wise, either ill-advisedly or purposely, sprang the question of the re-annexation of Texas.[121] In

[118] September 23, 1843. *Van Buren MSS.*

[119] Hammond, *Political Hist. of the State of New York*, III., p. 447; Alexander, *Political Hist. of State of New York*, II., pp. 66, 67; Shepherd, *Martin Van Buren*, pp. 402-412.

[120] *Van Buren MSS.*, October 17, 1843.

[121] *Richmond Enquirer*, October 20, 1843; " Calhoun Correspondence," *Am. Hist. Asso. Rept.* (1899), II., p. 549.

his characteristic and exaggerated style Wise insisted that
immediate annexation was necessary to prevent Great
Britain from abolishing negro slavery in independent
Texas, and thus paving the way for the abolition of negro
slavery in the United States.[122]

At the time it was made, this revelation produced
scarcely a ripple and did not apparently cause Van Buren
to lose a single friend in Virginia. The leaders thought
it the proverbial straw in the sight of a drowning man. If
we had not already opened negotiations to acquire Texas,
they knew that we were about to do so.[123] " Since it had
probably become a matter for diplomatic consideration,"
Ritchie regretted Wise's indiscretion, but he insisted that
the midst of a presidential campaign was not a propitious
time for " the free discussion and calm consideration of so
vital a subject." [124] About the same time W. H. Roane
wrote to Van Buren that he had long " opposed the annexation of Texas," and that he now saw " nothing to change
his mind." [125]

Although hopeful that " it might come out all right," [126]
Van Buren's friends in Virginia could not dismiss Texas.
Like Banquo's ghost it was ever reappearing. They
feared the outcome and the probable attitude of their candidate toward it. They would have given anything to
know his position, but knew not how to draw him out. In
a statement which causes surprise, to say the least, coming
as it did from a man prominent in public life in 1836, when
Texas had been an issue, and purporting to speak for one
of the most sagacious journalists of the day, Roane informed Van Buren that " neither Ritchie nor I recollect

[122] *Richmond Enquirer,* October 20, 1843.
[123] A. Stevenson to M. Van Buren, October 8, 1843. *Van Buren MSS.;
Richmond Enquirer,* October 10, 1843.
[124] *Ibid.*
[125] October 17, 1843. *Van Buren MSS.*
[126] A. Stevenson to Martin Van Buren, October 8, 1843. *Van Buren MSS.*

your position in regard to it " (Texas), and assured him
that any information on that subject " would be regarded
with the strictest confidence." [127]   With an equal degree of
improbability as to their strict accuracy, Stevenson made
similar statements.[128]   The profound silence maintained by
Van Buren only increased the doubt and uncertainty of his
friends.

The stirring events of September and October, 1843,
brought forth opinions, which help to explain Calhoun's
unpopularity in Virginia.   Ritchie doubted his ability to
live down nullification.[129]   Actuated by the democratic
ideas of his illustrious grandfather, Patrick Henry, Wm.
H. Roane could not assent to " all the learned jargon "
(now termed philosophy) about " the rights of minorities."   With Calhoun in the presidency, he would have
been in " constant terror, expecting from him some
new-fangled scheme or view," and he was willing to
wager his life upon it that " the book he is now writing will be John Taylor of Caroline with metaphysical
variations." [130]

On the other hand, there is abundant evidence to lead
one to believe that Calhoun was then held, by a large
minority of the people, in that high esteem with which he
is now generally regarded.   The extent and accuracy of his
knowledge, the strength of his judgment, the brilliancy of
his genius, his bold and chivalrous discharge of duty, and
" the almost immaculate purity of his character " [131] made
for him warm and uncompromising friends, in the same
manner that these traits have made popular other Amer-

[127] October 17, 1843. *Van Buren MSS.*
[128] He had been speaker of the House of Representatives from December, 1827, to December, 1835. The annexation of Texas had been discussed in 1829 and in 1835-36.
[129] *Richmond Enquirer,* September 22, 1843.
[130] W. H. Roane to M. Van Buren, September 11, 1843. *Van Buren MSS.*
[131] *Richmond Enquirer,* February 4, 1844.

icans, who have been no more successful politically than was Calhoun.

After the meeting of Congress and the state legislature in December, 1843, Calhoun's popularity waned rapidly. He was unable to control the organization of or even a considerable party in either. Rumor had it that he would withdraw from the contest.[132]   Contrary to expectations, some of the southern states had decided against him,[133] and the more lukewarm among his followers in Virginia began to drift either to Clay or to Van Buren.[134]

The leaders of Calhoun's party did not despair and determined to fight to the last.   R. K. Crallé visited some of the western counties and tried to control their local conventions.[135]   The *Petersburg Intelligencer* continued to complain of the " petulance," " dotage," and " dictatorship " of Ritchie,[136] and finally it was decided to carry the fight into the Democratic state convention, which met at Richmond, February 1, 1844.

On the evening before the convention met, however, Calhoun's address to the " political friends and supporters " came and gave an unexpected turn to events. It was the opinion of many that this paper had been held back until this opportune time with the hope that it might turn the tide from Van Buren.[137]   In this " ultimatum " Calhoun condemned the plans of organization and the methods of choosing delegates to the proposed national convention, and he declared it to be his purpose to support for an election to the presidency no candidate of the Democratic party " who is op-

[132] *Ibid.,* December 27, 1843.

[133] *Ibid.;* " Calhoun Correspondence," *Am. Hist. Assn. Rept.* (1899), II., pp. 554, 556.

[134] *Richmond Enquirer,* January 13, 1844; *Ibid.,* January 27, 1844.

[135] *Ibid.,* January 11, 1844.

[136] *Ibid.,* January 18,. 1844.

[137] H. A. Garland to M. Van Buren, February 7, 1844. *Van Buren MSS.*

posed to free trade or whose prominent and influential friends are," or one " who gives his aid and countenance to the agitation of abolition in Congress, or elsewhere, or whose prominent friends and influential supporters shall." He also expressed a desire that his name be not used before the Baltimore convention in connection with the nomination for the presidency.[138]   The effect was entirely different from that expected or contemplated.   Immediately the friends of Calhoun held a caucus.   They decided that the address was a resignation of Calhoun's candidacy, that it released them from their duty to support him, and that they would support the nominee of the Democratic party.[139]

Thus the state convention became a Democratic love-feast.   In enthusiastic and patriotic speeches, R. M. T. Hunter, W. F. Gordon, and James S. Barbour announced the decision of their caucus, but placed the ultimate consequences of Van Buren's election upon his friends.[140]   Ritchie seized the opportunity and, in the only important political speech of his life, welcomed the return of political accord and assumed, for his faction of the party, the responsibility for the consequences.[141]   The convention adopted conciliatory resolutions and placed a number of Calhoun's friends upon the electoral ticket.[142]   The next number of the *En-*

[138] W. H. Roane to M. Van Buren, February 3, 1844. *Van Buren MSS.;* *Richmond Enquirer,* February 1, 1844; *Ibid.,* February 6, 1844.

[139] *Richmond Enquirer,* February 6, 1844. The friends of Calhoun issued an address. They could not remain neutral, and the dangers of the election of Clay were becoming so great that they could not remain inactive. They would therefore support Van Buren. *Ibid.,* February 10, 1844; H. A. Garland to Martin Van Buren, February 7, 1844. *Van Buren MSS.* In a letter to R. M. T. Hunter, dated February 1, 1844, Calhoun gave up all hope of success in Virginia. " Calhoun Correspondence," *Am. Hist. Assn. Rept.* (1899), II., p. 562.

[140] *Richmond Enquirer,* February 6, 1844.

[141] *Ibid.*

[142] *Richmond Enquirer,* February 8, 1844.

quirer proclaimed the Democratic party of Virginia " one and indivisible," and announced that " The Ark . . . which has been agitated on the billows of the sea of liberty . . . has now touched the summit of Mount Ararat—the rainbow of peace is brightening the Heavens—and the Dove has gone forth from the Ark to bring back the Olive Branch to all our party." [143]   It was currently rumored and generally believed that Ritchie and the Junta had committed themselves to Calhoun for the succession in 1848,[144] and Van Buren was informed that he could rely upon the vote of Virginia and South Carolina.[145]   On February 26, 1844, two days before the death of Abel P. Upshur on the ill-fated *Princeton,* and thus before Calhoun could have entertained a notion of becoming secretary of state, B. H. Rhett informed Van Buren that Calhoun was no longer a candidate for the presidency.[146]

With one accord the Democrats now directed their energies to the spring elections and to the necessity of preserving unity within their party.   Ritchie was also active in furthering the candidacy of Stevenson for the vice-presidency.[147]   With a view to the coming elections all reference to Texas was scrupulously avoided. With the greatest caution, lest they should either alienate the Democracy of the north or revive the Calhoun party or jeopardize the interests of Stevenson, the tariff was made the chief issue.[148]   Unavailing efforts were also made to have Van Buren commit himself upon this subject in more satisfactory terms than those

[143] *Ibid.,* February 3, 1843.

[144] To the day of his death Ritchie never ceased to deny the repeated assertion that he had made an alliance with Calhoun on this occasion.

[145] W. H. Roane to Van Buren, February 3, 1844, and H. A. Garland to Van Buren, February 7, 1844. *Van Buren MSS.*

[146] P. H. Rhett to M. Van Buren, February 26, 1844. *Van Buren MSS.*

[147] *Richmond Enquirer,* February 13, 1844.

[148] *Richmond Enquirer,* January 11, 1844; *Ibid.,* February 23, 1844.

used by him in his response to the Democratic state convention of Indiana.[149]

Ignore it as they would, Texas continued to be the one question of vital importance. The pending treaty for its annexation and the uncertainty of the final outcome, seemed to command silence on the part of both Democrats and Whigs. But it would not down. In March, 1844, the Northern prints and the *National Intelligencer* discussed almost nothing but Texas. About the same time Senator Walker's famous letter on its reannexation found its way into the press.[150] Silence on the part of Virginians was no longer possible or expedient.

Practically every prominent Democrat of Virginia favored the " reannexation of Texas." [151] Since 1829 Ritchie had lost no opportunity to support it,[152] and Roane now saw both the wisdom and expediency of such a course.[153] With born expansionists and with a people who had a larger surplus quantity of slave property, which would find a ready market by the extension of the southwest, it was not strange that the desire for Texas became a passion.

But there is little or no evidence that their enthusiasm for slave territory or their fears of his probable attitude toward Texas caused Mr. Van Buren's friends to think, at this time, of abandoning his candidacy. On the other hand, they tried to bring him to their way of thinking and thus promote his ultimate success. To this end Ritchie

[149] Thomas Ritchie to H. A. Garland, January 8, 1844; H. A. Garland to Van Buren, January 12, 1844; S. B. French to Van Buren, February 18, 1844. *Van Buren MSS.*

[150] *Richmond Enquirer,* March 23, 26, 29, 1844.

[151] The opposition made by the Whigs was largely for the sake of politics, and was directed against the manner of acquiring and not the policy.

[152] *Richmond Enquirer,* March 22, 1844.

[153] Letter to Van Buren, April 20, 1844. *Van Buren MSS.*

wrote to Silas Wright, Van Buren's closest political adviser, as follows:

" I send you the following extract of a letter I received last night from Washington:

" ' March 17—The Texas question is destined to succeed. I think the treaty when made will certainly be ratified. . . . To-morrow evening a decisive article will appear in the *Globe*. General Jackson is most heartily with us, and *will go the whole*. He is the originator of this movement and *will see it through*— Unless forced to do so we must not make this a party question— Unless there is great imprudence or folly, Van Buren will be elected—but if he goes against Texas (which I deem impossible) all is lost.'

" I would send you the original letter, but it is marked ' confidential.' The writer is a member of Congress and a friend of Mr. Van Buren.—Be so good as to consider its contents confidential, with the reservation only, that if you think it best, you may communicate them to Mr. V. B. I leave that disposition of them to your own discretion." [154]

Two days later Ritchie published, under date of February 12, 1844, General Jackson's letter of February 12, 1843, to Aaron V. Brown of Tennessee, in which the annexation of Texas was urged on the ground of military necessity.[155] About the same time and in keeping with the nation-wide demand to know the opinion of public men, W. H. Hammett of Mississippi interrogated Martin Van Buren regarding his opinions on the proposed annexation of Texas.[156] The typographical error in the publication of a letter of such vital interest and upon such a delicate subject, which had been kept from the public for more than a year, and the interrogation of Van Buren by a slave-

[154] Ritchie to Silas Wright, March 20, 1844. *Van Buren MSS.*

[155] *Richmond Enquirer*, March 22, 1844.

[156] W. H. Hammett to Martin Van Buren, March 27, 1844. *Van Buren MSS.* Jefferson Davis of Mississippi had interrogated him two days earlier. *Van Buren MSS.*

owner in the secrets of the Democratic party have caused historians to give credence to the alleged existence of a plot, mentioned above, to keep the nomination from going to Van Buren.[157]. Writers who have accepted this interpretation and implied, or asserted, that Van Buren's friends in Virginia were parties to it, were certainly ignorant of the fact that W. H. Roane had, five months before the publication of Jackson's letter to Brown, informed Van Buren of the existence of such a letter and of the use proposed to be made of it.[158]   They have also overlooked the fact that Ritchie corrected, in the next issue of the *Enquirer,* the typographical error made in the original publication of the letter from Jackson to Brown, and called attention to the fact that an error had been made.[159]

While other public men were daily giving their opinions regarding the annexation of Texas,[160] the Democrats of Virginia waited impatiently to hear from Van Buren upon that subject.   It is evident from their correspondence that they appreciated the difficulties which confronted him in the north and that they would have preferred to keep the Texas question out of the campaign entirely.   After a month's delay and after the exchange of many opinions with Silas Wright[161] regarding the expedient course to pursue, Van Buren replied to Hammett in an able and carefully written letter.[162]   He opposed immediate annexation on the ground that it would be

[157] Alexander, *Political Hist. of State of New York,* II., p. 66; Hammond, *Political History of State of New York,* III., p. 447; McLaughlin, *Cass,* p. 215; Shephard, *Van Buren,* pp. 401-406, etc.

[158] W. H. Roane to Van Buren, October 17, 1843. *Van Buren MSS.*

[159] *Richmond Enquirer,* March 26, 1844. This correction was made before it had been suggested by Mr. Niles or any other editor.

[160] Clay came out against the annexation of Texas on April 17, 1844. He had just returned from a tour of the southern states.

[161] See *Van Buren MSS.,* for March and April, 1844.

[162] Van Buren to W. H. Hammett, April 20, 1844. *Van Buren MSS.; Richmond Enquirer,* April 30, 1844.

a breach of neutrality, as Texas and Mexico were then at war with each other, but he thought it within the constitutional powers of Congress to acquire territory. This letter came to Richmond on April 30th, when the Democrats were receiving the returns from an unsuccessfully contested election for members of the General Assembly.[163] Its effect is best described in a letter from Roane to Van Buren:

"Your letter to Mr. Hammett," said he, "is just received here and has caused a sensation and is likely to produce an *effect* which no paper has caused or produced in my knowledge."[164] He also informed him that the publication of his letter two weeks earlier would have given the House of Delegates of the Assembly to the Whigs by 30 or 40 majority and added, "you cannot (I am grieved to the heart to think) carry this state next fall. Whether any Democrat can, God only knows."

The members of the Junta were at a loss to know what to do. Various courses were suggested. Finally the Shockoe Hill Democratic Association was called to meet the following day. At this meeting Ritchie drew, offered, and secured the adoption of resolutions, which declared that the immediate reannexation of Texas to the United States was a measure required by the best interests of the Union, that such a course was consistent with the soundest principles of international law, that the efforts then being made in the north by Albert Gallatin and others to prevent the acquisition of more slave territory would, if successful, place the south under the ban of the republic, that the commercial and abolitionist activities of Great Britain in Texas furnished strong and additional grounds why we should repossess ourselves of that country, that Clay's letter opposing annexation was an attack upon the institution of

---

[163] W. H. Roane to Van Buren, April 30, 1844. *Van Buren MSS.; Richmond Enquirer,* May 2, 1844.

[164] April 30, 1844. *Van Buren MSS.*

negro slavery, and that the Democrats of Virginia be at once urged to express their opinions on the subject of Texas and on " the propriety of relieving their delegates to the Baltimore convention from their instructions, leaving them to the exercise of a sound discretion, or even to instruct them, if they deem it expedient to do so, to cast the vote of Virginia in favor of men known and pledged to be for annexation." [165]

While the Democrats were openly and publicly repudiating Van Buren by elaborate resolutions, which did not refer to him by name, but contained a detailed refutation of his letter on Texas, the following anonymous letter was written to him: [166]

Richmond May 1, 1844.

MY DEAR SIR,—
    You are deserted. Ritchie, Roane, Stevenson are *all* against you on the Texas question; *positively, openly,* and *unequivocally* against *you*. Arrangements are *now,* at *this very hour,* being made to take up another candidate, and of this be assured, if there be a God in Heaven.

a faithful follower
and friend.

Q in the corner.
4 o'clock P. M.

Letters, telling why Van Buren could not carry Virginia, began to pour in upon Ritchie from all sides.[167]   On May 5th he sent to Mr. Van Buren a number of these letters and a long personal letter, from which the following interesting and suggestive extracts are taken:

" I have refrained from writing you a single letter during the present campaign, and I deeply regret that the first one which

[165] *Washington Union,* April 3, 1847.
[166] *Van Buren MSS.*
[167] Ritchie to Van Buren, May 5, 1844. *Van Buren MSS.*

I shall have to write would be one, which gives me as much pain
to write, as any which ever came from my pen. I need not tell
you Mr. Van Buren the feelings which I entertain toward you.
Trusted at all times with a kindness and liberality and a distinction far beyond my merits, I have conceived a sentiment toward you, which partook not more of confidence in you as a
politician, than of attachment to you as a man. I have received
from you a hundred evidences of good feeling, which have left a
reciprocal impression upon my heart. But I will not dwell upon
particulars, nor will I deal in any profusion. You must know
me well enough to believe that unnecessary.

"The last ten days have produced a condition of political
affairs, which I did not believe to be possible. I am compelled
to come to the conclusion that we cannot carry Virginia for you.
We have lost, I now believe, the joint vote in the Legislature.
We have ten majority in the Senate, it is true, but in the House of
Delegates, where we had a majority of 16 at the last session,
the Whigs now have a majority of about 12. But I do not
attribute so much importance to this Revolution as some of my
friends—I have recovered from the temporary panic, which is so
natural with such circumstances. I assure you, I do not write
you under the influence of any feeling, which might cloud my
judgment. But I write you under the effect of what I have
heard from my friends and what they write me about your
prospects in November next. Judge for yourself, sir. If I did
not know that you were a man of honor, I would not put the
enclosed letters in your hands. Read them, my dear Sir, but
don't preserve their names—take no copies of them—but return
me the originals. I will have no half-confidence with you—some
of them are my best friends. They are all your warm friends.
I trust them in your hands—for I know that you will not abuse
the confidence I am now reposing in you. Read them, and judge
for yourself. I am most anxious to spare your feelings, if I
can, but I owe to you, as my friend, as the friend of our great
principles, to let you see what others have trusted to me, that
you may determine for yourself.

"Whom we can get to supply your place, I know not, if you
retire. You will see what my correspondents say upon that point.
I can only tell you that Mr. Calhoun's friends solemnly disclaim
any wish to run him—that I have solemnly protested and will
protest against any such idea as that. I am actuated by no other
motive under Heaven, than the desire to possess you of the views

which these letters express. It is the same opinion, which is entertained by gentlemen, as stanch republicans as any in the state, who are around me, who have been late and are now your personal and political friends."

Without a line of comment Van Buren returned the letters sent to him by Ritchie.[168]   Despite this cold rebuke of their frank and honest and patriotic conduct, his former friends in Virginia continued to speak kindly of him.   Geo. C. Dromgoole, his most enthusiastic supporter, went so far as to publish a long letter in which he condemned absolutely and unequivocally the repudiation of Mr. Van Buren.[169]   The friends of Calhoun issued an address in which they denied the alleged existence of an intrigue on their part to turn the tide against him by " lying down " in the spring elections or by allying with the " anti-Van Buren Clique " at Washington.[170]   The Democratic central committee in an " address to the people of Virginia " praised him as a conscientious " statesman " and " patriot," [171] and Ritchie pledged himself to support him for an election, should he be the nominee of the Democratic party.[172]   But the tide had ebbed never to return; the people were with their leaders.

Meanwhile the leaders were having difficulty to agree upon another candidate.   Ritchie would accept Calhoun under no conditions;[173] James Buchanan and Colonel R. M. Johnson had only small followings, and they were confined to isolated communities in the western counties,[174] and

[168] *Van Buren MSS.*

[169] *Richmond Enquirer,* May 10, 1844. He did not charge or imply in this letter that Mr. Van Buren had been deceived.

[170] *Richmond Enquirer,* May 10, 1844.

[171] *Ibid.*

[172] *Ibid.,* May 7, 1844.

[173] Ritchie to Van Buren, May 5, 1844. *Van Buren MSS.* Calhoun's friends made no effort to revive his candidacy.

[174] *Richmond Enquirer,* January 6, 1843; *Ibid.,* October 6, 1843.

the opinion prevailed that neither Silas Wright nor
Thomas H. Benton would accept the nomination so long
as Van Buren remained in the race.   Thus the choice fell
upon Lewis Cass, who already enjoyed much popularity in
Virginia.   He was favorably known in the western part
of the state, where he had intermarried with a family
widely and prominently known; [175] he was popular with
the former conservative faction of the Democratic party,
which had opposed Van Buren's independent treasury
scheme; [176] and, most important of all, he was sound on
the question of Texas.[177]   The vote of Virginia in the
Baltimore convention was given to him until the " dark-
horse," James K. Polk, dashed into camp and captured the
banner.

The subsequent contest between the Whigs and the
Democrats was spirited and in doubt to the end.   The
Whigs continued to attack the " despot," the " artful wire-
puller," and the " miniature Talleyrand," Ritchie; [178] they
insisted that he and others of the Junta were owners of
lands in Texas, and that they were willing to destroy the
Union for mercenary purposes; [179] they denominated the
resolutions of '98 " mere abstractions," [180] and insisted that
a national bank would make money plentiful and equalize
exchange; [181] they protested against the alleged use of British gold in an effort to make the United States a free-trade
country,[182] and expressed great fear lest the success of the
Democratic party and the consequent repeal of the tariff

[175] Ambler, *Sectionalism in Virginia*, p. 237.
[176] *Richmond Enquirer*, January 13, 1844.
[177] *New York Republic*, May 4, 1844; *Richmond Enquirer*, May 14, 21,
1844.
[178] *Richmond Enquirer*, September 10, 1844.
[179] *Ibid.*, September 6, 24, 1844.
[180] *Ibid.*, November 12, 1844.
[181] *Ibid.*
[182] *Richmond Enquirer*, October 5, 1844.

act of 1842 would make it necessary for the laboring classes of this country to live upon " free-trade bread," [183] a " black rye-bread used by the laboring population of Germany;" they believed that Great Britain would prefer free trade with the United States to the ownership of a dozen such countries as Texas,[184] and claimed that the annexation of that country would lower the price of land in and decrease the population of Virginia; [185] they went even so far as to invite John Quincy Adams to address a public meeting in Richmond.[186]

On the other hand, Ritchie, as spokesman for the Democrats, did not deny that he and other Virginians owned lands in Texas,[187] but he did insist that their interest in the preservation of the Union was paramount to all other interests; [188] he pronounced the rumors of disunion, which had followed the rejection by the Senate of the treaty for the annexation of Texas, to be " idle chimeras " started by some hasty resolutions in South Carolina, which Calhoun " regrets " and " reprobates;" [189] he proved the " black rye-bread" argument to be a fraud by showing that rye-bread was a wholesome and popular diet with all classes in Germany,[190] and held out the adoption of free trade in Europe as an example which we should follow; he pronounced the proposed visit of Adams a disgrace to the grand Old Commonwealth,[191] and almost daily insisted that Adams and Henry Clay had stolen the presidency in

[183] *Ibid.,* October 22, 1844.
[184] *Ibid.,* October 5, 1844.
[185] *Ibid.,* July 11, 1844.
[186] *Richmond Enquirer,* September 3, 1844.
[187] *Ibid.,* September 6, 1844.
[188] *Ibid.*
[189] *Ibid.,* June 18, 1844; *Ibid.,* August 6, 9, 1844; *Ibid.,* September 24, 1844.
[190] *Richmond Enquirer,* October 24, 1844.
[191] *Ibid.,* September 3, 1844.

1825;[192] above all things, he insisted upon the immediate annexation of Texas. Texas in the Union, he thought, would be a less fearful competitor than Texas in the British Empire. In either case, it would be populated largely from the United States, and would raise cotton. As a part of the United States, she would afford a ready market for "worthless negroes" at "high prices." The money from their sales could be used to make necessary improvements at home, and their removal would give a place for desirable whites and German immigrants in those mechanical and commercial employments from which a surplus of slave labor had driven them.[193]

Although the results of this contest were in doubt to the last the Democrats won by a popular majority of almost six thousand. The current of public opinion was in their favor, and they outgeneraled their opponents in both tactics and arguments. The slogan, "Polk and Texas," was popular with voters of all parties in eastern Virginia, and in the very last days of the campaign, Ritchie gave wide circulation, through the medium of the press, to the attacks made by the *Richmond Whig* in 1840, upon the alleged ignorance and stupidity of the "Suabian Dutch" of the Valley, who had caused the vote of Virginia to be cast against W. H. Harrison for the presidency. By these tactics he turned threatened defections from the Democratic party in the western counties into large majorities.[194]

CHARLES HENRY AMBLER.

[192] *Ibid.*, October 10, 12, 15, 1844.
[193] *Richmond Enquirer*, July 19, 1844.
[194] *Richmond Whig*, November 13, 1840; *Richmond Enquirer*, October 3, 1844.

THE SOUTHERN WHIGS, 1834-1854

IF we are to interpret correctly the character and career of any political party we must beware of expecting too complete a consonance between their logical interests as we look back upon them and their actions, alliances, and war-cries. The doctrine of some historians [1] that the whole course of the Whigs, north and south, hinged upon their championship of congressional power as a preventive of presidential autocracy could only have been reached by taking too seriously the rhodomontade of party platforms and congressional speeches, and neglecting the pamphlet, newspaper, and epistolary materials.

While the function of government is to adjust society to its environment and to adjust groups and individuals within society to one another, and the function of politics is to readjust society in response to changes in the conditions of life, the adjustment and readjustment are never perfect. Political problems are never fully solved, but always in the process of solution. They could be fully solved only if men's knowledge, intelligence, and self-control were perfect, and if men's conditions, interests, and aims were harmonious. Since these are never so, there is never a cessation of political strife, but only an occasional abatement. When, in a republic, relatively permanent differences of condition and interest set off one large element of the people against another, each lull in politics, each " era of good feeling," is likely to be succeeded by a revival of the same alignments as before, and a renewal of strife on much the same grounds.

[1] The most positive of these is Burgess, J. W., *The Middle Period*, N. Y., 1897, pp. 282, 283.

Politicians are not always aware of the character of the forces which cause and control their own actions, and even when so conscious, they are often prone to divert attention from the real conditions and motives by making appeal to theories and generalities.   Patriotism is the party cry of many who would use increased governmental power for their own particular behoof; the inherent rights of men are as much appealed to by those who would raise themselves as by those who would raise their brethren.   Radicals are easily caught by " general principles," and would often o'erleap the mark of soundness in their plans of social and political readjustment.   Conservatives, whether by native temperament or by the possession of vested interests, are skeptical of generalities and slow to indorse the proposal of any change from the established order.

The ante-bellum south was an entirely normal community so far as the play of political forces is concerned.   The negro-slave-plantation system created and maintained a huge special vested interest differentiated from and in more or less chronic conflict with the local " farming interest " and the farming, manufacturing, and commercial interests in the northern states.   But politicians and political interests must have bedfellows.   The southern planters were always a minority of the voting population in their several states and in the United States; and for the sake of security to their interests they were obliged to find and retain allies at home and abroad, and to decry the too sharp definition of real issues.   And they must be chary, also, of political shibboleths which might prove, for them, wolves in sheep's clothing.

The wave of Jeffersonian democracy and of Jacksonian democracy successively put the conservatives of the south (the planters and their allies) on the defensive.   Neither of these movements paid heed to the fact that southern industry and society were exceptionally constituted upon a peculiar basis, and each in turn threatened danger to the fabric. The champions of the established régime had to rally to its support against each of these waves, and to use for their purpose such means as were found at hand. Hence, the southern Federalists [2] of Jefferson's time, and the southern Whigs of Jackson's. With the latter we are here concerned.

When the propaganda of Jacksonian Democracy began to sweep the country, in the late eighteen-twenties and the early thirties, it bade fair for some years to destroy a variety of existing adjustments, and to injure a variety of interests. Its campaign for the idea that one man is as good as another threatened and then actually overthrew the historic property-holding qualifications for suffrage and office-holding. Its contempt for checks and balances promised a régime of government by impulse rather than by deliberation, in case of definitive Jacksonian victory. Its hostility to corporations, capital, privileges, and aristocracy drove all who were friendly to these things, as well as those who were temperamentally conservative, into resistance to all that was Jacksonian.

The only means conceivable for erecting substantial resistance to the Democratic surge, as well as to Jackson's arbitrary will, was to organize a country-wide party of opposition. And to give that party a prospect of success its numbers must be made as large, its membership as comprehensive, as possible. All resources to be found in the existing situation must be utilized, all dislike of Jackson or his lieutenants must be fanned, all old controversies which might be useful must be revived, all the local factions available for national purposes must be attracted, and the most talented leaders, old and new, must be brought into service and be given free opportunity to spar with the

[2] *Cf.* the writer's article, " The South Carolina Federalists," in the *American Historical Review*, Vol. XIV., pp. 529-543, 731-743, 776-790.

Administration in Congress and on the hustings, to expose Jacksonian weaknesses and develop opposition strength.

When in 1834 the first steps were taken to establish the Whig party, political conditions throughout the country were highly complicated, local considerations and local animosities ruled the day, and perhaps nothing short of a national emergency such as Jackson precipitated could have centralized politics and have simplified conditions into a national two-party régime.   The simplification, as we shall see, was more apparent than real, and each of the parties was destined to have chronic trouble in maintaining its own harmony and efficiency.   The Democracy was a unit in Jackson's day, it is true, but thereafter it was in frequent danger of splitting asunder.   The Whig party at large, as John Fiske has well shown,[3] was from its birth to its death a coalition of National Republicans, mainly northern, and state-rights men, mainly southern.   The present essay will show that the southern wing of the Whig party was itself a coalition of broad constructionists and strict constructionists, without the possibility of firm cohesion, beset with troubles, and achieving victories only at the peril of dissolution.   Nevertheless, the southern Whigs exerted a powerful influence upon their times and have left a strong impress upon later generations.

In the early eighteen-thirties in every southern state old enough to have begun to emerge from frontier conditions there prevailed some alignment of local factions opposing one another mainly upon local issues.   In Kentucky the principal questions of policy had been banking and debts, in Tennessee the taxation of lands, in Georgia the Indian relations, and in the Carolinas, Virginia, and Maryland the distribution of representation and the building of internal improvements.   Federal problems were of active influence

[3] "Harrison, Tyler, and the Whig Coalition," in his *Essays Historical and Literary*, Vol. I.

also, with the tariff issue focusing in South Carolina and the issue of Supreme Court jurisdiction in Virginia and Georgia; and finally the development and maintenance of state factions was greatly aided, particularly in Georgia and Tennessee, by the prevalence of personal feuds and friendships, and everywhere by the existence of more or less definite class-distinctions in society.[4]

In general in the late twenties and the thirties the bulk of the southern people tended to endorse the doctrine of state rights. This inclination was in part a traditional possession from the days of Crawford, Macon, Randolph, Roane, and John Taylor of Caroline;[5] but it had recently been strengthened by the Creek, Cherokee, and tariff issues and by the studious consideration of the semi-latent but rising issue of negro slavery. The producers of sugar, wool, hemp, salt, and iron were favorable to protective tariffs, and the people of certain districts were eager for federal roads, canals, and river improvements, which if built would specially benefit their localities. But the tobacco and cotton producers, the slaveholding interest in general, except where identified with sugar planting, were,

---

[4] These themes of developments within the several states have been treated with greater or less monographic fullness in the following works: Ambler, C. H., *Sectionalism in Virginia from 1776 to 1861;* Chandler, J. A. C., "Representation in Virginia," in Johns Hopkins University *Studies,* series XIV., Nos. 6, 7; Wagstaff, H. McG., "State Rights and Political Parties in North Carolina, 1776-1861," *ibid.,* series XXIV., Nos. 7, 8; Houston, D. F., *A Critical Study of Nullification in South Carolina;* Schaper, W. A., "Sectionalism and Representation in South Carolina," in the *American Historical Association Report* for 1900, I., pp. 237-463; Phillips, U. B., "Georgia and State Rights," *ibid.* for 1901, II., pp. 1-224; Phelan, James, *History of Tennessee;* Shaler, N. S., *Kentucky;* Steiner, B. C., "The Electoral College for the Senate of Maryland and the Nineteen Van Buren Electors," in the *American Historical Association Report* for 1895, pp. 129-167; and the theme of contemporary development in the northern states, in Charles McCarthy's "The Anti-Masonic Party," *ibid.* for 1902, I., 365-574.

[5] *Cf.* Turner, F. J., *Rise of the New West,* chap. xviii.

as a rule, hostile to federal paternalism; and these were of course by far the predominant interests in the south. The nullification episode, with McDuffie's " forty-bale " theory as an incident, had stressed the importance of free trade to the cotton planters, and Jackson's anti-nullification proclamation and the force bill spread and intensified the devotion to state rights among the planters and their friends.

The development of social cleavage and its influence in the cleavage of political elements is more difficult to trace and is impossible to demonstrate in brief compass.[6] Suffice it here to say that in every southern state in which a clear-cut alignment of local parties had developed during the " Era of Good Feeling," one faction in each state comprised most of the well-to-do and aristocratically inclined people, and the other was largely made up of the illiterates and unprosperous. The lines were not at all sharply drawn in this connection either in society or in politics; but a tendency nevertheless strongly prevailed. The lower classes were of course in most communities the first to welcome Jackson and Jacksonian Democracy. But in the presidential elections of 1828 and 1832, when the only choice lay between Jackson and Adams or Jackson and Clay, the two opposing factions in numerous states vied in their ardor in supporting Jackson. This was conspicuous in Georgia and North Carolina. But when the question of Van Buren's succession arose, opportunity was furnished for one local faction or the other to withdraw from the Jacksonian alliance and return to its favorite occupation of fighting its local antagonist. By 1840 party lines were so sharply drawn throughout the southern states, and the rank-and-file so firmly habituated to their neighborhood friendships and enmities, that oftentimes the leaders themselves could not remodel the popular alignment. When

---

[6] Cf. Flisch, Julia A., "The Common People of the Old South," in *Amer. Hist. Assn. Report* for 1908, I., pp. 133-142.

Tyler and Wise, for example, went from the Whig into the Democratic camp in 1841-42, their district continued to give Whig majorities.

The great central body of southern Whigs were the cotton producers, who were first state-rights men pure and simple and joined the Whigs from a sense of outrage at Jackson's threat of coercing South Carolina. With Calhoun and Tyler at their head, they entered an alliance with Webster, Clay, and the National Republicans as a choice of evils. For several years it was merely an alliance which was established, not a union; and, indeed, Calhoun and all of his following in South Carolina and some of it in Georgia and Virginia, withdrew from that alliance before the " hurrah campaign " of 1840 cemented the Whigs into a union. The basis of amity within the coalition was of course an agreement, partly implicit and partly expressed, that all questions as between paternalism and state rights should be waived for the sake of a joint campaign against presidential autocracy and irresponsible democracy. Successive arbitrary deeds of Jackson in the middle thirties drove to the Whigs still other politicians and constituencies,[1] until by the middle of 1836 there was in every southern state a strong anti-Van Buren organization, and in the election of that year the electoral vote of the south was evenly divided between Van Buren and the several Whig candidates.

The Whigs when defeated in the north by Van Buren in 1836 promptly realized that union instead of alliance was a condition of party success, and began to prepare for victory in 1840. But some of the anti-Van Buren allies when confronted with the demand that they take party pledges, revised their choice of evils and marched back to the Democratic camp. The Democratic movement had

[1] Cf. Tyler, L. G., *Letters and Times of the Tylers*, I., p. 604; *William and Mary College Quarterly*, IV., p. 239.

lost its momentum as a rise of the lower classes and was
no longer to be feared by conservatives, and Van Buren
was clearly not a Jacksonian autocrat. Calhoun, dreading
a revival of a paternalistic program by the Clay following, forsook the Whigs in 1837-38 and by gradual stages
became fully identified with the Democratic party, and R.
M. T. Hunter of Virginia and three Georgia congressmen, Mark A. Cooper, Walter T. Colquitt, and Edward
J. Black, followed Calhoun's example in 1839-40.

These Georgians were vigorously assailed at home as
turncoats; and they as vigorously defended their action.
Cooper as their principal spokesman issued in April, 1840,
an elaborate circular to his constituents [8] maintaining that
his whole career had been one of devotion to state rights
and contending that his state-rights principles must require
him and his colleagues to support Van Buren as against
Harrison. The Whig party he declared to be a coalition
against Van Buren, with no principle in common, but with
National Republicans predominating in its membership.
The course which he himself had adopted, he said, was
like that of Calhoun, not to commit his constituents to
either party in Congress but to apply to each the state-
rights test and to support those leaders who were most
likely to promote the state-rights cause. The Democrats,
he maintained, had now abandoned and repudiated the
Jacksonian exaggeration of federal powers, while the
Whigs were tending strongly to advocate centralization.
He urged that state-rights men should stand independently
as a third element in national politics, throwing their weight
into one scale or the other as might best serve their own
purposes. The Whigs, he concluded, were now to be opposed not only because of their federalistic tendency but
also because of the presence within their party of a strong

abolitionist wing at the north. With a defense of his vote for Hunter as speaker and for Blair and Rives as public printers, Cooper rested his case; and so far as his former constituents were concerned, he lost it.

The reasons and conditions which impelled the Georgia Whigs into the course which the bulk of them actually followed do not appear in a formal document, but must be gathered from the editorial policy of the state Whig organ, the *Southern Recorder* of Milledgeville, and from the proceedings of local Whig meetings and of the Whig state convention of 1840. On June 25, 1839, the *Southern Recorder* announced that it would support for the presidency in 1840 George M. Troup, the veteran fire-eating ex-governor of Georgia, whose name was of course one to conjure with among state-rights devotees; and other Whig papers followed the *Recorder's* example. The Democratic presses denounced this raising of Troup's banner as a ruse to carry Georgia's vote for Clay in case the election should be thrown into the United States House of Representatives. The *Recorder* in reply[9] repudiated such a purpose, declared its determination to secure Troup's election if possible, and made a counter charge that the Van Buren presses were attempting to discredit the nomination of Troup, because they knew that if the state-rights party, now commonly called Whig, should support Clay's candidacy it would throw the state irrevocably into the Van Buren column. The nomination of Harrison and Tyler in December by the Whig national convention at Harrisburg (in which Georgia was not represented) removed the danger of Clay's candidacy and relieved the need for an independent candidate in Georgia. Nevertheless, the *Recorder* continued to carry Troup's name at its "masthead" until the end of April, 1840, devoting its editorials, meanwhile, to the censure of both Van Buren and "feder-

[9] July 30, 1839.

alism," and incidentally scolding Cooper, Colquitt, and Black for their failure to rally to Troup's standard. But in April a series of local Whig meetings showed such a strong current in the state for Harrison and Tyler that on May 5 the *Recorder* announced its withdrawal of Troup's name. The resolutions adopted by one of these meetings—that at Macon on April 11—indicates the strong attachment to state rights which the Georgia Whigs still felt. In reply to the charge by the Democratic organs that Harrison was an enemy to state rights and southern interests, these resolutions said: " Would John Tyler consent to be identified with such a man on the same ticket? It cannot for one moment be believed." [10] On June 1 and 2, the " anti-Van Buren " or Whig convention of the state held its session at Milledgeville, with John M. Berrien as its president and Robert Toombs a leading member, deliberated very briefly, indorsed Harrison and Tyler, nominated a ticket of electors in their behalf, and adjourned to a nearby grove for a barbecue and jubilation. [11] Contemporaneously with this, a Georgia Democrat wrote to a colleague: " Two or three state-rights men that I know, and only two or three, will vote for Van Buren. It is impossible to beat it into the heads of the Nullifiers that Cooper, Colquitt, and Black are not turncoats, but sustain the same principles they have ever done, and those they were sent there to uphold." [12] Against the Harrison-Tyler movement further protests in the name of state rights were vain. The combination of state-rights protestations and Tippecanoe hurrahs carried the state in November by a

[10] *Southern Recorder,* April 21, 1840.

[11] *Ibid.,* June 9, 1840.

[12] Letter of James Jackson, Monroe, Ga., June 7, 1840, to Howell Cobb, Athens, Ga. This and all other letters quoted in this essay are from the MSS. correspondence of Toombs, Stephens, and Cobb, which will be published in the *American Historical Association Report* for 1910, report of the Historical Manuscripts Commission.

large majority; and as was usual in the ante-bellum period, as Georgia went, so went the nation.

The Georgia Democrats, however, were merely defeated, not routed, and they stood ready to profit by Whig blunders and misfortunes. Their position as regards state rights in 1840 was not appreciably different from that of the Georgia Whigs, and the basis of party divergence was not federal problems. Georgia Whigs voted the Whig ticket mainly because they were or aspired to be cotton-planting squires and because they or their fathers had voted for Crawford or Troup or Gilmer in preceding decades, while Georgia Democrats were Democrats mostly because they were non-slaveholding farmers of the mountains or the pine-barrens or perhaps, in the cotton-belt, traditionally opposed to the squirearchy.

The conditions in Alabama and Mississippi prior to 1840 are obscure, but all discernible indications point to developments closely parallel to those in Georgia. In North Carolina the course of affairs was also similar to that in Georgia up to the year 1836; but thereafter it happened for some obscure reason that the planters' party held fast to the Jackson-Van Buren organization in the country at large, while the farmers' party, including of course the mountaineers, went over to the Whig alliance, running thus precisely counter to the development in Georgia, Alabama, and Mississippi. In South Carolina the majority of the body politic was at Calhoun's bidding, and the electoral vote of the state from 1836 to 1848 was probably cast in each case as he directed. The presidential electors were chosen by the legislature in that state instead of by the people, and it is not practicable to plot the vote by counties nor to determine fully at any time the localities or the character of the Whig and Democratic constituencies. Kentucky was nearly as much a pocket borough of Clay as South Carolina of Calhoun.

In the rest of the southern states there were definite local interests more or less dependent upon the use of broad powers by Congress for the promotion of local prosperity; and in each of these states, on account of the demand for internal improvements in East Tennessee and portions of Virginia and Maryland and for sugar protection in Louisiana, as well as for wool and hemp protection in Missouri and Kentucky, the Whig party never professed full devotion to state rights but was a coalition at all times embracing a substantial body of National Republicans. Personal relations among the political and social leaders, of course, complicated the social and economic alignments in politics. In Tennessee, for example, Jackson was warmly supported by Grundy and Polk, and was bitterly opposed upon diverse grounds by John Williams, Hugh L. White, John Bell, David Crockett, and William G. Brownlow. On the surface of things the campaigns seem personal and confused. But when the votes are plotted on maps of the state it is revealed that practically every county which lay on the Tennessee, the Cumberland, or the Mississippi rivers and prospered in the possession of rich lowland soil gave steady Whig majorities, while the counties lying in the more sterile highlands and mountains tended to be steadily Democratic. Williams, White, and Bell were moderate state-rights men, Brownlow an extreme nationalist, and Crockett merely a personal enemy of Jackson. Probably most of the Whigs of middle and western Tennessee were of the state-rights brand, while most of those in East Tennessee were National Republicans partly because of Brownlow's influence, partly because of their dislike of negroes and slavery, but mainly because they wanted the federal government to build a national turnpike through the region and to build a canal around the Muscle Shoals of the Tennessee River. In Virginia the map of the vote shows the coalition character of the Whigs

to be still more conspicuous, and indeed obscures the social differentiation of the parties.   Nearly everybody in
the state was unprosperous alike, the plantation system was
decadent, and the gentry assiduously avoided the drawing
of class lines in politics.   The paramount factors in the
Whig alignment were local needs for transportation facilities and on the other hand the state-rights tradition.   The
people along the routes, actual or projected, of the Po-
tomac canal and the James River and Kanawha canal and
those of the upper Roanoke River basin and in the district
of the Dismal Swamp canal all gave Whig majorities in
the elections, for National Republican reasons, while by
state-rights arguments the same party had established a
firm control of much of the tide-water region, and particularly of the peninsular district between the James and
York rivers and the Accomac peninsula, which together
comprised the congressional district represented by John
Tyler and then for many years by Henry A. Wise.

To summarize: The southern people tended generally
to be Democrats unless there were special considerations
to the contrary; and the principal considerations operative
were the social class consciousness of the squires, the tradition of local party antagonisms, and the problem of federal
powers.   The squires almost with one accord joined the
Whigs throughout the south, except in North Carolina
where they went by chance into the wrong camp, and in
South Carolina where they followed Calhoun's plan and
were chary of party pledges on either hand.   Upon the
problem of federal powers the Democratic party exhausted
the patience of the extremists on both sides of the question and drove them into a coalition so uncongenial upon
questions of constructive policy as to require the constant
labors of the country's most talented statesman to secure
its preservation.

When Tyler acceded upon Harrison's death and vetoed

Clay's measures, the Whig coalition was promptly threatened with utter wreck, and the state-rights wing of it was confronted with much the same quandary as it had experienced in 1839-40. Tyler and Wise now foreswore the Whig allegiance, and enough of the floating vote was swung with them to give victories to the Democrats for several years. But after much searching of hearts the bulk of the State-Rights Whigs determined to hold fast to their party connections. These were times of severe economic adversity which tried men's souls, set them to questioning their traditional doctrines, and made them long for order and prosperity at almost any cost. When in 1842-44 cotton prices in the interior of the belt went down to five, four, and three cents, and planters by thousands were bankrupted, and remedial efforts by state legislation had proved abortive, radicalism became discredited at the south in all its phases, and many state-rights men became persuaded that a moderate protective tariff might be wholesome in steadying business conditions. N. A. Ware, who describes himself in his book as a slaveholding cotton planter, published a treatise in 1844 [13] with the advocacy of protection as its main burden. Alexander H. Stephens and Robert Toombs, the Damon-and-Pythias young Georgians who were now rapidly forging to the leadership of the southern Whigs, both committed themselves in their first years in Congress to the advocacy of a tariff discriminating for the sake of protection though with main regard to revenue. And many other straws showed the direction of the current. In a word, the State-Rights Whigs were in a fair way in the middle forties to subordinate sectional and state-rights policies to the cause of party and national harmony. But before the old problems had been fully put out of the way, new and crucial issues arose over abolition

---

[13] *Notes on Political Economy as Applicable to the United States, by a Southern Planter* (N. A. Ware). New York, 1844.

petitions in Congress and the annexation of Texas and the war with Mexico, which precipitated the great slavery struggle and promptly threatened to wreck both of the parties and the Union itself. In the minds of southerners the states as such were of course much less concerned in the negro-slavery issue than was the south as a section; and after 1844 the term " state rights " became much less frequently used than before. The phrase and the idea gave place in general use to " Southern rights "; and the adjective " Southern-Rights " became as commonly applied to pro-slavery Democrats as to pro-slavery Whigs.

The historians have often related how the issues of the middle forties split each of the great parties into two sectional wings. It would probably be more accurate to say that these sectional issues caused each of the two parties to fall into three divisions, anti-slavery, neutral, and pro-slavery, with the several groups possessing no sharp lines of demarcation but shading into one another like the colors in the rainbow. The Whigs and Democrats alike came to comprise men ranging all the way from downright fire-eating abolitionists at one extreme to downright fire-eating secessionists at the other, while the great bulk of both parties continued to be neither abolitionist nor secessionist. The center of each party held party interests paramount over sectional ones; the sectional groups had as a main purpose the using of the party machinery for the furtherance of sectional ends. In pre-nomination debates each sectional wing was prone to express forebodings and threats of disaster and disruption in case its candidate and policies were not adopted by the whole party. After the convention had met and acted, however, the members of a defeated wing generally accepted the decision and supported the candidate, with a view to sharing in the spoils and to renewing the contest for the control of the party prior to the next convention. But occasionally some members of a sectional wing proved irreconcilable to the defeat of their purposes by their colleagues and bolted the party after an adverse decision.

In 1844, Clay was accepted by all the Whigs as inevitable and was nominated, though with little enthusiasm. Van Buren seemed equally inevitable for the Democrats until Tyler presented the Texas annexation treaty to the Senate in April. John B. Lamar, an excellent spokesman of Democratic opinion in Georgia, wrote to Howell Cobb on April 19:

" If Van Buren favors Annexation and Clay opposes it, either directly or indirectly, and the Democrats in the House will at last stand by the bill of the Committee of Ways and Means, without material alteration, I tell you we can carry Georgia. But if Van Buren comes out in a milk and water way on Annexation, and the bill of the Committee is lost in the House, then ' Good-night to Marmion ' in this quarter. And the same effects, if not to the same extent, will be produced throughout the South."

Two weeks later Lamar's hopes were dashed. He wrote to Cobb on May 4:

" The letter of Mr. Van Buren . . . in the *Globe* . . . was like a flash of lightning from a clear sky, changing brightness into gloom. Our party here is like a routed army, with no leaders and no rallying point. All is confusion. Some propose to run Calhoun, some Tyler, but all unite in damning Van Buren. In their fury they are getting up a Texas meeting, and what they propose doing I can't tell you. But this much is certain, to run Van Buren is to throw ourselves into an irrecoverable minority in Georgia." [14]

A southern block was promptly formed which defeated Van Buren in the Baltimore convention, nominated Polk, a southern dark horse, and carried his election on a pro-Texas platform. The campaign of 1844, in which Polk was outspoken for annexation and Clay was endeavoring to

---

[14] On the effect of Van Buren's letter in Virginia see the essay by Professor C. H. Ambler in this volume.

straddle, had the effect of attaching all the extreme pro-
slavery men to the Democratic party and of making the
Whigs decry sectional agitation; and this anomalous condition persisted for years afterward. T. W. Thomas of El-
berton, Ga., remarked to Howell Cobb in a letter of May
8, 1849: "What folly to ask the Democrats to get into
an excitement about ' niggers ' when not one in a hundred
of us own one; " but within a twelvemonth afterward
Thomas was himself shouting with the best of the fire-
eaters.

The abolition petitions and the Wilmot Proviso widened
the schism in both parties and drove many impetuous southerners, and later a number of thoughtful ones, to an attitude of aggressive resistance. As early as February 2,
1844, John W. H. Underwood of Georgia wrote Howell
Cobb:

"I am as ardently attached to our Union and institutions as
any man, but when our Northern brethren, forgetful of ' the
spirit of compromise which resulted in the formation of our Constitution, and regardless of our rights as members of this Union,
force issues upon us which were intended by the framers of
our government to be buried and closed forever, it is time that we
should hold them as we hold the rest of mankind, ' enemies in
war, in peace friends.' I am opposed to any temporizing on
this question. . . . Sir, the negroes in Georgia are already saying to each other that great men are trying to set them free
and will succeed, and many other expressions of like import.
And if the agitation of the subject is continued for three months
longer we will be compelled to arm our militia and shoot down
our property in the field. If the thing is not already incurable,
tell the agitators we had rather fight them than our own negroes,
and will do it too."

Many other expressions of fire-eating sentiment may be
found in the private correspondence of the period.[15]

[15] *E.g.,* letters to Calhoun, in "The Correspondence of John C. Calhoun," edited by J. F. Jameson, in *The American Historical Association*

The preaching of harmony by the Whigs in the early forties had already driven most southerners of impatient disposition into the Democratic party. But by 1848 a large element even of the southern Whigs, and the very leaders of the party in Congress, were beginning to adopt fire-eating doctrines, either in actual despair of southern rights in the Union or in feigned despair intended to impress their northern Whig allies with the danger of pressing anti-slavery policies too far. It was common knowledge that the Whigs at the north had much stronger anti-slavery leanings than the northern Democrats, especially after Van Buren's withdrawal into the Free Soil party. The southern Democrats could dictate the nomination of a " Northern man with Southern principles " and maintain a strong show of party accord in 1848, but the Whigs were driven to the device of a colorless military-hero candidate, the avoidance of a platform, and the confession of party schism. Yet by the adroitness of the Whig leaders the party succeeded in electing Taylor over Cass. Toombs, Stephens, Bell, Rives, and Crittenden had co-operated to nominate Taylor and Fillmore, to Clay's exclusion, and then stumped their states with arguments prepared strictly for local consumption. A Georgia Democratic campaign worker, W. H. Hull, wrote to Howell Cobb, July 22, 1848:

"One great advantage the Whigs have in argument is that they have no common platform. We are compelled to take a moderate compromise ground because our party must be satisfied in all sections, while they, in the South, take the most ultra Southern ground and abuse us as traitors to the South for not going as far as they do, and in the North vice versa. They don't care a fig what you prove on them about their Northern allies. They don't profess to think alike, and they will give up the

Report for 1899, II., pp. 952, 954, 963, 1046, 1102, 1128, 1144, 1157, 1177, 1193, 1210.

Northern Whigs freely (except Fillmore) if they can involve the Northern Democrats in the same odium."

The key to the southern Whig policy in the campaign of 1848 was, of course, that they, and particularly Toombs and Stephens, expected to control Taylor after electing him. Congress seemed likely to pass the Wilmot Proviso in spite of southern resistance, and the assurance of a presidential veto was regarded as the only southern safeguard in prospect. But Taylor resisted the pressure, refused to promise to veto the Proviso if passed, and gave the southern Whigs the same sort of unpleasant surprise as Tyler had given the northern Whigs in 1841. As a final resort, the southern-rights men, Whigs as well as Democrats, were driven into a headlong and desperate championship of the extreme southern claims in Congress in order to prevent the passage of the Proviso.

The southern leaders in both parties were now brought squarely to confront the double quandary which troubled nearly all southern party men from time to time between 1844 and 1860,—the quandary whether southern interests and rights could by any means be permanently maintained within the Union, and if so whether the most feasible way of establishing that security would be by organizing a southern phalanx regardless of old party ties or by maintaining the existing régime of two parties, preaching magnanimity, and diverting popular attention from sectional issues. Yancey, Rhett, and Quitman were sectionalists throughout; Benton, Clay, Brownlow, and Botts were nationalists throughout; but Calhoun, Toombs, Stephens, Cobb, Berrien, Clingman, Holden, Hunter, Foote, Davis, Soulé, and most other southern leaders between 1845 and 1860 found it very hard to decide between these alternatives. Several of them, in fact, made more than one shift of position in the premises, their devotion to their section waxing with the waxing of its dangers and waning with the returning prospect of inter-sectional peace.

In the winter of 1847-48 Calhoun reluctantly reached the decision that a southern phalanx was essential to southern safety in the Union, and he invited his southern colleagues at Washington to join him in a movement toward its organization. Most of the southern Democrats in Congress indorsed his proposal of an address to the south to awake the people to a sense of their dangers, but most of the southern Whigs, together with a few of the southern Democrats, Howell Cobb among the number, opposed the movement, contending that the uniting of the south would invite a union of the north into a phalanx against the south and would hasten the very ills which the signers of "the Southern Address" were dreading. Toombs wrote to Crittenden, from Washington, December 3, 1848:

"Almost every man of the Southern Democrats have joined Calhoun's movement. After mature consideration we concluded to go into the meeting in order to control and crush it; and it has been a delicate business, but so far we have succeeded well, and I think will be able to overthrow it completely on the 15th Inst."

On January 22, 1849, Toombs wrote to Crittenden again in more vehement strain:

"We have completely foiled Calhoun in his miserable attempt to form a Southern party. We found a large number of our friends would go into the miserable contrivance, and we all then determined it was best to go in and control if possible the movement. We had a regular flare-up in the last meeting, and at the call of Calhoun I told them briefly what we were at. I told him that the Union of the South was neither possible nor desirable until we were ready to dissolve the Union,—that we certainly did not intend to advise the people now to look anywhere else than to their own government for the prevention of apprehended evils,— that we did not expect an administration which we had brought into power would do any act or permit any act to be done which it would become necessary for our safety to rebel at, and that the Southern opposition could not be sustained by their own friends in acting on such a hypothesis, and that we intended to stand by the government until it committed an overt act of aggression upon our rights, which neither we nor the country ever expected. We then by a vote of 42 to 44 voted to recommit his report (we had before this tried to kill it directly but failed). . . . We are opposed to any address whatever, but the Democrats will probably outvote us to-night and put forth the one reported; but it will not get more than two or three Whig names."

But their disappointment in Taylor's attitude and their increasing realization of the strength of the anti-slavery menace at the north brought many of the southern Whigs before the end of 1849 to indorse the position which they had denounced at the beginning of the year. At the opening of Congress in December, 1849, Toombs and Stephens in particular proclaimed that southern rights were in imminent danger and could be saved only by a mighty show of stern resolution to resist aggressions. The situation was so critical that a large number of southerners, whether impulsive or thoughtful, resolved in this period to advocate withdrawal from the Union as the only means of southern safety. Henry L. Benning, an extraordinarily clear-sighted Democratic leader at Columbus, Ga., wrote Howell Cobb, July 1, 1849:

" It is apparent, horribly apparent, that the slavery question rides insolently over every other everywhere. . . . It is not less manifest that the whole North is becoming ultra anti-slavery and the whole South ultra pro-slavery. . . . Hunkerism is manifestly giving way—it has already yielded—throughout the North. Old associations, old pledges, old hopes, perhaps convictions, may for awhile keep a few old leaders of the Northern Democracy in their old position on the slavery questions, but the body and the present leaders of the party are gone, gone forever. What inference do I ask you to draw from all this? The inference that your long cherished wish to keep up the unity of the Democratic party is now vain, and that you ought not to sacrifice yourself

and your usefulness to your state in holding on to a chimera. . . .
Surely . . . it can be but a little time . . . before, owing
to the causes now at work, the North and the South must stand
face to face in hostile attitude. What I would have you consider
is this: is it not better voluntarily to take at once a position, however extreme, which you know you must and will sometime take,
than to take it by degrees and as it were on compulsion? . . .

"I think . . . that the only safety of the South from abolition universal is to be found in an *early* dissolution of the Union.
I think that the Union by its *natural and ordinary* working is
giving anti-slavery-ism such a preponderance in the Genl. Government, both by adding to the number of free states and dimin-
ishing the number of slave, that it (anti-slavery-ism) will be able
soon to abolish slavery by act of Congress and then to execute
the law. I no more doubt that the North will abolish slavery
the very first moment it feels itself able to do it without too much
cost, than I doubt my existence.

"I think that as a remedy for the South, dissolution is not
enough, and a Southern Confederacy not enough. The latter
would not stop the process by which some states, Virginia, for
example, are becoming free, viz., by ridding themselves of their
slaves; and therefore we should in time with a Confederacy again
have a North and a South. The only thing that will do when
tried in every way is a *consolidated* republic formed of the Southern states. That will put slavery *under the control of those most
interested* in it, and nothing else will, and until that is done nothing
is done. You see therefore that I am very extreme in my opinions, and that you must weigh them as you weigh what I recom-
mend to you. During the last six months I have given much
attention to this problem of problems to the South, and have
made up my own mind in my own way. I am no Calhoun man.
He in fact is off the stage; the coming battle is for other leadership than his, a leadership that is of this generation, not of the
past."

There was in fact in this period a very strong movement
for immediate secession in the states from South Carolina
to Mississippi, the history of which has never yet been
published.[16] The non-secessionist southern-rights con-

[16] *Cf.* Claiborne, J. F. H., *Life and Correspondence of John A. Quitman,* II., pp. 21-52, 114-175; Phillips, U. B., "The Economic and Political

gressmen had a delicate task of steering the ship of state between the Scylla of anti-slavery aggressions and the Charybdis of southern secession, but they succeeded adroitly in obviating the crisis. Toombs, Stephens, and Cobb made use of the secessionist sentiment in South Carolina and the Gulf States to impress the north with the danger to the Union, while Clay, Calhoun, and Webster appealed for inter-sectional magnanimity in the Senate. By these means the Compromise of 1850 was enacted. Then the issue arose as to whether the people would accept it.

The Compromise of 1850, which was largely wrought by the southern Whigs, was the beginning of their undoing. The thunderings of their congressmen against northern aggressions, while intended to drive the north into acceptance of the Compromise, so alarmed the rank and file when published in the newspapers, that when Congress adjourned " the Lower South " was near the verge of secession. The congressmen now hastened home to stem this tide of sentiment. They stumped their states for the Constitutional Union cause, and for the better securing of their object, urged the repudiation of old party ties and the fusion of Whig and Democratic friends of the " finality of the Compromise " into a new Union party. This party was actually established in Georgia, Alabama, and Mississippi, attracting to its membership most of the Whigs and many Democrats. It won the critical elections in each of these three states in 1850-51,[17] and even per-

Essays of the Ante-bellum South," in *The South in the Building of the Nation*, VII., pp. 173-199; *Charleston Mercury*, January 23, February 27, March 1, 3, 24, 29, April 11, October 15, November 4, 1851.

Dr. Melvin J. White of Tulane University has a monograph nearing completion on " The Secession Movement of 1847-1852."

[17] Phillips, U. B., *Georgia and State Rights*, pp. 161-170; Mellen, G. F., " Henry W. Hilliard and W. L. Yancey," in the *Sewanee Review*, XVII., pp. 32-50; Garner, J. W., " The First Struggle over Secession in Mississippi," in the *Mississippi Historical Society Publications*, IV., pp. 89-104.

suaded the body politic of South Carolina to relinquish for
the time its determination to secede.   But as a country-
wide movement the Union party project was abortive, and
it left its leaders in danger of political stranding.   The
southern-rights men in " the Lower South " had not indorsed the assertion of the Unionists that the old parties
were dead, but had preserved their regularity as Democrats, and now denied regularity to the Unionists, who
wished to return to the Democratic fold.   Meanwhile the
northern Whigs were becoming increasingly undesirable as
party colleagues for such southerners as did not wish to
join the Democrats.   The vehement denunciation at the
north of Webster's Seventh of March speech and of Fillmore's signature of the Fugitive Slave bill, enabled the
anti-slavery element to capture the northern Whig organization, and to make it impossible for any considerable number of southerners to resume or continue the affiliation.   A
final effort, however, was made during the presidential
campaign of 1852.   A caucus of the Whig senators and
congressmen was called in April to decide upon a time and
place for the national convention, and at it Mr. Marshall
of Kentucky introduced a resolution indorsing the finality
of the Compromise.   The chairman ruled the motion out
of order, and the meeting adjourned in confusion.   The
caucus reconvened on the night of April 24, with a considerable number of southern Whigs absent.[18]   Marshall
renewed his motion, appealed from the decision of the
chair, and was defeated by a vote of 56 to 18.   Then
arose a clamor of southern indignation, followed by se-
cessions from the caucus.

" Mr. Marshall said, as the Chair had decided the Compromise
principles of the Whig Administration out of order, this was no
place for Whigs to remain, and he then withdrew. . . .

[18] This account is taken from the *Federal Union,* May 4, 1852.

Mr. Outlaw wished to be understood. If the Compromise Resolutions were thrust out of the Whig Caucus, it was thrusting him out and the Whigs he represented; and he withdrew.

Mr. Moore (La.) said such action ruled the Southern Whigs out of the caucus; and then he and his colleague (Mr. Landry) withdrew.

Mr. Brooke (Miss.) would like to know, before he went to the Whig National Convention, what company he was to keep; he then left.

Mr. Strother said the Whigs of Virginia had in substance instructed him to leave when the Compromise was thrown out. Left.

Mr. Cabell said the previous decision of the Chair caused many Southern Whigs to be absent to-night—and he and others came hoping for the reverse of such a decision—the confirmation of such a decision would leave the caucus with only the Northern men and eight or ten Southern Whigs. He left with Senator Morton.

Mr. Clingman after some remarks left also.

Messrs. Williams of Tennessee, and Gentry, made some subsequent remarks; and of the Tennessee delegation there was in the chamber only Cullom and Jones. . . .

Mr. Morehead (N. C.) said he staid behind only because he hoped that the Whig Convention would adopt the Compromise; and it was certain that North Carolina would vote only for the Compromise. . . .

A sharp controversy ensued between Messrs. Brooks, Stanley, and Truman Smith, and the caucus separated amidst great excitement, near midnight."

At the national convention at Baltimore at the middle of June, a last effort was made to accomplish the impossible and preserve the national Whig party. The southerners by adroit manœuvering secured the adoption of a mild finality plank in the platform, in spite of the clamorous northern opposition; but the candidate nominated was one for whom the south had little confidence and could have no enthusiasm. In the election in November, Scott was given the normal Whig vote in " the Upper South " except Virginia, but in " the Lower South " he received little more than half the normal.   In the whole country he secured the electoral votes of no states but Kentucky, Tennessee, Massachusetts, and Vermont; and the Whigs never rallied from the defeat.   Northern Whigs and southern Whigs no longer made any pretense of co-operation in federal politics, though they each retained their organization for state elections until the Know-Nothing movement and the Kansas-Nebraska issue in 1854 drove all but a scattered and forlorn remnant of the Whigs, north and south, to enter either the Know-Nothing, the Republican, or the Democratic parties.   Sporadic efforts were made by men who longed for the old régime to reorganize the " Old Line Whigs " as a national party, but they received faint response.[19]   The Bell-Everett movement of 1860 was a last flicker of Whig Union-saving effort which falls beyond our present scope.

In the lowland parishes of South Carolina the Episcopal Church is sometimes defined as " a company of gentlemen, religiously inclined."   Paraphrasing this, the southern Whigs may be described as a company of gentlemen, politically inclined.   As a type they were honest, high-toned, and patriotic, and not more controlled by opportunism than is usual in American politics.   Nearly all of them throughout the Whig period were anxious not only to safeguard southern control of southern affairs, but to preserve the " Union of the Fathers," and, in fact, a main function of their party throughout its life was to postpone the disruption of the Union.[20]

In a letter to Howell Cobb, September 2, 1852, Henry L. Benning, whose insight we have previously had occasion to praise, made an analysis and forecast which may well serve to conclude this essay:

[19] Quincy, Josiah, *Whig Policy Analyzed and Illustrated*, Boston, 1856.
[20] *Cf.* Johnson, Allen, " The Nationalizing Influence of Party," in the *Yale Review*, XV., pp. 283-292.

"You know well that it has been my conviction for the last two or three years that nothing we could do, short of general emancipation, would satisfy the North. Your idea was that the measures of the Compromise would substantially effect that object, and you went for them for that reason chiefly, I think. Should it turn out that I am right and you are wrong it will not be long before it must be known. And it is therefore now time for you to be making up your mind for the new 'crisis.' Suppose the Whig party shall be beaten, and especially at the North, will not that disband it and send the elements of which it has been composed into union with this late Pittsburg free-soil anti-slavery concern? Manifestly. What then? That concern takes the North. The Democratic party there, in conjunction with pretty much the whole South, may be able to make one fight, say in 1856—a grand Union Rally—but then the thing will be out. Is it not so? You must have thought of all this. Have you made up your mind as to what is to be done?"

ULRICH B. PHILLIPS.

THE BEGINNINGS OF SPANISH-AMERICAN
DIPLOMACY

THE decadence of Spain as a colonial power with the corresponding rise of new nations in the Spanish Indies constitutes a spectacular drama in modern history. At the opening of the nineteenth century the king of Spain and the Indies claimed title to the territory in the New World which stretched from the sources of the Mississippi River to Cape Horn. This domain, which covered about seven million square miles, included almost one-half of the area of the Americas—a patrimony from which could be carved thirty-five states as large as Spain. It had been gradually divided for administrative purposes into viceroyalties and captain-generalships, both of which were composed of provinces. Legally this glorious heritage was not the property of the Spanish people, but of the Spanish monarch. The relation between Spanish America and the mother country was not an organic union but a personal union. His Catholic Majesty was the connecting link.

The diplomacy of Spanish America, in a sense, originated in the era of discovery and colonization. In a more vital sense, it began during the revolution which ultimately rent the patrimony of Spain in America into fragments. This revolution was accompanied by attempts of the revolting provinces to enter into political and commercial relations with neighboring provinces and with foreign governments. This study will consider, so far as the opportunity permits, the most significant efforts of the Spanish-American insurgents to initiate diplomatic relations with foreign nations from 1810 to 1816 with

231

special attention to Venezuela which was for a time the storm-center of the early revolution.

Attempts had indeed been made before the second decade of the nineteenth century to arouse sympathy for the cause of Spanish-American emancipation in the United States, France, and England. Alexander Hamilton became interested in the liberation of Spanish America about 1783 by listening to the glowing representations of Francisco de Miranda, a native of Venezuela who had fled from the Spanish military service in disgrace. The awakening interest in the Spanish Indies was illustrated later by the attitude of filibusters and of statesmen who wished the United States to grow at the expense of the crumbling empire of Spain in America.

France took an interest in the Spanish estate in America as early as the middle of the eighteenth century. After the treaty of Paris in 1763, which transferred Louisiana to Spain, the re-establishment of the colonial glory of France became a perennial ambition of French statesmen. Napoleon planned in vain to make the magnificent domain of Louisiana the base of a new Franco-American colonial empire. Schemes for the separation of part or all of the Spanish dominions in America from the parent country were urged upon the governments of France and England at propitious moments by private memorialists, by governmental officials, and by elusive adventurers who claimed to represent the oppressed colonists of Mexico or South America. The enthusiastic patriot-filibuster, Miranda, urged his elaborate schemes for the revolutionizing of Spanish America upon various ministers from 1790 to 1808 and sought particularly the aid of England. Miranda's plans were eagerly listened to when that nation was at war with Spain and when the belief grew in official circles that France, the implacable enemy of England, entertained designs upon the Spanish dominions. English officials in the West Indies were instructed to keep a watchful eye upon the dissensions in Spanish America and to foster trade with the neighboring Spanish colonies. In 1806 and 1807, when England and Spain were at war, English soldiers made unsuccessful attacks on the viceroyalty of Buenos Aires. In the summer of 1808, when Napoleon dominated Spanish politics and when many Englishmen despaired of checking the victorious French arms on the European continent, an English expedition was preparing to sail for America to prevent the Spanish Indies from becoming the prey of Napoleon.[1]

At this juncture Napoleon's continental ambitions lured him into that continental policy which was greatly to change the political geography of Europe and America. The irruption of French troops into Portugal in 1807 forced the royal family of Braganza to flee to Rio Janeiro under the escort of a British squadron—a measure which anticipated the independence of Brazil. The odious intrigues of Napoleon in Spanish affairs were perhaps partly due to a desire to force the Spanish royal family likewise to seek a refuge in their transatlantic empire. If this idea was entertained by the Spanish Bourbons, it was rudely banished by a passionate tumult of the populace.[2] The seizure of fortresses in northern Spain by French troops, the abdication of King Charles IV, and the enforced renunciation of the Spanish crown by his son, the idolized Ferdinand VII, provoked a national uprising, the beginning of the war of the peoples. Juntas, or local councils of

[1] For the projects of European governments in regard to Spanish America and for the attitude of statesmen in the United States on various occasions see Robertson, W. S., "Francisco de Miranda and the Revolutionizing of Spanish America," *American Historical Association Report*, 1907, I., pp. 189-414.

[2] Cevallos, P., *Exposición de los hechos y maquinaciónes que han preparado la usurpación de la corona de España y los medios que el Emperador de los Franceses ha puesto en obra para realizarla*, pp. 11, 31, 40, 65, 66.

government, sprang up, as if by magic, from Oviedo to
Granada. On June 6, 1808, Napoleon arrogantly proclaimed his brother Joseph king of Spain and the Indies [3];
while the patriots soon formed a central junta to exercise
the national authority.

From the mediæval fortress of freedom in the Asturias,
a patriotic junta stealthily hurried two deputies across
the water to solicit aid from Napoleon's inveterate foe.
After conferences with the great minister, George Canning,
they were promised speedy succor.[4] On July 4, 1808,
England accordingly published a formal proclamation of
peace with Spain.[5] In the king's speech to Parliament on
that day it was declared that because of the resistance of
Spain to the usurpations of France, the Spanish nation
could "no longer be considered as the enemy of Great
Britain," but was recognized by his Majesty as "a natural
friend and ally." It was expressly declared that the king
had "no other object than that of preserving unimpaired
the integrity and independence of the Spanish monarchy." [6]
Hence, English officials in the West Indies soon transmitted to the Spanish colonies the news of the national
uprising in Spain and of the pivotal change in English
policy.[7] The British redcoats that had been bivouacking

[3] Lafuente, M., y Valera, J., *Historia general de España*, XVII., pp.
456, 457.

[4] The declaration of the king of England to the envoys of the Asturias,
June 12, 1808, is found in the *Annual Register for 1808*, pp. 321, 322. In
the speeches of Sheridan and Canning in the house of commons on June
15 are found hints of the negotiations, Hansard, T. C., *Parliamentary Debates*, XI., pp. 886-892. See also Hume, M., *Modern Spain*, pp. 131, 132.

[5] *London Gazette*, July 2-July 5, 1808; *London Times*, July 7, 1808.

[6] Hansard, T. C., *Parliamentary Debates*, XI., pp. 1140, 1141; *Journals
of the House of Commons*, LXIII., pp. 481.

[7] Draft of dispatches to the governor of the Windward and Leeward
Islands, June 22 and July 7, 1808, *Public Record Office, Colonial Office
Correspondence, Windward and Leeward Islands, 25;* Cockburn to
Castlereagh, August 1, 1808, describes the mission sent from Curaçoa to
Caracas to transmit the news, *ibid., Colonial Office Transmissions,*

on the shores of Ireland in readiness for a South American
expedition were now sent, under Sir Arthur Wellesley,
to fight France in the Iberian peninsula.[8] This movement
was crowned by the convention of January 14, 1809, by
which the central junta of Seville, in the name of Ferdinand
VII, and the English government agreed to confirm these
new relations by a " formal Treaty of Peace, Friendship,
and Alliance." [9]

The identical circumstances which transformed England
into the firm ally of Spain started a protracted drama in
a spacious theater beyond the Atlantic. After Napoleon
had usurped the government of Spain, he hurried confidential emissaries to the Spanish Indies to announce the
dynastic change and to secure the allegiance of the colonists to his brother Joseph. The emissaries sent to the
province of Venezuela were spurned by many inhabitants
of the city of Caracas. The news of the startling changes
in the Peninsula caused great excitement and much display
of fidelity to Ferdinand VII.[10] In July, 1808, the *cabildo*,
or municipal council, of Caracas, influenced by Spanish
example, framed a project for the establishment of a local
junta.[11] In December, 1808, a few of the nobility vainly
petitioned the captain-general, Vicente Emparan, to establish a governmental assembly.[12] Rumors of reverses to
the Spanish cause in the Peninsula helped to set Venezuela
into a state of fermentation. Hence, when agents arrived

Curaçoa, 668; Vane, C., *Memoirs and Correspondence of Viscount Castlereagh,* VI., pp. 374-376.

[8] Robertson, W. S., " Francisco de Miranda," *Am. Hist. Assn. Rept.,* 1907, I., pp. 404-414.

[9] *British and Foreign State Papers,* I., part 1, pp. 667-673.

[10] Smyth, W. H., *Life and Services of Captain Beaver,* pp. 334-339; Blanco, J. F., *Documentos para la historia de la vida pública del liber-tador de Colombia, Perú y Bolivia,* II., pp. 160-166.

[11] Blanco, J. F., *Documentos,* II., pp. 171-174.

[12] Memorial of the Count of Tovar to the captain-general of Caracas, December 1, 1808, *P. R. O., Colonial Office Transmissions, Curaçoa, 670.*

in Caracas from Spain with orders to recognize the supremacy of the regency, to which the central junta had transferred its authority, an extraordinary *cabildo* peacefully deposed the captain-general and, on April 19, 1810, established a provisional junta, which publicly professed to be acting on behalf of the exiled Ferdinand VII.[13] This provisional government soon deported the chief colonial officials, organized rudimentary administrative departments, and decreed various social and political reforms.[14] It soon directed a manifesto to the regency boldly disavowing its authority.[15] The creation of this new government in Venezuela was in reality a revolution in disguise.

A revolutionary spirit soon swept over other provinces of Spanish America. In May, 1810, in the city of Buenos Aires Viceroy Cisneros was quietly succeeded by a junta which was formed ostensibly to conserve the authority of Ferdinand VII.[16] A similar junta was set up about two months later at Santa Fé de Bogota, the capital of the viceroyalty of New Granada.[17] In September, 1810, in the city of Santiago de Chile, Captain-General Carrasco was replaced by a governmental junta which loudly proclaimed allegiance to the beloved king.[18] In the insurrection which broke out in the viceroyalty of Mexico in the same month under the leadership of the sagacious curate, Miguel Hidalgo y Costilla, the name of Ferdinand was a favorite battle-cry.[19] About a year later a council

[13] Blanco, J. F., *Documentos*, II., pp. 391, 407, 408. On the revolution see also Rójas, A., *Los hombres de la revolucion, 1810-1826*.

[14] *Caraccas Gazette* in *London Times*, July 2, 1810; the regulations on the liberty of the press are found in Niles, *Weekly Register*, I., pp. 21, 22.

[15] Blanco, J. F., *Documentos*, II., p. 410.

[16] *Registro oficial de la república argentina* (Buenos Aires, 1879 ff.), I., pp. 22-24.

[17] Blanco, J. F., *Documentos*, II., pp. 555-559.

[18] *Ibid.*, pp. 639, 640; Barros Arana, D., *Historia jeneral de Chile* (Santiago, 1884-1902), VIII., pp. 215-237.

[19] Alamán, L., *Historia de México* (México, 1883-1885), I., pp. 331-335.

which styled itself " the supreme governmental junta of America " was created in the picturesque Mexican village of Zitácuaro.[20]

In this essay there is opportunity only to suggest the animus of some of the leading actors in the kaleidoscopic scenes in which viceroys and captain-generals were often succeeded by provisional juntas. It must not be forgotten that there were many devoted loyalists who followed the Spanish standard on many widely-separated battlefields. Opportunists there were not a few. The historian of the future may indeed seek a partial explanation of this uprising in the psychology of a group or a " race." Some Spanish Americans were loyal to Ferdinand VII, but agitated because of the chaotic conditions in Spain and loath to yield allegiance to the changing authorities in the Peninsula. In certain regions the people were apparently affected by the contagion of example. Some argued that the dethronement of the Spanish king had broken the connecting link between Spain and the colonies,[21] a plea resembling one made at times by the men of 1776. Many Spanish Americans were discontented because of inherent evils in the colonial régime. A few were animated by the doctrines of the revolution in France; some were influenced by the militant policy of England with respect to Spanish America; while many conceived the United States to be their grand exemplar. To these nations the chiefs who entertained thoughts of independence naturally turned with great expectations.

What was the policy of distracted Spain towards this movement in her transatlantic dominions? On January 22, 1809, the central junta declared the American pos-

[20] Hernández y Dávalos, J. E., *Colección de documentos para la historia de la guerra de independencia de México de 1808 á 1821*, III., p. 340.

[21] As a specific illustration of this constitutional plea, see the letter of J. G. Roscio to Andrés Belo, June 29, 1810, in Amunátegui, M. L., *Vida de Don Andrés Bello*, p. 83.

sessions of Spain to be not colonies, but an integral part of the Spanish nation with the right to representation in the junta.[22]   But the regency decreed in August, 1810, that because of the establishment of the provisional government by Venezuela, its ports were to be rigorously blockaded.[23]   On January 21, 1811, after fruitless negotiations with the Venezuelans,[24] an agent of the regency from a coign of vantage in the West Indies, rashly ordered the enforcement of the blockade.[25]   On the other hand, the Spanish Cortes, which met in September, 1810, soon decreed that the Spanish dominions in both hemispheres comprised one nation, that the inhabitants of the ultramarine provinces had equal rights with the peninsular Spaniards, and that the American insurgents would be pardoned as soon as they recognized the legitimate sovereign authority in Spain.[26]   Decrees were passed ostensibly to encourage industry, commerce, and equality of classes in the Spanish Indies.[27]   These measures, however, did not conciliate the American deputies in the Cortes, who presented a strong remonstrance on American affairs.[28] The proceedings of the national peninsular authorities hence did not heal the widening breach between Spain and her colonies.

The quixotic junta of Caracas was meanwhile trying to

[22] Blanco, J. F., Documentos, II., p. 230.

[23] Walton, W., An Exposé on the Dissentions of Spanish America, appendix, document D.

[24] Blanco, J. F., Documentos, II., pp. 693-696, 699-703.

[25] A copy of the order is found in P. R. O., Foreign Office Correspondence, Spain, 120.

[26] Colección de los decretos y ordenes que han expedido las cortes generales y extraordinarios desde su instalación en 24 de setiembre de 1810 hasta igual fecha de 1811, p. 10.

[27] Ibid., pp. 72, 73, 87, 90, 61-63.

[28] Aláman, L., Historia de México, III., pp. 451-471, for comment on the proposals see Walton, W., An Exposé, p. 291.   The eleven propositions on American affairs can be found in Guerra, J., Historia de la revolución de Nueva España, II., pp. 647-655.

establish friendly relations with foreign governments. It
soon communicated with English officials in the West
Indies. Early in May, 1810, the junta sent an account
of the separatist movement in Venezuela to Governor
Layard of Curaçoa, who at once dispatched his aide-de-
camp, Captain Kelly, to London with the news that the
junta was preparing to send envoys to England.[29] An
agent of this junta, Juan Ewardo, soon arrived in the
island with messages of friendship for Great Britain. He
was graciously received by Layard, who declared that he
cordially approved of every step which had been taken,
and that the manner in which the junta had been established would be " the admiration of all future ages."
Governor Layard also expressed his intention of sending
his secretary, John Robertson, to congratulate the junta
and to promote friendly relations between Curaçoa and
Caracas. The sympathies of the governor were so
strongly enlisted that he even offered to furnish the Venezuelans with muskets from the governmental ordnance
in the island.[30] The junta of Caracas also sent a message
to Governor Manchester of Jamaica " expressing a desire
to enter into the strictest alliance and freest commercial
intercourse with the British Nation." [31]

The actions of Governor Layard were not in perfect
harmony with the wishes of the English cabinet. The
mission of Captain Kelly to England with the news of the
changes in Venezuela was approved [32]; but the virtual
recognition of the governmental junta was disapproved.[33]

[29] Layard to Liverpool, May 8, 1810, *P. R. O., Colonial Office Transmissions, Curaçoa, 671.*

[30] Layard to José de Llamosas and Martin Tovar Ponte, May 14, 1810,
ibid.

[31] The Duke of Manchester to Lord Liverpool, June 10, 1810, *P. R. O.,
Colonial Office Correspondence, Jamaica, 71.*

[32] Layard to Liverpool, June 29, 1810, *P. R. O., Colonial Office Correspondence, Curaçoa, I.*

[33] Layard to Liverpool, July 23, 1810, *ibid.*

On June 29, 1810, Lord Liverpool, the English minister for war and the colonies, thus described the conduct which England wished its representatives in the West Indies to observe:

"The great object which His Majesty has had in view from the first moment when intelligence was received in this Country of the glorious resistance of the Spanish Nation against the Tyranny and Usurpation of France, was to assist by every means in His Power this great effort of a brave, loyal, and high spirited People, and to secure if possible the Independence of the Spanish Monarchy in all Parts of the World. As long as the Spanish Nation persevere in their resistance to their Invaders, and as any reasonable Hope can be entertained of ultimate Success to their Cause in Spain, His Majesty feels it to be his Duty according to every obligation of Justice and good Faith, to discourage any proceeding which may have the effect of separating the Spanish Provinces in America from the Parent State in Europe;—the Integrity of the Spanish Monarchy upon principles of Justice and true Policy, being not less the object of His Majesty than of all loyal and patriotic Spaniards." [34]

Before this dispatch was written, the junta of Venezuela had sent Simón Bolívar, Luis Lopez Mendez, and Andrés Bello on the important mission over-seas. Bello, a scholarly and talented Venezuelan, acted as the secretary of the commission; [35] Mendez was a member of a leading insurgent family; and Bolívar, the chief of the trio, was the scion of an illustrious family of Caracas, who had been educated in Venezuela and in Europe. [36] Like other chiefs

[34] Layard to Liverpool, June 29, 1810, *P. R. O., Colonial Office Correspondence, Curaçoa, I.* An indorsement on Manchester's dispatch to Liverpool, June 21, 1810, states that a copy of these instructions was sent to Manchester, *ibid., Jamaica, 71.*

[35] Velasco y Rojas, marqués de, *Simón Bolívar,* p. 15.

[36] Larrazábal, F., *La vida y correspondencia general del libertador Simón Bolívar* (New York, 1901), I., pp. 4-41, sketches the early career of Bolivar.   In Rójas, A., *Historia Patria, Estúdios, Históricos, Orígenes Venezolanos,* I., appendix, p. 106, is material on Bolívar's ancestry.

of the Spanish-American rebellion, Bolívar had served
under the Spanish banner of blood and gold, for in January, 1797, he had enlisted in a militia company of the
valley of Aragua.[37]   His revolutionary ardor, which was
to make him a " liberator " of South America, had apparently just been aroused.[38]   These envoys from the New
World to the Old were brought to England in July, 1810,
in the corvette *Wellington,* which seems to have been sent
for that purpose from the English squadron in the West
Indies.[39]   They took advantage of the ambiguous clause
in their instructions regarding their compatriot Miranda,[40]
soon consorted with that apostle of South American emancipation,[41] and thus probably received hints regarding the
policy of England towards Spanish America.   Bolívar and
Mendez brought with them an address from the Venezuelan junta to King George III, in which it was suggested that England was destined " to complete the grand
work of confederating the scattered sections of America,
and to cause order, concord, and rational liberty to reign
therein." [42]

The circumstantial instructions to the commissioners,
which are preserved in the archives of the English gov-

[37] *Ibid.,* appendix, pp. 119-122, are printed the official records of
Bolívar's military services.

[38] In regard to the selection of Bolívar as the leader of this deputation
see Ducoudray Holstein, H. L. V., *Memoirs of Simon Bolivar,* p. 28;
Velasco y Rojas, marqués de, *Simón Bolívar,* p. 13; Petre, F. L., *Simon
Bolivar,* p. 45.

[39] Velasco y Rojas, marqués de, *Simón Bolívar,* p. 13; on the attitude of
Admiral Cochrane see also his correspondence with the junta in the *Alexandria Gazette,* July 23, 1810.

[40] Robertson, W. S., " Francisco de Miranda," *Am. Hist. Assn. Rept.,*
1907, I., p. 432, note a.

[41] Dispatch of Apodaca (number 155), July 17, 1810, *Archivo General
de Simancas, Estado, 8173;* J. Tovar to M. Tovar (copy), November
6, 1810, *Archivo Histórico Nacional, Estado, 3549;* Wilberforce, R. I.
and F., *Life of Wilberforce,* III., p. 4.

[42] Walton, W., *An Exposé,* appendix, xxv.

ernment, suggest more fully the Venezuelan state of mind.
The agents were told how to answer certain queries of
the English ministers regarding Venezuela.   The changes
in that province were to be justified because of the ille-
gitimacy of the Spanish junta and the arbitrary administration of the colonies.   The establishment of juntas by
the peninsular Spaniards was to be cited as a justification
for the proceedings of the Venezuelans.   It was asserted
that there was a universal sentiment in Venezuela for
adhesion to Spain if the patriot cause in the Peninsula was
triumphant, and for the establishment of independence
if the French arms were victorious.   Venezuela was declared to be still an integral part of the Spanish empire.
Bolívar and Mendez were also instructed to ask England
to aid them to procure arms, to protect their commerce,
to enjoin the English officials in the West Indies to respect
their government, and to favor whatever might promote
their peace and happiness.   The envoys were directed
to conduct themselves with decorum towards the Spanish
embassy in London.   They were also to solicit the
beneficent influence of the English government in paci-
fying any disagreements which might arise among themselves or with the neighboring provinces in America.[43]

The English secretary for foreign affairs at this time
was the brother of Sir Arthur Wellesley, Marquis Wellesley, a builder of the English empire in India.[44]   The
Venezuelan commissioners soon sought the marquis.   At
the first interview, which was perhaps at the minister's
house,[45] the agents were informed that the English government could enter into no " formal or official communi-

[43] June 2, 1810 (copy), *P. R. O., Colonial Office Transmissions, Curacoa,*
672.

[44] Brodrick, G. C., and Fotheringham, J. K., *The Political History of*
England, 1801-1837, pp. 68, 397-400.

[45] Amunátegui, M. L., *Andrés Bello,* p. 88; Larrazábal, F., *Simón*
Bolívar, I., p. 77, note.

cation " with them because of the alliance with Spain.[46]
A tradition exists that on this occasion Bolívar forgot his
instructions and made an eloquent plea for Venezuelan
independence.[47] The English minister evidently soon
divined that these emissaries wished to negotiate an alliance with England even against the mother-country.[48] The
assertion of the Venezuelans, however, that they still adhered to Ferdinand and that they were willing to aid
Spain during the struggle with France furnished the
marquis a convenient excuse for holding conferences with
Bolívar and Mendez, in which Wellesley sounded them
in regard to Spain, and enunciated the policy of England.
To quote a felicitous passage from the official memorandum of the English government:

" In affording to the Deputies from Venezuela the reception to
which they were entitled, Lord Wellesley considered it however,
to be his Primary Duty to represent to them, without reserve, the
danger to which the general Interests of the Spanish Monarchy,
and of the Allies, were exposed, by the Separation of Venezuela
from the Central Authority acknowledged in Spain; and he
therefore endeavored, in the first instance, to inculcate the urgent
Expediency of pursuing such conciliatory Measures, as might
tend to re-unite the Province to the authority actually exercising the
Government of the Parent State, in the name of their Common
Sovereign.

Lord Wellesley stated this union to be highly important to all
the objects, which the Province had avowed; to the immediate
Preservation of the Rights of Ferdinand VII, and of the Monarchy, in complete integrity, harmony and order; to the vigorous

[46] "Memorandum of the Communication between Marquess Wellesley and the Commissioners from Venezuela," *P. R. O., Foreign Office
Correspondence, Spain, 106.*
[47] Amunátegui, M. L., *Andrés Bello,* II., p. 89; Larrazábal, F., *Simón
Bolívar,* I., p. 77.
[48] "Notes on the Caraccas, July, 1810," *P. R. O., Foreign Office Correspondence, Spain, 106.* These notes, made while the conferences were
being held with Bolívar and Mendez, embody the impressions of the
English officials.

Prosecution of the contest against France by an effectual & systematic Combination of the whole Power and Resources of the Empire, and especially to the main purpose, professed by the Province of Venezuela, of contributing the most efficacious aid to the Parent State in the Crisis of her Fate; Towards the attainment of this End, no means could be deemed more useful, than the Strength which the Central Government would derive, in the administration of the general Resources of the Monarchy, by the continued connection and uninterrupted Support of Every Province and Colony:—With respect to any local or temporary Grievances, of which the province complained under the Provincial Government established in Spain; Lord Wellesley stated, that these considerations were rather Grounds of urgent Representation to that Government of amicable adjustment, or of the interposition of the good offices of the Allies, than any Justification of a positive and abrupt Separation from the General Government of the Empire." [49]

While Bolívar and Mendez admitted the " Principle of these Representations," they " resisted the practical Conclusion." They maintained that Venezuela could more effectually promote the cause of Ferdinand VII and of Spain under its existing government than by a closer union with the Spanish authorities. They expressed their " utter despair " of obtaining the needful redress of grievances, except through the provisional government which they had constituted as the " only Organ by which they could hope to preserve the Rights of Ferdinand VII in the province of Venezuela against the Usurpation of France. . . . They further declared, that they possessed no authority to negotiate for any reunion of the Province to the Central authority in Spain; that they were merely the Agents of the Government which had been formed at the Caraccas; and were not authorized further

[49] " Memorandum of the Communication between the Marquess Wellesley and the Commissioners from Venezuela," *P. R. O., Foreign Office Correspondence, Spain, 106.*

than to state the sentiments and views of that Government to His Majesty and to receive His Majesty's reply." [50]

Two courses were now open to Wellesley, either to allow Venezuela to take her own measures without any interposition by England, or to offer his good offices " for the purpose of preventing common danger to Spain, to South America, and to the Alliance." The marquis chose the latter course. He accordingly requested the envoys to state, " in an unofficial form, the views and objects of that Province, in the Mission, with which they were charged." [51] Bolívar and Mendez then made four proposals. First, as Venezuela, " as an integral part of the Spanish Empire," was threatened by France, they asked for the maritime protection of England in defending the rights of Ferdinand VII and in completing the " measures of security against the Common Enemy." Second, as the decision of Venezuela might become the cause of " unpleasant dissentions " with the provinces which had recognized the regency, and perhaps with the parent country, they asked " the high Mediation of H. B. Majesty, in order to preserve their relations of peace and friendship with their brethren of both hemispheres." Third, as the maintenance of commercial relations between Venezuela and Spain required some stipulations between the two governments, they wished to make " such stipulations under the Guarantee of H. B. Majesty." Fourth, they wished to have instructions sent to the English naval commanders in the Antilles so that they might promote the desired ends. [52]

[50] *Ibid.*

[51] " Memorandum of the Communication between the Marquess Wellesley and the Commissioners from Venezuela," *P. R. O., Foreign Office Correspondence, Spain, 106.* A Spanish translation of this memorandum in Velasco y Rojas, marqués de, *Simón Bolívar,* pp. 26-28, states that the commissioners were asked to state their views " de un modo oficioso," which is undoubtedly incorrect.

[52] " Propositions from the Commissioners of Venezuela," July 21, 1810,

In reply to these requests, Marquis Wellesley assured
the envoys that the naval protection of England would be
given to Venezuela to enable her to defend the rights of
her " legitimate Sovereign," and to secure herself " against
the common Enemy," France. That province, however,
was " earnestly recommended " to seek a reconciliation
with the government existing in Spain and the good offices
of England were offered for that purpose. That nation
promised to employ " every effort of friendly interposition " to prevent war between Spain and Venezuela, and to
" preserve Peace and Friendship between Venezuela and
her Brethren of both Hemispheres." The marquis recommended that Venezuela should maintain " the relations
of commerce, friendship, and communication of succors
with the Mother Country " during the war with France,
and agreed to employ the good offices of England to
promote an amicable adjustment between Venezuela and
Spain. Instructions, said Wellesley, had been sent to
English officials to promote these objects in " the full
Confidence that Venezuela will continue to observe her
Allegiance towards Ferdinand 7th, and will co-operate
with Spain and with His Majesty against the common
enemy." [53]

These negotiations, therefore, did not meet the expectations of the Venezuelans. Three weeks after the
conferences were over, Bolívar and Mendez informed the
English government of their intention of soon returning
to South America.[54] When the news of the blockade of

P. R. O., *Foreign Office Correspondence, Spain, 106.* A Spanish translation of these is found in Velasco y Rojas, marqués de, *Simón Bolívar,* pp.
21, 22.

[53] " Note in Reply to the Propositions from the Commissioners from
Venezuela," *P. R. O., Foreign Office Correspondence, Spain, 106;* in
Spanish, Velasco y Rojas, marqués de, *Simón Bolívar,* pp. 22, 23. The
London Packet, March 4-March 6, 1811, prints the circular letter of Lord
Liverpool to the English officials in the Antilles.

[54] Velasco y Rojas, marqués de, *Simón Bolívar,* pp. 30, 31.

the Venezuelan ports by the Spanish regency reached London, the commissioners apparently appealed to Marquis Wellesley to keep his pledge and to prevent a rupture between Spain and Venezuela.[55] Perhaps this crisis caused Mendez and Bello to remain in the English metropolis when Bolívar embarked for America. One important result of the mission of Bolívar and Mendez was the immediate return of Miranda to his native land. The objects of England in these negotiations, as suggested in contemporary official notes, were: "that by making a skillful use of the bond of allegiance to Ferdinand," England might "prevent a total or sudden separation from Old Spain," might "compel the latter to alter her Colonial system," and might "preserve the Colonies from the influence of France."[56] Between the lines of the official memorandum one may indeed read the desire of the English to foster their commerce in Spanish America.[57] In the opinion of the writer, the English ministers in 1810 were consciously framing a policy which would enable them to develop profitable commercial relations with the Spanish Americans if France should triumph on the European continent or if some of the Spanish-American provinces should ultimately secede from the mother-country.

The English memorandum of these unofficial negotiations emphasizes that interpretation of the negotiations which England wished her ally, Spain, to accept. The Spanish minister in London, Juan Ruiz de Apodaca, was

[55] *The Baltimore American,* January 12, 1811, prints, evidently from Caracas papers, a dispatch of Bolívar and Mendez to the government of Venezuela.

[56] "Notes on the Caraccas, July, 1810," *P. R. O., Foreign Office Correspondence, Spain, 106.*

[57] See Liverpool to Layard, June 29, 1810, "secret and confidential," *P. R. O., Colonial Office Correspondence, Curaçoa, 1;* Henry Wellesley to Bardaxi y Azara, December 30, 1811, *ibid., Foreign Office Correspondence, Spain, 115.*

at once furnished by Wellesley with a copy of this memorandum which was to serve Spain as a guide to the conduct that England proposed to pursue in regard to the revolting colonists.[58] It was soon made clear to Spain that, in the case of Venezuela, the English ministers had reached a decision which they would follow in regard to the other Spanish-American colonies. In 1811 the English ambassador, Sir Henry Wellesley, was instructed to inform the Spanish government that: " Particular care was taken to avoid any direct or formal recognition of the governments or official authorities constituted in Spanish America; nor was any such official communication sanctioned with them, as could be construed into an indirect acknowledgment of their legitimacy. . . . The Principles stated with regard to Venezuela were expressly stated to you and to the British authorities in South America to constitute the general rule of conduct which It was intended by Great Britain to observe with respect to every other Province of Spanish America." [59]

While England was formulating her policy towards Spanish America, emissaries from the insurgent provinces were trying to elude the royalists who beset them on the way to the goal of their highest hopes in North America. The first commissioners formally appointed to the United States from Venezuela were Juan Vicente Bolívar, an obscure relative of Simón Bolívar, and Telésforo de Orea, whose biography has yet to be written. Like the agents

[58] " Memorandum of the Communications between the Marquess Wellesley and the Commissioners from Venezuela," bears the indorsement: " Memorandum presented to the Commissioners from Caraccas and to the Spanish minister, August 9th, 1810," ibid., 106.

[59] Marquis Wellesley to Henry Wellesley, May 4, 1811, P. R. O., Original Correspondence, War Office, 45. For other accounts of the mission of Bolívar and Mendez cf. Becerra, R., Ensayo histórico documentado de la vida de Don Francisco de Miranda, I., pp. 75-77; Baralt, R. M., y Díaz, R., Resúmen de la historia de Venezuela desde el año de 1797 hasta el de 1850, I., p. 42.

sent to England, Bolívar and Orea were inexperienced in diplomatic procedure. Their credentials stated that the Venezuelan government wished to improve its relations of friendship and commerce with friendly or neutral nations.[60] In the midsummer of 1810 these venturesome commissioners, who probably expected a speedy realization of their dreams of aid and recognition, disembarked at the friendly haven of Baltimore and proceeded to the city of Washington.[61] Bolívar and Orea, who at times evidently forgot that they represented only a junta which had not yet discarded the mask of allegiance to the king of Spain, were probably amazed at their reception. Only a few fugitive notices of these commissioners appeared in the newspapers. They were not officially received by the government of the United States, although Bolívar gave an inkling of his mission to the department of state.[62] This agent also tried to ship munitions of war to South America, but his efforts in this direction were apparently hindered by Luis de Onis, the vigilant Spanish minister in the United States.[63] A rumor reached distant Venezuela that the latter had even persuaded Bolívar to favor the recognition of the Spanish Cortes by his compatriots.[64]

[60] Robertson, W. S., "Francisco de Miranda," *Am. Hist. Assn. Rept.,* 1907, I., p. 527; Juan de Escalona to the secretary of state of the United States, March 18, 1811, declared that Bolívar was the head of the embassy, *State Dept. MSS., Bureau of Rolls and Library, Papers Relative to the Revolted Spanish Colonies.*

[61] *The Baltimore Evening Post,* as quoted in the *American Daily Advertiser,* June 7, 1810, mentions the arrival of these deputies. See also in *The London Packet,* July 25-July 27, 1810, an extract of a letter from Washington, June 15, 1810.

[62] Lowry to Smith, Baltimore, July 10, 1810, mentions meeting Bolívar; an indorsement on this letter reads, "Mr. Bolivar, the young man who was here," *State Dept. MSS., Bureau of Indexes and Archives, Letters from Consuls, La Guayra, I.*

[63] *Ibid.,* Hunt, G., *Writings of James Madison,* VIII., p. 106, note 1; Alamán, L., *Historia de México,* III., pp. 498-503.

[64] Amunátegui, M. L., *Andrés Bello,* p. 110.

Perhaps this rumor caused a change in the mission, for, unlike Silas Deane, Bolívar soon vanished from court without having even found a Beaumarchais.

The secretary of state of the United States during the gathering storm which preceded the war of 1812 was Robert Smith, characterized by John Quincy Adams as " a sleepy Palinurus at the helm." [65] The arrival of the Venezuelan commissioners probably stimulated Smith to appoint agents to investigate conditions in Spanish America. Robert K. Lowry was selected as agent of the United States to Venezuela about the time that Joel R. Poinsett of South Carolina was made agent to Buenos Aires.[66] No copy of the commission given by Secretary Smith to Lowry, which President Madison hoped would be adapted to the " unsettled state of things in Caracas " [67] has been found in the archives of the United States. According to the agent's own recapitulations of his instructions, Lowry was made marine and commercial agent of the United States to Venezuela, and was " directed to correspond with the Department of State, from time to time communicating such particulars as may interest touching the state of this Province " [68]; he was also directed " to correspond with Mr. Shaler in Mexico and Mr. Gelton in Buenos Ayres did opportunity present,

---

[65] Adams, H., *Life of Gallatin*, p. 391.

[66] On Poinsett see Paxson, F. L., *The Independence of the South-American Republics*, pp. 107-109.

[67] Hunt, G., *Writings of James Madison*, VIII., p. 106. On the relations between Secretary Smith and President Madison see *ibid.*, pp. 137-149.

[68] Lowry to the secretary of state of the United States, June 9, 1811, *State Dept. MSS., Bureau of Indexes and Archives, Letters from Consuls, La Guayra, I*. The reception of Lowry as " agente Maritimo y Comercial " is mentioned by Juan de Escalona in a letter of March 18, 1811, to the secretary of foreign affairs of the United States, *State Dept. MSS., Bureau of Rolls and Library, Papers Relative to the Revolted Spanish Colonies*.

and was furnished with a means of doing so in cypher." [69]

Lowry will live in the annals of American diplomacy as the first agent of the United States to serve his country in Spanish America. He reached his destination long before Poinsett. In the autumn of 1810 Lowry caught glimpses of the mountain-peaks of Venezuela, and located at the port of La Guayra.[70] In spite of the fact that the revolutionary partisans considered the authorization of Lowry unsatisfactory, they entered into friendly relations with him, and, in the autumn of 1811, asked him to procure aid for them from the great republic of the North.[71] In February, 1812, Lowry reported that he had been invited to the city of Caracas to confer with the leaders of the revolutionary government regarding an appeal which they wished to make to his government for assistance in " arms and money." He declared that he had urged upon them the necessity of making " a candid statement of the resources of the country." According to the account of the agent, the independent chiefs even implored him to embark for the United States in order to inform that government of the actual condition of Venezuela and to present their supplications.[72] In the spring of 1812, some time after the appointment of a consul to Buenos Aires,[73] Lowry received his commission as consul for the

[69] Lowry to Graham, November 30, 1816, *State Dept. MSS., Bureau of Indexes and Archives, Letters from Consuls, La Guayra, I.*

[70] Lowry to the secretary of state, September 6, 1810, *State Dept. MSS., Bureau of Indexes and Archives, Letters from Consuls, La Guayra, I.*

[71] Lowry to Monroe, August 21, 1811, *ibid.*

[72] Lowry to Monroe, February 2, 1812, *ibid.* Macgregor to Perceval, January 18, 1812, speaks of Lowry watching over the interests of the United States with "no common care" and "circulating reports unfavorable to the British," *P. R. O., Foreign Office Correspondence, Spain, 171.*

[73] Paxson, F. L., *The Independence of the South-American Republics,* p. 109.

United States to " the Port of La Guayra in Caracas and such other ports as shall be nearer thereto than to the residence of any other Consul or Vice-Consul of the United States within the same allegiance." This commission, said Lowry, was forwarded to the patriot officials at Caracas, who received it gladly, but calamitous circumstances prevented the " usual forms of recognition " from being completed.[74]

The revolutionary party in Venezuela was evidently chagrined at the attitude of the United States. On March 18, 1811, Juan de Escalona, president of the provisional government of Venezuela, addressed, at " the palace of government," a communication to the United States, in which the failure of that government to make a generous response to the approaches of Bolívar was contrasted with the cordial reception accorded to Lowry. The United States was informed that Telésforo de Orea and, in a subordinate capacity, José R. Revenga, a Venezuelan who thus began a noteworthy public career,[75] were now made the commissioners of Venezuela to the United States to promote the " fraternal union and reciprocal usefulness of North and South America." An alliance was again proposed between that province and the United States.[76] After July 5, 1811, when the United Provinces of Venezuela declared themselves free, sovereign, and independent,[77] an example which was soon emulated by other

[74] Lowry to Monroe, June 5, 1812, Lowry to Graham, November 30, 1816, *State Dept. MSS., Bureau of Indexes and Archives, Letters from Consuls, La Guayra, I.*

[75] Azpurúa, R., *Biografías de hombres notables de hispano-américa*, IV., pp. 317-330, sketches Revenga's career.

[76] Addressed to the secretary of state of the United States, *State Dept. MSS., Bureau of Rolls and Library, Papers Relative to the Revolted Spanish Colonies.* The arrival of Edwardo at Philadelphia with dispatches from Caracas is mentioned in *The Baltimore American*, July 2, 1810.

[77] The declaration of independence may be conveniently found in *The Annual Register* for 1811, pp. 331-336.

Spanish-American provinces, Orea and Revenga became the first diplomatic representatives accredited to the government of the United States from a Spanish-American state which formally claimed independence. The news of the adoption of the first formal declaration of independence by a Latin-American neighbor reached North America on the eve of the war with England. This helps to explain the surprising fact that this announcement evoked less enthusiasm in the newspapers of the United States than had some filibustering expeditions.[78]

The Confederation of Venezuela soon invested Orea with the title of " extraordinary agent " to the United States. In the meantime Robert Smith had been succeeded by James Monroe, who was thus the secretary of state of the United States when one Spanish-American state assumed a free and independent condition. According to his instructions,[79] on November 6, 1811, the agent of Venezuela addressed Monroe, enclosing the design of the tricolored independent flag and a copy of the declaration of independence. " Although the action of Venezuela," said Orea, " is grounded upon the natural rights of men, nevertheless the respect due to other nations has inspired that Confederation to make manifest the causes which have put an end to the deference that she has hitherto generously observed towards Spain. Thus justified in every respect, Venezuela does not doubt that the United States will recognize that new Confederation as a free and independent nation. The uniformity of principles and the reciprocity of interests of both nations make

[78] Newspaper comment on Venezuelan independence may be found in Niles, H., *Weekly Register*, II., p. 71; *The Aurora*, September 3, 1811; *National Intelligencer*, December 12, 1811; extracts from the *Virginia Patriot* are found in *The Alexandria Gazette*, August 11-August 22, 1810.

[79] The credentials dated July 27, 1811, are found in *State Dept. MSS., Bureau of Rolls and Library, Papers Relative to the Revolted Spanish Colonies.*

Venezuela hope that such recognition will be the precursor
of treaties of amity and commerce founded upon equitable
and mutually useful bases." [80] The favorite project of
an alliance between Venezuela and the United States was
again broached.[81]

The presentation of this evidence concerning the status
of the revolution in the province where the movement had
made most progress, was not without an influence on the
United States. In President Madison's message to Congress on November 5, 1811, he referred to " the scenes
developing " in the " great communities which occupy the
southern portion of our own hemisphere, and extend into
our neighborhood, " and declared that it was a national
duty to take a " deep interest " in their destinies.[82] This
part of the message was referred to a special committee
of the house of representatives to which Secretary Monroe
also sent, by request, the Venezuelan declaration of independence. On December 10, 1811, this committee reported a resolution, which, however, was not acted upon;
that Congress beheld, " with friendly interest, the establishment of independent sovereignties by the Spanish provinces in America," that the United States felt " a great
solicitude for their welfare," and that when these provinces
had attained " the condition of nations, by the just exercise
of their rights," the Congress of the United States would
join with the president to establish with them, as " sovereign and independent States," amicable relations and
commercial intercourse.[83] A few days later Monroe referred the envoy of Venezuela to this resolution as evi-

[80] *State Dept. MSS., Bureau of Rolls and Library, Papers Relative to
the Revolted Spanish Colonies.*

[81] Undated (marked number 9), *ibid.*

[82] Richardson, J. D., *Messages and Papers of the Presidents*, I., p. 494.

[83] *American State Papers, Foreign Relations*, III., pp. 538-539. This
resolution was printed in Spanish in the *Aurora de Chile*, May 28, 1812.

dence of American interest in his cause, and informed him that President Madison had received the Venezuelan declaration of independence " with the interest which so important an event was calculated to excite." Orea was also told that the ministers of the United States in Europe had been " made acquainted with these sentiments of their government, and instructed to keep them in view, in their communications " with the courts where they resided.[84] Indeed Monroe had already informed Joel Barlow, the minister of the United States to France, that a " very friendly and conciliatory answer " had been given to the proposals of the Venezuelans. Barlow was instructed that the ministers of the United States in Europe were to avail themselves of " suitable opportunities to promote their recognition by other powers." [85]

France, as well as the United States, was viewed by some Venezuelans in this critical period as a possible ally. At the very time when the attention of French ministers in Paris was being directed to Venezuelan affairs,[86] Telésforo de Orea approached Sérurier, the French minister, who had recently arrived in the United States, in the hope of establishing relations with France. Sérurier soon informed Orea that " direct communications " could not be established between the French empire and the Venezuelan republic until he had received instructions from Paris.[87] Like Marquis Wellesley, however, Sérurier entered into unofficial negotiations with Venezuela. Hence, early in December, 1811, Orea asked the French diplomat for a

[84] December 19, 1811, *State Dept. MSS., Bureau of Indexes and Archives, Notes to Foreign Legations, II.*

[85] Hamilton, S. M., *Writings of James Monroe*, V., p. 364.

[86] Roederer to Napoleon, August 21, 1811; Dauxion Lavaysse to Count d'Hauterive, December 21, 1811, *Affaires Étrangères, Memoires et Documents, Amérique, Colonies Espagnoles, 33.*

[87] Orea to Sérurier, December 4, 1811, states that he was thus informed on November 15, 1811, *Affaires Étrangères, États-Unis, 66.*

pledge that Venezuelan emissaries to Napoleon would be received with " the esteem due to friends and with the consideration which the representatives of a free and independent nation had a right to expect." He also asked if, in case of necessity, France would generously protect the efforts of Venezuela to secure her liberty. The agent predicted that these queries would be made the object of direct communications between the agents of Venezuela and the ministers of France.[88] In the reply of Sérurier he declared, unofficially, that each day strengthened his conviction that a Venezuelan minister would be well received in France, that he believed that Venezuela would not " appeal in vain to so powerful a monarch," and that she would find in Napoleon's general policy all the support which she could desire. Orea was also told to inform his government that until a Venezuelan minister arrived in Paris, Sérurier would serve as the medium of communication between Venezuela and France.[89]

On December 9, 1811, Sérurier sent a dispatch to his government which described a long and interesting conversation that he had held with the Venezuelan agent. According to this dispatch, the French minister had informed the latter of the " generous views " of Napoleon with regard to Venezuela. Orea had declared that it was not probable that the English and the Spaniards would permit the Venezuelans to live long in peace. " Our first thoughts," said Orea, " in this state of uncertainty turned to France. We hope that perhaps she will now do for South America what she so generously did thirty years ago for North America." The agent affirmed that in case of war the republic of Venezuela would accept with

---

[88] Orea to Sérurier, December 4, 1811 (copy), *ibid.*

[89] Sérurier to Orea, December 6, 1811, *Affaires Étrangères, États-Unis,* 66.

gratitude whatever protection and assistance the emperor might grant, and declared that he would immediately inform his government of the flattering communication of Sérurier. Orea soon expected to be able to inform the latter what kind of succor was most needed by the revolutionists of Venezuela. The French minister also conversed with Orea about the revolt in other parts of the Spanish patrimony in America. The South American now asked Sérurier for a document which he might transmit to his government as indicative of the intentions of France in regard to Venezuela. Although the experienced French diplomat felt that such a paper might be used to injure France, he could not utterly refuse to comply. As a compromise, and unofficially, he cautiously agreed to express in general terms what he believed to be the intentions of his government. So favorable an impression was made on Orea by these unofficial assurances that, in the words of Sérurier: " The envoy of Venezuela believed that on the arrival of his dispatches in Caracas the minister designed to convey to his Majesty the wishes of his republic would at once leave for France, if indeed he had not already departed." [90]

But Orea was not to be shrined in history as the Benjamin Franklin of the Venezuelan revolution. This zealous envoy, who in the last days of February, sent to Secretary Monroe a copy of the federal constitution that had just been adopted by Venezuela in the hope that this measure might accelerate the action of the United States in regard to his republic,[91] saw his plans spoiled by unforeseen calamities. The ruinous earthquake which vis-

[90] Sérurier to Maret, December 9, 1811, *Affaires Étrangères, États-Unis,* 66. On the attitude of France at this time see also Hunt, G., *Writings of James Madison,* VIII., p. 171.

[91] February 27, 1812 (translation), *State Dept. MSS., Bureau of Rolls and Library, Papers Relative to the Revolted Spanish Colonies.*

ited Venezuela on March 26, 1812,[92] checked the recognition of Consul Lowry, retarded progress with Sérurier, and altered the nature of Orea's supplications to the United States.

The Venezuelan agent now made a pathetic plea to that government " to preserve the melancholy remains of the most horrible earthquake." He asked that the embargo which had been laid on the commerce of the United States be raised so as to permit the exportation of supplies to his stricken countrymen.[93] The distressed envoy soon learned that the sympathy of the United States had been aroused by the reports of the earthquake, and that Congress, with characteristic generosity, had passed a law by which President Madison was authorized to present provisions to the government of Venezuela " for the relief of the unfortunate sufferers." Orea was informed that arrangements had been made for carrying this act into effect at once, and that Alexander Scott, " a very respectable citizen of the United States," had been intrusted with the execution of the commission, and would soon sail for South America.[94]

Alexander Scott of the District of Columbia had apparently been selected as " a political agent to Venezuela " in 1811, but being detained in port by the embargo, he did not leave the United States until the spring of 1812.[95] The instructions to Scott of May 12, 1812, intrusted him with more duties than the delivery of the supplies. Like Lowry he was to investigate conditions. For guidance

---

[92] Robertson, W. S., "Francisco de Miranda," *Am. Hist. Assn. Rept.,* 1907, I., pp. 460-462.

[93] Orea to Monroe, April 28, 1812, *State Dept. MSS., Bureau of Rolls and Library, Papers Relative to the Revolted Spanish Colonies.*

[94] Monroe to Orea, May 14, 1812, *State Dept. MSS., Bureau of Indexes and Archives, Notes to Legations, II.* For the law see *Annals of Congress, 12th Congress, 1st Session,* p. 2294.

[95] *House Report No. 72, 20th Congress, 2d Session,* p. 3.

Scott was given a copy of the instructions of June 28, 1810, to Poinsett.[96] Alexander Scott, however, was instructed by Secretary Monroe that the " independence of the Provinces of Venezuela forms an essential difference between their situation and that of the other Provinces of Spain in America; but still, until their independence is more formally recognized by the United States, it cannot materially affect your duties." Until such acknowledgment was made, he was given " credential letters " like those held by Poinsett. Scott was told that a " principal motive in delaying to recognize in greater form " the independence of Venezuela arose from a desire to ascertain how far the Venezuelans had actually committed themselves to independence. " Nothing," said Monroe, " would be more absurd than for the United States to acknowledge their independence in form, until it was evident that the people themselves were resolved and able to support it. Should a counter-revolution take place after such acknowledgment, the United States would sustain an injury, without having rendered any advantage to the people." Scott also was instructed to cultivate friendly relations with the Venezuelans. He was told that the United States was disposed to render good offices to Venezuela in her relations with foreign powers, and that instructions had been given to the ministers at Paris, St. Petersburg, and London to inform these courts that the United States took " an interest in the independence of the Spanish provinces." [97]

But no glad tidings of a royalist surrender in Venezuela enabled her envoys to cement relations with foreign powers.

[96] Poinsett's instructions are found in *ibid.*, pp. 7, 8; cf. Paxson, F. L., *The Independence of the South-American Republics*, pp. 107-109. On the relations between the United States and Spanish America at this time, see also Lyman, T., *The Diplomacy of the United States*, II., pp. 424-433. Latané, J. H., *The Diplomatic Relations of the United States and Spanish America*, pp. 55-58.

[97] *House Report No. 72, 20th Congress, 2d Session*, pp. 8, 9.

Alexander Scott had only begun his labors in Venezuela when a counter-revolution actually triumphed, and the patriot soldiers, under the dictator Miranda, laid down their arms to the jubilant royalists, commanded by Domingo Monteverde.[98] The designs of Miranda for new diplomatic missions to the United States and England [99] were thus frustrated; his confidential emissary, Thomas Molini, reached the court of London in time to plead only for the liberation of his master from a Spanish dungeon.[100] The harassed Mendez now prayed for relief from the dire financial embarrassments of his agency,[101] and vainly petitioned Lord Castlereagh, the English minister of foreign affairs, to intervene in behalf of the proscribed Venezuelan patriots.[102] In the autumn of 1813, Telésforo de Orea was granted a passport to leave the United States; [103] José R. Revenga soon emerged in South America as the trusted secretary of Simón Bolívar; [104] while Messrs. Lowry and Scott were forced by the tyrannical Monteverde to leave Venezuelan soil.[105] The alluring hopes of foreign recognition that had been cherished by some South Amer-

---

[98] Rojas, marqués de, *El General Miranda*, pp. 750-753, prints the capitulations.

[99] Robertson, W. S., "Francisco de Miranda," *Am. Hist. Assn. Rept.*, 1907, I., pp. 466, 467.

[100] Molini to Richard Wellesley, March 11, 1813, *P. R. O., Foreign Office Correspondence, Spain, 151.*

[101] Amunátegui, M. L., *Andrés Bello*, pp. 129, 207, 208. See also Vansittart to Miranda, March 19, 1811, *Miscellaneous Correspondence of Lord Bexley* (British Museum), *Additional MSS., 31.230.*

[102] Mendez to Castlereagh, October 14 and November 28, 1812, *P. R. O., Foreign Office Correspondence, Spain, 157.*

[103] Monroe to Orea, October 19, 1813, *State Dept. MSS., Bureau of Indexes and Archives, Notes to Legation, II.*

[104] Amunátegui, M. L., *Andrés Bello*, p. 215; Azpurúa, *Biografías*, IV., pp. 319-334.

[105] Scott to Monroe, December 1, 1812, January 14, 1813, *State Dept. MSS., Bureau of Indexes and Archives, Letters from Consuls, La Guayra, I.*

ican patriots vanished, and with these hopes faded the dreams of foreign gold, and arms, and fleets, and armies. The appeals of the Venezüelans to the United States during this period typify the aspirations of many Spanish-American patriots. In 1810 Miguel Hidalgo y Costilla, the father of Mexican independence, dispatched " a pleni-potentiary and ambassador " to the United States.[106] Early in 1813 Ignacio L. Rayón, president of the junta of Mexico, selected an agent who was to initiate relations of commerce and alliance with the United States.[107] Manuel Palacio, an expatriated Venezuelan, informed the secretary of state of the United States in the same year that he had been commissioned to seek aid and protection for the independent province of Carthagena in South America.[108] On March 22, 1811, the provisional government of Chile addressed to the president and the Congress of the United States a communication regarding the opening of Chilean ports to American commerce.[109] The junta on the banks of the River La Plata in June of the same year instructed two agents, bearing assumed names, to secure arms from the generous republic of the North.[110]

[106] Alamán, L., *Historia de México*, II., pp. 466, 467. The fate of the agent is suggested by Romero, M., *Mexico and the United States*, p. 323.

[107] Alamán, L., *Historia de México*, III., pp. 505, 506. See further the proclamation of I. L. Rayón, June 18, 1814, on the arrival at Nautla of a certain General Embert, a supposed envoy of the United States, "our generous neighbors of the North," *ibid.*, IV., pp. 564, 565.

[108] M. Palacio to the secretary of state of the United States, December 26, 1813, *State Dept. MSS., Bureau of Rolls and Library, Papers Relative to the Revolted Spanish Colonies.* *Ibid.*, No. 18, is an appeal from one subscribing himself Pedro de la Lastra to James Monroe on behalf of New Granada, asking for the formation of close political relations with the United States; *ibid.*, No. 19, is a communication (undated) from the junta of Santa Fé to the president of the United States, proposing an alliance. On Palacio see Azpurúa, R., *Biografías*, II., pp. 186-193.

[109] *State Dept. MSS., Bureau of Rolls and Library, Papers Relative to the Revolted Spanish Colonies;* see also the *Aurora de Chile*, March 5, 1812.

[110] The credentials to these agents, Diego Saavedra and Juan Pedro de

The attitude of Venezuela towards the United States, therefore, was not peculiar. To describe the diplomacy of Venezuela towards the United States and Europe during this epoch is to depict Spanish-American diplomacy in miniature. Signs are indeed found of the desire of other nascent Spanish-American states to enter into relations with European nations. Early in 1812 a nondescript agent in the city of Washington wrote a letter to the French minister Sérurier regarding Buenos Aires.[111] The junta of that city at once opened communications with Lord Strangford, the influential English envoy at Rio Janeiro,[112] and soon dispatched its able secretary, Mariano Moreno, on an ill-starred diplomatic mission to England.[113] In August, 1812, the warrior-priest, J. M. Morelos, attempted to interest British officials in the Mexican struggle for independence.[114] About two years later an alleged agent of New Granada sent an exposition to the English chancellor of the exchequer in which he directed attention to the climate, population, and resources of Venezuela and New Granada.[115] In December, 1814, the provisional

Aguirre, are found in *State Dept. MSS., Bureau of Rolls and Library, Papers Relative to the Revolted Spanish Colonies.* On Martin Thompson, who appeared in Washington in 1816 to represent Buenos Aires, see *American State Papers, Foreign Relations,* IV., p. 174.

[111] January 9, 1812, *Affaires Étrangères, États-Unis, 67.* The English government appears to have believed that Palacio was making approaches to Sérurier, see Henry Wellesley to Labrador, April 28, 1813, *P. R. O., Foreign Office Correspondence, Spain, 144.*

[112] Calvo, C., *Recueil complet des traités, conventions, capitulations, armistices, et autres actes diplomatiques de tous les états de l'Amérique latine,* VII., pp. 227-229.

[113] *Registro oficial de la república argentina,* I., p. 98; see also Mitre, B., *Historia de Belgrano y de la independencia argentina* (Buenos Aires, 1902), I., pp. 322, 323, II., p. 1.

[114] Morelos to "Exmos. Sres. Almirante de Marina ó Ministros de la Gran Bretaña," Tehuacán, August 27, 1812, *Archivo General de México, Historia, 116;* (British Museum), *Additional MSS., 31.231.* See further Alamán, L., *Historia de México,* III., pp. 488-493.

[115] (Translation), *Miscellaneous Correspondence of Lord Bexley* (Brit-

government of Buenos Aires sent the well-known leaders Manuel Belgrano and Bernardino Rivadavia on a diplomatic mission to England and Spain which culminated in an interesting project to found a European principality in South America.[116]   In the benighted city of Asunción the mysterious consul José Gaspar Rodriguez de Francia, eulogized by Carlyle, apparently tried to initiate the bizarre diplomacy of Paraguay by commissioning an English merchant to present a parcel of Paraguayan produce to the house of commons, and to negotiate with England a treaty of " commerce and political alliance." [117]

But neither the appeals of revolutionary partisans nor significant political events greatly modified the policy of certain nations towards Spanish America.   After hostilities broke out between Spain and America, England carefully watched the fluctuations of the war through her officials,[118] and repeatedly tried to induce Spain to accept her mediation in the hope that the revolting colonists might thus be amicably reconciled with the peninsular Spaniards.[119]   Strict injunctions were sent from London to English officials in America not to supply either the royalists or the insurgents with munitions of war.[120]   During the struggle England aimed to secure new markets for her manufactures,[121] but steadfastly resisted the crafty

ish Museum), *Additional MSS., 31.231.* On the attitude of Simón Bolívar in 1814 see Velasco y Rojas, marqués de, *Simón Bolívar*, p. 113.

[116] *Registro oficial de la república argentina*, I., p. 299; Calvo, *Traités*, VIII., pp. 234-291, 341-355.

[117] Robertson, J. P. and W. P., *Letters on Paraguay*, II., pp. 279-287.

[118] English governors in the West Indies and naval officers made many reports on conditions in Spanish America. So did agents, as J. Pavia to Peele, August 10, 1812, *P. R. O., Spain, 140*, which deals with Venezuela and New Granada.

[119] Stapleton, A. G., *The Political Life of George Canning*, II., p. 10. Correspondence regarding these attempts is found in *P. R. O., Spain, 156.*

[120] Draft of dispatch to General Morrison, March 5, 1812, *P. R. O., Jamaica, 77;* Manchester to Bathurst, July 17, 1813, *ibid., 79.*

[121] This is illustrated by article four of the treaty of July 5, 1814, be-

suggestions of the Spaniards that she join hands with them
in the subjugation of the insurgents in return for commercial concessions.[122] Even after Napoleon had been
humbled, England formally pledged herself to Spain to
take " the most effectual measures " to prevent her subjects from furnishing military supplies to the Spanish-
American rebels,[123] a convention which was apparently
accompanied by an agreement that English merchants
were still to carry on the trade with the Spanish colonies
which had been secured during the Napoleonic wars.[124]
In 1817 a formal proclamation was issued by England,
enjoining her subjects to remain neutral in the struggle
between Spain and Spanish America.[125]   After the end of
the war with England, in 1814, the United States did not
much alter her policy, for the negotiations with
Spain over the Floridas soon checked any tendency to
favor the Spanish-American rebels. On September 1,
1815, President Madison issued a proclamation warning
all citizens not to enlist in any military expeditions or
ent prises against the Spanish possessions.[126] About the
same time, by the orders of the government, vessels from
the insurgent provinces were freely admitted into the
ports of the United States, regardless of the flag flying
from the mast-head.[127]

tween England and Spain, which provided that if commerce with the
Spanish colonies was thrown open, England was to be the most favored
nation, *British and Foreign State Papers,* I., part I., p. 275.

[122] Henry Wellesley to Lord Bathurst, February 14, 1815, *P. R. O., Foreign Office Correspondence, Spain, 173.*

[123] See article three of the additional articles between England and
Spain, August 28, 1814, *British and Foreign State Papers,* I., part I., p. 293.

[124] Stapleton, A. G., *The Political Life of George Canning,* II., pp.
10, 11.

[125] November 27, 1817, *British and Foreign State Papers,* IV., pp. 488,
489.

[126] *American State Papers, Foreign Relations,* IV., p. 1.

[127] Moore, J. B., *Digest of International Law,* I., pp. 170-176, see especially the instructions to the collector Duplessis, July 3, 1815.

A contemporary might well have prophesied early in 1816 that the Spanish-American revolution was over. The idolized Ferdinand had been restored to the throne of his father. The indomitable viceroy, Calleja, had almost stamped out the insurrection in New Spain. The royalist commander, Morillo, dominated Venezuela and New Granada. The provinces of La Plata had not even framed a declaration of independence.

But the historian can detect some harbingers of independence. In the ancient capital of the Aztecs the intrepid but discredited royalist commander, Agustín de Iturbide, was brooding over his fancied wrongs, and perhaps planning that coup d'état which caused him to be hailed as liberator of Mexico.[128] In the seclusion of the West Indies, Simón Bolívar was dreaming of an American state system and of an international congress on the soil of independent Colombia.[129] Down in a province of La Plata the valiant José de San Martín was quietly recruiting the brave army of the Andes, which was destined to eclipse in the New World the achievements of Hannibal.[130] The Congress of Tucumán, in the autumn of 1816, after adopting a declaration of independence for the United Provinces of Rio de La Plata, enjoined the chief executive, Juan Martín de Pueyrredón, to send an agent to the United States to negotiate for aid and recognition, and likewise directed him to instruct their agents in Brazil

---

[128] One of the complaints against Iturbide is found in [*Rocafuerte,* V.] *Bosquejo ligerisimo de la revolución de Mégico,* pp. 22-39; Iturbide's own account of the affair, written several years afterwards, is found in *Breve diseño crítico de la emancipación y libertad de la nacion mexicana* (Mexico, 1827), pp. 7, 8.

[129] Larrazábal, F., *Simón Bolívar,* I., pp. 400-403.

[130] Miller, J., *Memoirs of General Miller,* I., pp. 88-104; Mitre, B., *Historia de San Martín y de la emancipación Sud-Americana* (Buenos Aires, 1907), II., pp. 5-210.

and England to initiate similar negotiations with European nations.[131]

The period from 1808 to 1816 was indeed only the prelude to the era in which the revolutionary party in Spanish America triumphed and various provinces were recognized as independent states.[132] It was during this period that Spain entered upon a misguided policy towards her American colonies. France, which had displayed a keen interest in the revolutionizing of Spanish America, sank, after the battle of Waterloo, from her high international position. England, the ally of Spain, desirous of balking French designs and anxious to promote her own commercial interests, formulated that neutral and mediatory policy which she followed, in the main, until after the proclamation of the Monroe Doctrine. The United States adopted a cautious and neutral policy towards Spanish America, which, however, occasionally contemplated the recognition of Spanish-American independence. The United States listened, unofficially, to emissaries of the insurgents, sent agents to investigate conditions in Spanish America, and in time allowed the revolting provinces belligerent rights. Sympathy, at least, was enlisted for the independent cause on both sides of the Atlantic. Prominent European and American statesmen, notably George Canning and James Monroe, were led to meditate upon the relations of Spanish America to Europe and the United States.[133] The diplomacy of this period symbol-

---

[131] *Registro oficial de la república argentina,* I., 381.

[132] It was not until 1836 that Spain reluctantly recognized Mexico as a free, sovereign, and independent state, see Olavarría y Ferrari, V., *México independiente, 1821-1855* (México á través de los siglos, volume IV.), pp. 392-394 and note 2. The treaty of Córdoba, August 24, 1821, by which General O'Donojú recognized the independence of the Mexican empire, was declared illegal and void by the Spanish government.

[133] See Adams, C. F., *Memoirs of John Quincy Adams,* III., p. 352, on the attitude of J. Q. Adams towards Spanish America.

izes the early attitude of many Spanish-American patriots towards those nations which profoundly influenced their political ideals; even San Martín occasionally stretched out his hands expectantly towards Anglo-Saxondom. At this time Spanish America appeared in the guise of a suppliant, stumbling at the threshold of national life. Although the student of law may hold that the Spanish-American peoples did not, during this transitional period, constitute sovereign and independent states, yet the student of history can discern new nations arising in the western hemisphere— nations which strove in vain to initiate those diplomatic relations with Europe and the United States that acquire more significance with each passing year.

WILLIAM SPENCE ROBERTSON.

SOME NOTES ON THE STUDY OF SOUTH AMERICAN HISTORY

THE first requisite for the fruitful and truly scientific study of South American national history lies in an understanding of the European and colonial background of South American life, as well as in an appreciation of the special factors introduced through the physical and ethnical character of South America during the process of colonization. The active elements in the colonizing process, the warriors, priests, and colonists proper, must be studied from the point of view of their social and economic position in the countries from which they came. The present status of the scientific study of Spanish and Portuguese history leaves much to be desired in this respect, yet it is of the first importance that we should have this accurate understanding of the materials which composed the colonizing forces.

On the whole, it may perhaps be said with justice, that more work of permanent value has been done in South America in connection with colonial history than upon the later developments of national life. National history in South America is too often written from the point of view of political argumentation, or, at any rate, under the dominance of political views which cause the materials to be presented one-sidedly and with a distinct *parti pris*. The historical value of the notable writings of such men as Mitre is vitiated by this fact. In the treatment of colonial institutions and development, political passions are not so apt to control, and though so far few studies of definitive authority have been produced, a good deal of useful work has been done and documentary material has been collected as well.

The first desideratum concerning the student of South American history is that he should keep his mind free from misleading analogies, and that, appreciating the distinctive characteristics of the South American world, he should allow his conclusions to develop naturally from the original materials at hand. In this respect, too, much of the history writing in South America is defective. It frequently happens that some European genius, like Le Bon, Lombroso, or Comte, gains such an ascendency over the mind of a South American writer, that the latter begins to see the history of his own society entirely in the terms of European thought. While the books thus produced are usually interesting reading, the luminous explanations in which they abound, are often dangerously deceiving because they do not truly result from a complete and impartial study of South American facts.

The serious student will next attempt to form some idea as to the conditions imposed upon social development by the physical environment of South America. He will not deal with that continent as a unit, but will appreciate that the highlands of Colombia impose conditions of life essentially different from those obtaining in the vast river basin of the Amazon, the heart of the Tropics, or the arid heights of the Peruvian Mountains, or the narrow coast line belt of Chili, or the broad, level, and immensely fertile plains of Argentina. Nor will he forget that South America is the only continent in which the representatives of the white race live side by side, and in a political community with native Indians and imported Africans, and that in the regions north of the La Plata River these racial conditions must, in the nature of things, always continue to exercise a determining influence.

As the investigator is dealing with new societies, it is

indeed true that many of the problems which make the interest of North American history will receive fresh elucidation from scientific study in the south.   The effect of free land and of frontier conditions upon social life may here be studied in new phases.   All the results of a transplantation of European stock to new regions and the vast economic problems that arise with the gradual development and subjugation of these regions may here be traced.   The effect of the presence of a permanently inferior population upon social life and institutions, as well as upon the character of the white *élite,* receives most abundant illustration in South American experience.   But it will be dangerous on any of these points to approach South America with preconceived ideas.   Situations differ so much from country to country, that while the problem will fire the curiosity and enthusiasm of the investigator, he ought to be sure not to reflect in his work solutions derived from the study of other parts of the world.

It is a common opinion that the political history of South America is most unprofitable and devoid of real interest, and, indeed, it must be confessed that a book like Akers' *History of South America,* with its monotonous succession of revolutions, battles, truces, dictatorships, and changes in constitutions, is rather dreary reading.   The shifting kaleidoscope of revolutions soon becomes tiring when the historic process, decade after decade, seems to reveal no real, progressive development of social and political life.   So many persons, after dipping into South American history for a while, turn away discouraged in the belief that the anarchical succession of revolutionary leaders exhausts South American historical experience, and that there is nothing valuable to learn from such a catalogue of adventitious and fortuitous events.   This is, indeed, a great mistake.   But, on the other hand, it is true that purely political history, dealing with the superficialities of public action, is not by itself very profitable.   Political development in South America has been hindered and beclouded by many factors that have not allowed the true needs and aspirations of the respective societies to come to their own.

We meet here in the first place the uncritical imitation of foreign institutions and political theory.   At the time of the separation from Spain, the people of the colonies lacked practically all political experience and education. Government had resolved itself into administration by representatives of the mother country.   There were no legislative bodies in any of the colonies.   The only institutions which contained a germ of self-government were the *cabildos,* or town corporations.   So, looking for guidance, the men who became the leaders of the South American revolution were inspired largely by the theories of Rousseau as embodied in the French Revolution.   The early constitutions, therefore, placed emphasis entirely on the ideas of independence and democracy, making scarcely any effort to construct institutions and legal relations corresponding to the special situations and the varying degrees of advancement in which the peoples of South America then found themselves.   The influence of French ideas was especially strong in the Caribbean countries, where, under the influence of Nariño, the entire French " Declaration of the Rights of Man " was embodied in the New Granada Constitution of 1812.   But throughout, French theories exercised a profound influence upon South American thought and constitution-making during the first half century of independence.

The United States appeared to the South Americans as the elder sister, the country which had successfully solved the problem of republican government.   The knowledge of its institutions came to them by way of Europe, especially through France.   Of the actual conditions in the

United States, a rather shadowy conception prevailed; and its institutions were taken as the ultimate embodiment of reason tested by experience, as a solution of all political difficulties, and one which could be relied upon to lead South American states to greatness and true freedom. It is but natural that countries confronted by the problem of giving themselves a national political organization should look about and study the experience of others. But the acceptance of the North American model was usually uncritical and unaccompanied by a positive consideration of local needs and conditions. Thus the imitation of this model became in many ways a hindrance to the spontaneous development of South American life; and it, therefore, also introduced many elements that will prove puzzling to the investigator. Being a superficial adoption, it makes a cumulative contribution to that impression of superficiality which one so easily obtains from the study of South American political life.

Even in those countries where conditions were more favorable to the establishment of representative institutions, as in Argentina, the uncritical imitation of the federal form of government brought many evils in its train. The Argentinian leaders were tolerably free from purely theoretical considerations. The original act of independence of 1810 contains no enunciation of general principles nor declaration of rights, and carries within it only the germ of representative government in the invitation directed to the *cabildos* to have themselves represented in a national council. After Argentina had passed through three or four decades of anarchy and purely personal government, after the downfall of Rosas, actual constitution-making began. Alberdi, the most original thinker on politics whom South America has produced, had a positive view of the political relations, and, therefore, urged upon his contemporaries the necessity of adapting constitutional rules

to the actual conditions of the nation.   His point of view
is expressed in the following words: [1]

" South American constitutional history has two periods.   One
covers the period of the wars of independence.   In this the constitutions were originally adopted.   Since then the same constitutions have been variously modified; either central power has been
strengthened in behalf of order or weakened in behalf of liberty.
The exercise of power has been centralized, at other times it has
been localized, but never has constitutional law been looked at
from the point of view of present necessities.   The original constitutions emphasized liberty and equality as was natural when
the countries separated from a monarchical state, but no attention
was given to matters of progress in the action of economic interests.   The model of the French Revolution affected us.   This
Revolution was weak on the economic side, as it did not recognize liberty of commerce.   The Convention used the customs
duties as an instrument of war.   Napoleon followed with his
continental blockade.   The United States, too, early adopted a
restrictive system.   What is important for us in South America
is to have free movement of population, immigration, free
commerce, and a general guarantee of progressive reform.   Political constitutions of to-day have the duty to organize practical
means for leading emancipated America out of the obscure and inferior condition in which she finds herself.   So, as before we
placed in our constitutions independence, liberty, and religion,
to-day we must place there free immigration, liberty of commerce, railways, free industry; not in place of those grand principles but as essential means to bring it about that they may cease
to be words and become realities.   To-day we must promote population and railways, the navigability of our rivers and the wealth
of our states.   We must elevate our population to the habit of
a free government which necessity has imposed upon us.   We must
give them the aptitude which they lack for being republican, make
them worthy of the republic which we have proclaimed and
which to-day we can neither practice nor abandon.   The Chilean
Republic has found in the energy of the presidential power the
public guaranty which monarchy offers for order and peace, with-

[1] In his *Bases y puntos de partida para la organización política de la
República Argentina.*

out abandoning the nature of the republican government. Bolivar said: 'The new states of America need kings with the name of presidents.' A republic can have no other form when it exists immediately after a monarchy. The new régime must connect with the old. You cannot advance by leaps."

The Argentinian constitution of 1853 was influenced largely by this point of view. It contained the federal form of government copied from that of the United States, but with such modifications as adapted it to a country where national unity was clearly demanded, and where the provinces or states had not achieved a distinct existence as commonwealths as they had with us at the time of the formation of the Union. This constitution was unacceptable to the statesmen of Buenos Aires, and Sarmiento criticised it as not following closely enough the North American precedent. It was his opinion that:

"If our country constitutes itself under the federal system and if in its constitutional charter, it adopts to the letter that other constitution already settled and approved, the result will be that all the labor of that society, all its science and experience, will act, together with the constitution, to serve and support our own."

He, therefore, favored the adoption not only of the text of the constitution, but of the doctrines developed by North American statesmen and legal authorities. In opposition to this, the point of view of Alberdi was that constitutions " should not express the necessities of yesterday or of to-morrow, but those of to-day." And when the constitutional commission of 1860, which had reformed the constitution in the direction of further approximating it to that of the United States, argued deprecatively against originality in constitution-making, saying that " it would have been extravagant to depart from what is recognized and admitted in the nations most free and most civilized, and to pretend to produce an original work; " Alberdi answered that " there could not have been a greater extravagance than to try to apply the constitutions of the most free and most civilized countries to a small and ill-prepared population."

" Originality in constitution making [he says] is the only kind to which we can aspire without immodesty or pretension. It does not consist in a newness, superior to all known perfection, but in an adaptability to the special case to which it is applied."

His judgment of the situation culminates in the sentence:

" In order to dissolve the unity of the Argentine Republic, it would be sufficient to apply strictly the United States constitution, treating as sovereign states those units which hitherto were provinces within a state."

As to the Constitution of 1860, the drafting commission in its report stated:

" Federalism is the only form of government possible in our republic in the present state of its civilization. As up to the present, the democratic government of the United States is the highest result of human logic; because its constitution is the only one which has been made by the people and for the people without having in view any alien interest, without compromising with any illegitimate fact; there would be as much presumption as ignorance in attempting to make innovations in constitutional law, ignoring the lessons of experience."

Similar expressions of a high admiration for the American government have been common down to the present. Vélez Varsfield, in comparing the Constitution of 1853 with the amended form which was adopted in 1860, says:

" The Argentinian legislators [1853] took the American Constitution as their model, but they did not respect this sacred text and an ignorant hand made in it suppressions and alterations of great importance. The Commission [1860] has restored the constitutional law of the United States in the part in which it had been changed."

And yet a recent writer on Argentinian federalism [2] pronounces the opinion that it has become

" an obstacle to that internal peace which at first it served. It has fomented provincial revolutions, political disagreements, and fratricidal struggles, destructive of every guarantee of liberty, of justice, and of personal security. All of which has resulted in the depopulation of the provinces and our discredit before Europe."

This judgment is perhaps exaggerated in its severity, but it admits of no doubt that many of the evils of Argentinian public life may be traced to this lack of correspondence between the institutions of the written law and the actual conditions and practices of political life. The federal constitution of the United States is the most complicated political system ever developed by man. It includes the three cardinal institutions of a popular electorate, representative government, and a federal union, in which, with a high centralization of national power, there goes respect for local legislative autonomy. The introduction of this system into a country which at the time had no training in self-government, which had seen only an intermittent practice of popular election, and in which the local units, while filled with a spirit of particularism and insubordination, lacked experience in commonwealth action, of necessity led to a grave contradiction between the theory and the practice of public life. And while publicists may believe that Argentinian public life will gradually grow up into its institutions so as to correspond more fully with them, the historian will find in the artificiality of accepted institutions one of his greatest difficulties.

[2] Rivarola, *Del régimen federativo al unitario,* Buenos Aires, 1908, p. 121.

A very striking account of political fictions in Argentina was given by ex-President Carlos Pellegrini in a discourse in the Chamber of Deputies on May 9, 1906. In discussing the demands of the political situation, he said:

"We have a nation independent, free, organic, and we live in peace; but we lack something essential: we are ignorant of the practices and habits of a free people and our written institutions are only a promise or a hope. . . . Our régime is neither representative, nor republican, nor federal. It is not representative because the vicious practices growing day by day have allowed the men in the government to constitute themselves as grand electors and to take the place of the people in its political and electoral rights. . . . It is not republican because the legislative bodies formed under this personal régime do not have the independence which the republican system demands. They are instruments handled by those who have created them. It is not federal because every day we witness the suppression of provincial autonomy."

He then refers to the selection of provincial governors by the political leaders in Buenos Aires. The overpowering need of unity in national affairs has led to extra-legal arrangements through which the action of the provinces can be controlled by the central government.

The federal states of Brazil, too, are an artificial creation of a constitution modeled upon that of the United States. There was indeed at the time of the foundation of the Brazilian Republic a great deal of separatist and localist feeling, but it was not organized politically in the form of self-governing commonwealths. The situation is thus described by Felisbello Freire:[3]

"In the preliminary work which preceded the organization of the states to which the legal prescriptions of the decree apply, these were absolutely passive. The federal government was the

[3] *Historia constitucional da Republica dos Estados Unidos do Brasil,* Vol. II., p. 36.

propelling force. Through the union they were organized. They did not organize themselves. The entire movement of the new political life into which they were entering flowed from the center towards the periphery. The federation was nothing but the political organization of the states. Until then they had lived as provinces without the least portion of autonomy."

It is not surprising that these artificial creations should give rise to uncertainties in constitutional practice. The North American states were living organisms: they had developed their field of legislative and administrative action when the national union was founded, and the division of powers between them and the central government therefore rested on a historic and practical basis. In Brazil, where no such traditions existed, the creation of states has led to constant conflicts of jurisdiction, which are accentuated by the fact that the federal supreme court does not have a complete power to adjudicate upon state constitutions. Nor have the states on their part respected municipal autonomy.

It must be noted that in those South American countries which have adopted the North American system, the significance of *federalism* is exactly the opposite of what it is in the United States. With us *federal* goes with *union,* and refers to a bond constantly growing stronger between commonwealths that have developed, and preserve, a certain individuality. In South America *federal* imports usually *separation* and local independence, because in all cases the point of departure was the unitary system of the colonial government, or, in Brazil, of the empire, under which the states or provinces now existing were merely administrative circumscriptions. The adoption of the federal system, therefore, has usually meant a tendency toward the growth of local independence and in some cases of anarchy, rather than the strengthening of national unity. It must also be remembered that most of these adoptions fall in the time when the states' rights theory was still strong with us, and before national unity had been incontestably established through the Civil War. In Central America, indeed, federalism led directly to separation, and in other regions separation and anarchy were prevented only by resort to personal government, often of a despotic character. The effects of the system are thus portrayed by a Colombian writer: [4]

"We need only rapidly run through the history of the short period between 1863 and 1885 to see how there existed in Colombian institutions, and, as a consequence, in its political customs, an accumulation of the elements of disorganization, arbitrary rule, and anarchy, which rendered all good government impossible. Anarchy existed in the ideas, in character, and in political action, as well as in the institutions; and society maintained itself solely by force of its natural and historic elements of cohesion. The contradiction between social facts on the one hand and constitutions and laws on the other was notorious; [a contradiction] between the union and solidarity of the interests of the people, and the division and breaking up which necessarily resulted from the federal disorder, the sovereignty of the states, and the absolute theory of individual rights."

Conditions such as these did not result solely from the imitation of the American constitution and of our political experience, but from a failure to apply that experience with discrimination to the special conditions of South American societies. And while the American will naturally be proud of the influence which the institutions of his country have exercised in the southern republics, the historical investigator will find the difficulty of his problem increased by the complexity and artificiality thus introduced into South American public life.

This artificiality of political institutions in itself accounts to some extent, as has already been suggested, for the

[4] José María Samper, *Derecho Publico Interno de Colombia,* Bogota, 1886, Vol. I., p. 296.

chronic unrest to which many South American states have been subject, and for the numerous revolutions by which nearly all of them have been visited. Where written constitutions plainly do not correspond with the facts and needs of national life, legal authority is weakened and a constant uncertainty exists inviting appeals to force. The serious student of history, of course, will not be satisfied with any superficial study of these phenomena, nor will he ascribe them entirely to racial characteristics, as do many South American writers who have unfortunately fallen into the error of trying to explain these complex situations with reference to some national psychological trait or racial characteristic.

It is further vitally important that we should note the cardinal difference which separates the original revolutionary movement in South America from that of the United States. The thirteen colonies revolted because they had grown strong, because they had developed a self-sustaining life that made them desire independence. The Spanish colonies moved for separation because the home government was weak and disorganized by the French invasion. What was at first only a movement for supplying the absence of direction from the *metropole* grew by degrees into an actual and definitive separation from Spain. But there was lacking in the Spanish colonies that complete political organization including all the functions of government and communal action which was found in the north. Moreover, the wars of independence were nearly always civil wars, in the sense that, within the colonies themselves, parties differed as to the wisdom of separation from the mother country. From the United States the loyalists were expelled, leaving behind them a unified people agreed on the fundamental question of independence. In South America, on the contrary, the struggle frequently ended in a drawn battle in which neither party carried off a decisive victory, with the result that there did not come a definite and complete break with the political system of the past. Separation, indeed, was achieved, but true independence and self-government were not simultaneously established from within. There was no thorough change in the conception of government and in administrative methods. To the mass of the population government still remained something imposed from without or above, the power to tax, to grant privileges, and thus to enable its incumbents to practice all manner of exploitation. The commonwealth idea did not engraft itself with the revolution because its coming had not been prepared for during the colonial era.

Another factor of the highest importance which distinguishes the historical development of South America from our own and adds elements which have a tendency to shroud and conceal the real movements of national evolution, lies in the disproportionate importance of city life. The colonial cities, the centers of activity from which strong influences went out over the surrounding country and into which wealth was gathered, retained their predominant position under the new régime. Thus it came about that in these new countries, rural or frontier conditions never came to exercise that importance which they have held in our own national history. It was really Buenos Aires, Lima, Santiago, and Bogota that determined the ideas and the temper of South American civilization, rather than the country regions. In this manner European ideas continued to control, and the civilization of South America was dominated primarily by the feeling and standards of city existence. The back country, from having been the colony of Spain, became the colony of Buenos Aires, of Santiago, of Lima. Argentinian national history, in fact, plays almost entirely about the struggle of the metropolis to make permanent her ascendency.

Alberdi was a believer in the rude but regenerative forces of the life in country regions. He resisted the pretensions of Buenos Aires to the dominant position in all Argentinian affairs. In 1860 he wrote: [5]

" Buenos Aires revolted against Spain, not in behalf of the other Argentinian provinces but for the profit of its own province, which erected itself into a colonial mother country over its sisters. The provinces have ceased to be colonies of Spain in order to remain colonies of Buenos Aires. They are governed by the metropolis and produce for her, not for themselves. Their condition has become worse than under the Spanish domination. They have remained entirely alien to their own government, because lacking a national authority emanating from their own election, their sovereign powers have been exercised by the local power of Buenos Aires without the nation taking any part. The province of Buenos Aires has negotiated for them with the world, and has placed them in peace or in war according to its convenience. Under the government of Spain, the revenue produced in the provinces was applied in their own service, Spain taking merely the excess. Under the domination of Buenos Aires, the customs contributions have remained entirely in the hands of the local metropolis which collects them in its ports, and they have been applied exclusively in its service. The port has remained the only one in all the provinces, in conformity with the old Laws of the Indies. The Argentinians have become tributaries of Buenos Aires."

Dr. Carlos Pellegrini, in an address, August 25, 1897, spoke of this matter in the following language:

" Buenos Aires, the city of the viceroys, governed the colony for centuries, during which time it became her habit to command. With the revolution, the colony became a nation and Buenos Aires, following this custom of centuries, wished to continue governing and directing, notwithstanding the resistance of the people of the interior. These two forces and tendencies have, under different names and through thousands of instances of varied aspects, formed the woof of our entire political history."

[5] Alberdi, *Escritos postumos*, Vol. XII., p. 326.

The men of Buenos Aires looked upon the interior as arrested in its development and given over to barbarian practices and impulses. Sarmiento in his *Facundo* developed this theory in this manner:

"Many philosophers have believed that plains prepare the road for despotism. This extension of plains gives to life in the interior a pronounced Asiatic color. . . . From the conditions of pastoral life grave difficulties arise for any political organization and much greater for the triumph of European civilization, its institutions, and the wealth and liberty which are their consequence. In this society cultivation of the spirit is useless and impossible, municipal affairs do not exist, the common weal is a word without meaning. . . . In the Argentinian Republic we see at the same time two distinct civilizations; the twelfth and the nineteenth centuries living together, one in the cities, the other in the country regions."

Alberdi combats the idea of localizing civilization in the cities and barbarism in the country, and censures such a view as a source of anarchy and of artificial antipathy between localities which mutually need and complement each other. He considers it perfectly natural that the country regions should be less cultured than the cities. But he does not recognize the existence of barbarizing influences in the frontier districts. On the contrary, he has confidence in the worth of the simple and primitive country folk, and considers it an insult to Argentinian nationality that a character like Facundo Quiroga should have been selected as a personification of rural ideals—"the greatest insult which could be offered to this country, honest and good, which has the misfortune of attempting the creation of the republic while having only the most imperfect elements therefor." He sees in *caudillaje* or political bossism, a natural result of primitive conditions and of the colonial past which it is the purpose of natural development to overcome, but not by setting the city over against the country.

The fact to which we have here referred, the preponderance of city ideas in South America, may also account for the absence of that feeling of freshness and energy, in a word, of youth, which is characteristic of North American democracy.   In a sense the South American societies were born old.   The dominance of European ideas in their intellectual life, the importance of the city as a seat of civilization, never allowed the pioneer feeling to gain the importance which it has held and still holds in our life.   It is, of course, not entirely absent, and many traces of it will be encountered in South American literature, but it is not an original all-pervading force.

The South American country in which history has been most normal and logical is Chili.   In the hundred years of its independence it has indeed seen a few revolutions; such movements, however, were not mere personal struggles for a temporary ascendency, since the main motive in them was an attempt to settle some question of public policy or of constitutional principle.   Chilean society is governed by a closely-organized aristocracy, based upon the natural fact of social differences between it and the body of the people. Its leaders, in the early course of national history, established firmly that respect for authority, that rule of law and order which has always characterized the republic. It is a political society which discusses and works out its problems; having achieved the solution of some difficulty, it retains the advantages of any sacrifices that may have been made, and moves on to new developments and higher positions.   Chilean history, therefore, has something of the logical unfolding that makes the evolution of English nationality so fascinating a study.   This society has a great deal of political consciousness and self-confidence. Though composed of varied racial elements, in which, of course, the Spanish is the main stock, it has a strong assimilating power, and it has succeeded in evolving a very

distinct type of Chilean nationality. As a development
of the historical sense always accompanies the growth of
national feeling, it is not surprising that we should en-
counter in Chili more interest in historical studies, more
sentiment for historical facts than in other South American countries. The most substantial, if not the most brilliant, South American historian, Barros Arana, as well as
the greatest bibliographer and collector of materials, José
T. Medina, are Chileans. The list of Chilean historians
is long, and while there are many among them who view
national history from the position of their own interests
and political party, yet it may be said, on the whole, that
Chilean history is comparatively free from these influences
and is, or at least attempts to be, truly national and
scientific.

From what has been said above, it will be apparent how
easy it is to get a superficial view of South American history. Any presentation which confines itself to the changing aspects of political ascendency, to the shifting
modification of legal forms and institutions, or to political
actions and ideals as seen from the point of view of the
various *metropoles,* must necessarily lack depths and contact with the realities of social development. Considered
by themselves these changes are an unmeaning procession
of events; and so, in fact, they have thus far generally
been presented. But when once they are seen in their
relation to the deeper forces of social and economic life,
these apparently uninteresting facts immediately gain in
importance and significance. Of course, the study of
South American political theory is, in and of itself, an
interesting matter when rightly undertaken, as is also that
of the city as a center of civilization and political influence.
But a presentation of the complete historical development
of these nations requires a more comprehensive and deeper

grasp of social and economic facts which underlie political action. Their politics considered by itself seems to be anarchical or composed of extra-legal arrangements, such as executive interference in elections and local government, or the power of political bosses, *caciques, caudillos,* or *gamonales,* and of political clubs, arrogating to themselves public authority, such as the " Democratic Societies " of Colombia. Between the formal theory of the institutions and the sordid facts of political action, the investigator is apt to lose his interest unless he studies more fundamental relations. Dr. Freire, in the preface to his *Historia territorial do Brazil,* expresses himself as follows:

" Without the study of the interests, economic, political, or religious, which accomplished the conquest along the seacoast and then in the interior, opening roads for peopling the country and then forming centers of population here and there; without the study of the origin of the political and administrative units into which the country gradually divided itself in consequence of this peopling which, passing through successive phases, finally took form as organized political and administrative life; without a study of all these facts which formed part of the basic process of development, the history of Brazil would be nothing but a congeries of facts without logic, without harmony, without causality." [6]

Echevarria in his *Plan Economico,* and Alberdi in his *Estudios Economicos,* both held that it would be futile to treat of the development of Argentinian nationality without a previous careful study of the initial steps in economic life. And later Argentinian writers like Juan A. Garcia and José Ingegnieros have emphasized the importance of social and economic factors.

Humanity is always interesting; in its steady development and in unusual situations. It is in the latter that

[6] See also an article by José Oiticica in the *Revista Americana,* Rio de Janeiro, April and May, 1910.

South American history abounds. The conquest and colonization of a continent largely tropical by the European race; the meeting with the aborigines, and with the negroes brought from Africa; the intermingling of races, as well as the fusion of their ideas, customs, and institutions; in view of all this it seems that the interaction of physical, moral, and intellectual forces is nowhere illustrated in a greater variety of aspects than in South America. Nowhere in the world has there been such a wealth of elements in such multiform relationships and mixtures of races and folklores. The Christianized Indian superadds to his inherited customs rude forms of European beliefs and practices, as is so well depicted for us in books like Juan A. Garcia's *Ciudad Indiana.* The negro imported from Africa into the tropical world of South America, bringing with him the complex folklore of his native land, though enslaved, soon felt himself at home among his new surroundings. Then there is the *gaucho,* or, as this type is called in other countries, the *huaso* or *lacero,* the descendant of the poorer white settlers, usually with a strong admixture of Indian blood. This backwoodsman of South America has not achieved the national and estimable position of our frontiersman. The whole point of view in South America was so different; these people were never looked upon as the vanguards of civilization, but rather as its most backward sons, obliged by an unkind fate to dwell in uncultured regions far away from the hearths of civilization. To some extent, indeed, the poetry of the life of these battlers with crude nature has been realized and the *sabor criollo,* the creole zest, has had its poets and historians. But these picturesque types are rapidly disappearing, giving way to more humdrum forms of existence. Transformations wrought in the white race itself through settlement in tropical and subtropical regions may here also be studied—the effects of climate on race, and of natural conditions on institutions and ideas brought from different regions of the world.

The genital absence of political cohesion and harmony, during the first half century of independence, was due very largely to the lack of a definite economic organization. Under the colonial régime the economic policy had been one of undisguised and unmitigated exploitation.[7] Men came not to build themselves homes and to till the soil with their own hands, but to gain wealth rapidly and through the labor of others. The natives were reduced to the level of slavery, and when they were exhausted or their numbers proved insufficient, blacks were imported from Africa. Extensive and exhaustive modes of cultivation were employed without any thought that nature too needs to replenish her forces. The chief governmental action with respect to economic life was to grant exclusive privileges and monopolies. Industries were present only in a rudimentary form, and all economic life had the instability inseparable from that feverish hunt for fortunes which would exhaust one field of exploitation in order to turn elsewhere for greater gains. When the movement for independence came there was not in existence a stable, self-sustaining economic order upon which government could be based. Government, indeed, continued to be looked upon chiefly as the imposer of financial burdens upon the many and the source of privileges and gain to those in power. Thus the vices of economic life were directly translated to the political field and stood for a long time in the way of the up-building of suitable and responsible national government.

This lack of economic stability inevitably led to a permanent financial dependence upon Europe. It was, of course, natural that efforts should be made to supply the

---

[7] M. Bomfim in his book *America Latina*, Rio de Janeiro, 1905, calls the colonial society of South America "parasitic."

needs which existed in a new country for capital by inviting European enterprise. Unusual advantages and privileges were granted in order to attract it, and for decades national economic life in these countries came entirely under the tutelage and control of European financiers. While this resulted in the introduction of elements and influences favorable to law and order, it manifestly stood in the way of developing the feeling of complete national independence and responsibility. A fact which will soon arrest the attention of the historical investigator is the influence which the belief in the inexhaustible natural resources had upon the political and economic life in some of these countries. The effect seems to have been not so much to stimulate enterprise but to induce over-confidence in the economic capabilities of the country, leading men to plunge into debt and in every way to discount the future.

All through South American history, from the earliest missionary efforts of the *padres* to the discussions of our day as to the proper relation of Church and State, religion, with all its observances and institutions, has been a main element in South American social history. But, only this year has an attempt been made to study comprehensively this development in all its extension.[8]

The close relationship of South America with Europe and its dependence upon the older continent affected especially its intellectual life. This contact gave to literary forms an expression of notable finish; nor did Latin-American litterateurs allow any movement of thought to pass in Europe without giving it full attention. Accordingly, there has been far more of literary criticism here than in the north, and it is far better informed as to the various phases of European thought and artistic life. But generally speaking, there is a lack of originality. Individual writers may indeed see life and experience from a

[8] Quesada, V. G., *Derecho de patronato,* Buenos Aires, 1910.

special and new point of view, but no great national or
continental types have been created.   There are many
Lowells, but no Walt Whitman or Mark Twain.   Portrayal of local and national life is the work mostly of
artists who, in the middle of the century,[9] saw through
the lenses of romanticism, or, more recently, who attempt
to interpret things on the basis of the realism of Zola,
or the psychological analysis of Bourget.   As many South
American writers pass a large part of their life in Europe,
especially in Paris, it is but natural that they should seek
directly to portray European life, or to bring to bear upon
the intellectuality of their respective countries, European
ideas.   But even those who reside in American cities will
frequently, rather than to look about them and to interpret for us their varied and interesting surroundings, take
their subjects from the traditions of literature and from
European sources.   This is true of the notable writings of
Rodo, when he deals with *Motivos de Proteo,* and of
Leopoldo Lugones, in his *Piedras Liminares.*   Ernesto
Quesada, who is eminently qualified to produce a scientific
history and sociological study of his own country, has preferred to write learned disquisitions about the sociologists
of Europe.   There are indeed exceptions.   Thus in Brazilian literature we have a number of works that constitute
the most striking portrayal of tropical life in existence.
Such is the notable novel *Chanaan* of Graça Aranha.
In Argentina, Roberto Payro has given us some able
studies of popular life and character; and the Argentinian
theater, crude as many of its productions may be, is faith-
fully holding up a mirror to nature and portraying the
local life of city and country.   These are but a few of
many examples; but after all, they are exceptional com-
pared with the general currents of thought.   From all this
it is apparent that the historical student will receive com-

[9] *E.g.,* the *Maria* of Isaacs and the *Amalia* of Marmol.

paratively little help from the *belles lettres* of South America.

Juristic studies have always been attractive to South American minds. The clearness of reasoning, the *sensatez*, of jurisprudence accord admirably with the mental constitution of Latin-Americans. In this great science, of course, the contact with Europe has also exercised a predominant influence; although of late many original tendencies have appeared, and a persistent effort is being made to allow to purely South American conditions their due influence in the development of law. As has already been indicated, the study of philology has received much attention. And it is interesting to note that the field of Americanism which has been most sedulously cultivated is the study of American neologisms, adaptations of Spanish, and the use of Indian words introduced into the Spanish dialects. The natural and the applied sciences have thus far not been given such prominence in South America as in other parts of the world. Although, with the transformation which is now going on in South American temper, the scientific and technical point of view is distinctly gaining in importance.

One of the most interesting problems that invites the attention of the historical investigator is connected with the development of the divers national entities in South America. That in this comparatively short time there should have grown from the same Iberian stock, nationalities so totally divergent in their social institutions and political development as are Brazil, Argentina, Chili, Peru, Colombia, and Mexico is indeed a notable fact. The great Liberator, with all his enthusiasm for an united America, foresaw in his famous prophecy the different political tendencies and destinies of these countries. But it is not only superficial political traits that distinguish them. On the contrary, they differ radically in ideas of conduct, the aims of life, the social and political constitution of society. The Chilean aristocracy, securely established and confidently working out its national policy, is widely different from the congeries of races and the cosmopolitan society in the neighboring Argentina, which, on its part, contrasts fundamentally, in institutions and aims, with the imperial republic of Brazil. Before these differences all confident generalization comes to naught. Humanity is no less complex there than elsewhere. The conditions under which it lives are even more varied, and the great unity that makes its essence has taken on a multitude of divergent institutional forms. It is their very complexity which makes it a fascinating field for historical endeavor when once we look beneath the surface of ephemeral political movements and appreciate the deeper bases of institutional life in its many phases.

PAUL S. REINSCH.